RICHMOND, VIRGINIA 23234-3698

GENERAL LEE'S CITY

To Dr. Hugo J. Mueller,
Professor Emeritus of Linguistics and German
at American University, Washington, D.C.—
a distinguished scholar and gentleman
who contributed so much to this book
in countless, valuable ways.

GENERAL LEE'S CITY

An Illustrated Guide to the
Historic Sites of Confederate Richmond

Richard M. Lee

EPM Publications, Inc.
McLean, Virginia

Library of Congress Cataloging-in-Publication Data

Lee, Richard M. (Richard McGowan)
    General Lee's city.

    Bibliography: p.
    1. Historic sites—Virginia—Richmond—Guide-books.
2. Lee, Robert E. (Robert Edward), 1807–1870—Homes
and haunts—Virginia—Richmond—Guide-books. 3. Richmond
(Va.)—Description—Guide-books. I. Title.
F234.R565A24 1987   917.55′23   87-643
ISBN 0-914440-99-3

Copyright © 1987 Richard M. Lee
All rights reserved
EPM Publications, Inc., 1003 Turkey Run Road,
McLean, Virginia 22101
Printed in the United States of America

Book Design by Tom Huestis

TABLE OF CONTENTS

AN OVERVIEW—Richmond in Wartime 1861–1865	15
War Comes to Richmond—1861	17
Fighting Comes Close—1862	21
High Tide—1863	26
The Onslaught—1864	29
The Unthinkable Happens—1865	35
Evacuation Day—April 2, 1865	36
How to Use This Guide	41
FIRST TOUR—Capitol Square	45
1. *Capitol Square*	46
2. *The George Washington Statue*	48
3. *The Virginia State Capitol*	50
4. *The Governor's Mansion*	52
5. *The Bell Tower*	53
SECOND TOUR—Broad Street, Shockoe Hill and Court End	55
6. *Confederate Government Stables*	57
7. *Broad Street*	57
8. *The Richmond, Fredericksburg & Potomac Railroad Depot*	59
9. *The Richmond Theater*	59
10. *St. James Episcopal Church*	60
11. *The Powder Magazine*	60
12. *City Alms House*	61
13. *Shockoe Cemetery*	62
14. *Hebrew Cemetery—Shockoe Hill*	63
15. *Richmond Female Institute*	64
16. *The Egyptian Building*	65
17. *The First African Baptist Church*	65
18. *The Old Monumental Church*	66
19. *The First Baptist Church*	67
20. *Twelfth Street*	69
21. *The Confederate White House*	69
22. *Corners of 12th and Clay Streets*	72
23. *The Maury House*	73
24. *The James Caskie House*	73
25. *The Wickham-Valentine House*	75
26. *The Grant House*	76

27.	*The Broad Street Methodist Church*	77
28.	*Provost Marshal's Headquarters in Richmond*	78
29.	*The City Hall*	80
30.	*The Powhatan House*	81
31.	*John Moncure Daniel House*	82
32.	*Wartime Railroad Tracks Down Broad Street*	83

THIRD TOUR—Eastern Quarter 85

33.	*The Virginia Central Railroad Depot*	86
34.	*Mechanicsville Turnpike*	89
35.	*Church Hill*	89
36.	*Crenshaw House*	91
37.	*Oakwood Cemetery*	92
38.	*Richmond Dueling Grounds*	92
39.	*Chimborazo Military Hospital*	93
40.	*Libby Hill Park and Confederate Soldiers and Sailors Monument*	94
41.	*Rocketts Landing*	96
42.	*Confederate Navy Yard Sites and the James River Squadron*	97
43.	*Luther Libby House*	98
44.	*The Van Lew Mansion*	99
45.	*The Wilkins Home*	101
46.	*Seabrook's Warehouse (General Hospital No. 9)*	102
47.	*The Oldest Part of Richmond*	103
48.	*The First Market, Watch House and Public Hall*	105
49.	*William H. Grant Tobacco Factory (General Hospital No. 12)*	105
50.	*The Federal Pontoon Bridge*	106
51.	*The City Gas Storage Tanks and the Confederate War Balloon*	108
52.	*Castle Thunder and Castle Lightning*	109
53.	*Libby Prison*	109
54.	*The York River Railroad Depot*	111
55.	*General Lee's Railroad Gun*	111
56.	*The Second Alabama Hospital and Mrs. "Judge" Hopkins*	112
57.	*Richmond's Horsecars*	114
58.	*Trooper Boykin Retreats Down Main Street*	114
59.	*The Travail of Rebecca Jane Allen*	115
60.	*The Old Stone House*	116
61.	*The Bread Riots*	117

FOURTH TOUR—Area of the Evacuation Fire		119
62.	*Mayo's Bridge*	121
63.	*President Davis Leaves Richmond*	122
64.	*Shockoe Warehouse*	123
65.	*The Business District*	124
66.	*Kent and Paine Dry Goods Warehouse (General Hospital No. 5)*	124
67.	*Confederate Reading Room*	126
68.	*President Davis's Executive Offices*	126
69.	*High Jinks at the YMCA Hospital*	127
70.	*Mechanic's Hall*	127
71.	*How the Evacuation Fire Was Put Out*	128
72.	*St. Paul's Church*	129
73.	*St. Peter's Catholic Church*	131
74.	*Franklin Street*	132
75.	*Headquarters Department of Richmond*	133
76.	*General Lee's Richmond Home*	133
77.	*The United Presbyterian Church Burns*	134
78.	*The Fire and Mrs. Stannard*	134
79.	*The Corner of Franklin and 9th Streets*	135
80.	*Shoot-Out on Bank Street*	136
81.	*The Transportation Quartermaster*	137
82.	*The Federal Courthouse*	137
83.	*Belvin Block*	139
84.	*Clifton House*	140
85.	*A Heroine Stops at the Ballard House*	140
86.	*Vannerson Studio*	142
FIFTH TOUR—Gamble's Hill, Hollywood Cemetery and Monroe Park		145
87.	*A Memorable Parade Down Main Street*	147
88.	*The Spottswood Hotel*	148
89.	*The Richmond and Petersburg Depot*	148
90.	*Arlington House*	150
91.	*Hoge House*	151
92.	*Second Presbyterian Church*	152
93.	*Palmer-Caskie House*	154
94.	*The Harold House*	154
95.	*Secretary Mallory's Home*	154
96.	*Robertson Home/Hospital*	155
97.	*Pratt's Castle and Snyder House on Gamble's Hill*	156
98.	*The James River and Kanawha Canal*	158
99.	*The Confederate Armory and Shops*	158

100.	*Explosion at the Confederate Laboratory*	160
101.	*Tredegar Iron Works*	161
102.	*The State Penitentiary*	162
103.	*Hollywood Cemetery*	163
104.	*Belle Isle Prisoner of War Camp*	164
105.	*Monroe Park and Stuart Hospital*	165
106.	*Monument Avenue*	166

APPENDIX

The Defenses of Richmond	171
Chronology	176
Acknowledgments	179
Source Notes	180
Bibliography	182

PREFACE

The experience of Richmond during the War Between the States is unique in the history of this country. No other major city has endured four long years of peril—periodic attack, frequent raids, siege, capitulation and partial destruction by fire—and survived. Her people faced the loss of loved ones, economic and physical deprivation and the fear that a treasured way of life was about to be extinguished.

This book hopes to recapture some of the atmosphere of wartime Richmond by relating stories that tell how its inhabitants coped with the escalating terrors. Many of the stories are told in their own words; all reveal courage, humor and compassion. Some authorities believe Richmond has changed so much since the war that the appearance and flavor of the old city are not recoverable. However, it is possible by using the approach of five tours through the city, illustrated by 18 maps and some 150 photographs and drawings, at least to get a glimpse of what 1861–1865 Richmond was like.

The author invites the assistance of his readers, especially in the identification of new information, discovery of inaccuracies, and above all in the uncovering of still more, yet untold stories about the city and its inhabitants. Such contributions would be welcome.

R.M.L.

Richmond was the "central stage of the drama of General Robert E. Lee's life."[1] As commander of Virginia's forces in 1861, it was he who took the first active measures in its defense. As Union forces in strength drew close to Richmond in the spring of 1862, it was he as the new commander of the Army of Northern Virginia who delivered Richmond from its enemies in his first brilliant campaign of "the Seven Days." Then, as the months of war passed, he saved the city and the Confederacy again and again. The security of Richmond and its people was never far from his mind, and when the end drew close in 1865 and he could no longer protect it, he was in despair.

Cooper de Leon tells of Lee's ride into Richmond after his defeat at Appomattox, April 14, 1865:

"Next morning a small group of horsemen appeared at the far side of the pontoon. It became known that General Lee was amongst them, and a crowd gathered along the way, silent and bare headed. There was no excitement—no cheering, yet as the great chief passed, a deep, loving murmur . . . rose from the very hearts of the crowd. Taking off his hat and merely bowing his head, the man passed silently to his own door."[2]

The people of Richmond knew how he felt, and they responded with their undying affection. In this sense the city truly was his.

MAP 1
Confederate Offices and Installations—Richmond.

Flag 1: Former U.S. Customs House—Offices of President Davis and Secretary of State.
Flag 2: Mechanic's Hall—Confederate War and Navy Departments.
Flag 3: Virginia State Capitol—Meeting place of Confederate Congress.
Flag 4: Grouping of Confederate Quartermaster, Commissary and Ordnance offices on Main and Bank Streets; some on Cary Street.
Flag 5: Military manufacturing, storage and distribution center.

Library of Congress

AN OVERVIEW

Richmond in Wartime 1861–1865

War Comes to Richmond— 1861

As the train from Petersburg puffed along the railroad cut through the high bluff bordering Manchester, writer Cooper de Leon peered eagerly out of the coach window for his first glimpse of Richmond. It was 1861, about a month since Richmond had become the capital of the new Confederate States of America and the time of full Virginia spring. Suddenly, just across the James River, Richmond lay before him, spread across her smiling, verdant hills, as he was to write, "with the evening sun gilding simple houses and towering spires—turning the city into a glory." Following the gentle curve of the James the town sat behind the fall line, and the rushing waters sparkled in the evening light. Bordering the city were fringes of dark woods "providing a blue background against the sky." De Leon thought no city in the South had a grander approach.[3]

By today's standards the city was small, only 38,000 people, about a third of them slaves. Richmond ranked third in population among southern cities. Her leading citizens were professionals, planters and well-to-do businessmen. These men knew about the management of plantations from the colonial past, and Richmond's industry as well as government tended to assume the patriarchal outlook of plantation life. The mayor, Joseph Mayo, venerable and popular, functioned more or less as a supervisor over the conduct of free and slave blacks residing in the city. Both lived under a system of restraints.

On the whole the white citizenry of the city were conservative. They were hospitable neighbors and lived productive, comfortable lives. Most of them were involved primarily in their families, and this meant not only the immediate family but a much broader group of relatives belonging to a common ancestry. Blood relationships were important, especially if one traced his descent back to one of the oldest colonial families of Anglo-Saxon origin. In such families upper class women knew precisely who was related to whom and could recite in detail the lines of descent. At the top of the social pyramid were the leading families of the Old Dominion, an aristocracy of birth, and sometimes of land, which everybody acknowledged. Even the most senior ladies of the new Confederate government deferred somewhat to the Virginia aristocracy, for the Old Dominion stood first in prestige among her southern sister states. None could equal Virginia's early, proud

Cooper deLeon entered Richmond on this railroad bridge. His first view of the city must have been something like this.

Virginia State Library

record of settlement at Jamestown or match the leaders she produced to guide the new nation through its early perils.

Virginia stood second in population among southern states, and Richmond stood first in heavy industry in the South. Indeed, Richmond was the only southern city with a significant war-making potential. Twelve large mills had for years produced flour and meal, mostly for export to Latin America from Richmond's docks. Over 50 tobacco warehouses serviced the world's largest tobacco industry; people said,"the city stank of tobacco."[4] Richmond's primary input to a war economy was its iron industry. Several iron works, especially the Tredegar Works, could produce the essential tools of war: cannon, weapons, ammunition, steel rails and similar items in quantity.

The tranquil life of the city was disrupted by South Carolina's secession from the Union in December 1860, followed shortly by five other states of the deep South. Most of the citizens of Richmond were troubled, for a majority were reluctant to leave the Union. As the weeks sped by, the pace of disunion accelerated. A new nation was being formed at Montgomery, Alabama, throughout February 1861, and the distinguished southerner, Jefferson Davis, was elected provisional president. Then violence erupted. South Carolinians fired on Fort Sumter in Charleston Harbor, and it fell in mid-April. Richmond could scarcely ignore that time was running out for a peaceful solution.

A few days later Lincoln, the new President, asked for 75,000 volunteers to quell the insurrection in the South. As the chain of events progressed, the people of the city and Virginia found themselves confronted with what appeared to be an armed invasion from the North. Their allegiance, with exceptions, had primarily been to Virginia first and the Union second. By mid-April a majority in the state had swung behind secession; an Ordinance of Secession was passed by a Virginia State Convention, and the evening of April 19 witnessed a giant torchlight procession through the streets of Richmond celebrating the momentous event.

Events hurried on; as spring advanced the citizens of Richmond found themselves living in the new capital of the Confederacy, a situation scarcely believable. The Confederate Congress had voted to relocate their capital at Richmond. Soon the city was paying a price for its new eminence. As one pleasant May day followed another, the city turned into an armed camp. Thousands of young men from Virginia and other Confederate states got off trains, some in gaudy uniforms, some in homespuns, many in ordinary garb—all determined to defend Virginia and the South from invasion. The

Richmond stood at the fall line of the James River and by 1861 her docks at Rocketts were loading ocean-going vessels for Latin American and European ports.
Virginia State Library

RICHMOND IN WARTIME 1861–1865

Its training at Richmond completed, an Alabama regiment marches through Capitol Square on its way to join General Beauregard's army near Manassas. *Virginia State Library*

new government housed them in camps around the city and in tobacco warehouses, factories and public buildings. Meanwhile Richmond had doubled in size and kept growing. The natives found themselves being hemmed in by strangers: soldiers, businessmen, speculators, contractors, gamblers, government cadres, office seekers and hordes of others. It was a chore for the quiet old city to absorb and adjust to all these newcomers, but hospitable Richmond did its best, and somehow all were accommodated.

People didn't know what to think about the coming war. Some said, "Pshaw! There will be no war!"[5] But the day after secession was ratified by Virginia voters (May 24, 1861), Union troops suddenly pounced upon the town of Alexandria in force—on Virginia soil. Blood was spilled on both sides. War had begun. Southerners soon realized, in a phrase of those days, that "the erring sisters (southern states) would not be allowed to depart (the Union) in peace."[6] But optimism dies hard. People wanted to feel that it would be a short, victorious war. After all, one would say to another, "One Southerner is equal to a half-dozen Yankees. Everyone knows that!"[7] President Davis, now in Richmond, tried to discourage this facile judgment; he warned that it would be a hard, long war, but few believed him.

On July 21 the war became real for everyone when a battle occurred near Manassas in Northern Virginia. It was learned that the South had won after a long day's fight. The Yankees had been routed and were fleeing back to Washington. Morale soared in the city, and again the optimists held sway. Perhaps the soldiers could return to their homes before the first frost. The Yankees would now surely give up.

Sobering thoughts came with the first trainload of wounded men from Manassas. The train pulled in the Virginia Central Station on a rainy evening a day or so after the battle. Large crowds watched the unloading of the unfortunate men, insignificant in number compared to the toll of later months. But this was the first time the people saw what war could do to the young men Richmond had seen off to the front in such high spirits a few weeks before.

The experience of seeing wounded men was only the beginning of a deflation of the patriotic fervor that had marked the spring months. There were other reasons for worry. As the fall passed, bad news came in from the western half of the state. The Union was winning there, and more than a third of Virginia territory was being lost behind a wall of Union troops. To Virginians it was bad enough to undergo the ordeal of leaving the Union; it was at least an equal blow to have so much of the state secede and be able to do little about it. Within a year West Virginia had become a new state in the Union.

There were other reasons for dissatisfaction, closer at hand. Among the newcomers in the city were criminals. Civilians and soldiers had been robbed, some even murdered in a city unaccustomed to serious crime. Also present were strange businessmen whose shabby practices outraged the Virginian sense of honor, men who traded with the enemy. Rumor had it that spies were everywhere. The Confederate Congress met for the first time in Richmond; it seemed unimpressive perhaps because people had expected too much from it. Observers also noticed that, though fine leaders and

The Gallego Flour Mill, seen here shortly before the war, was one of the largest in the world. Its flour was shipped overseas from Richmond—the South's major industrial and shipping center.
Virginia State Library

many upright men arrived, coteries of influence peddlers, lobbyists and hangers-on of dubious habits also crowded into the city. Taking over the bars, hotels and rooming houses, they could be seen lounging about the streets or frequenting the Capitol, bent on personal advantage. These hustling strangers avoided the beloved gray uniform. They dressed well, had money in their pockets and didn't mind crowding the natives away from the best the town had to offer. Some of them reminded old Richmonders of the very Yankees they were trying to escape.

Shortages in goods and groceries that had always been abundant in Richmond were felt for the first time; prices began to climb as the colder weather approached. Some trusted, familiar stores disappeared, and people found themselves shopping at new stores with inflated prices. Something seemed to be wrong, and it was. The Confederate dollar, detached from U.S. currency, was not backed by adequate reserves of gold and had already begun a spiral of depreciation. By December 1861 it stood at 20 percent below the level of the previous April.

By this time the excitement and optimism of the spring was largely gone. Family separations were hard to bear, and people sensed they were in for a long, hard war since everyone knew that Richmond had become the primary objective of the Union armies. Nevertheless, with all the uncertainties, dissatisfactions and disagreements among the citizenry, a consensus formed as to what they and their sister states of the South were fighting for.

People agreed that the cause they were ready to fight, and if necessary die, for was *not* the preservation of slavery. They hardly recognized the term "slave" in their vocabulary. People referred to "their servants," and indeed servants were an integral part of their cherished way of life. What was important was their conviction that the North, and this meant the Federal government in Washington, was trying to force them to give up this way of life.

For more than 200 years the South had developed its own economy based on cotton, tobacco and other warm climate crops. Southerners had acquired their own traditions, social values, behavior patterns and their own aristocracy. Their forefathers had left Europe in order to free themselves from restrictions on their choice of lifestyle. The issue to them was one that went to the heart of the Constitution, a document the sovereign state of Virginia and 12 others had created. The Federal government should not be permitted to encroach upon their individual freedom.

As late as mid-April Virginians had not been able to bring themselves to abandon the Union. Then, like a thunderclap, came President Lincoln's Proclamation calling for 75,000 militia to quell the insurrection in South Carolina. Obviously, Mr. Lincoln was prepared to invade the South to preserve the Union. The public swung toward secession, and Virginia seceded with feelings running very high. The protection of home and family was now involved.

Northerners held equally strong opinions; the vast majority became determined to preserve the Union, even if this meant forcing the southern states back in. A lesser but growing conviction held that it was morally wrong to continue the enslavement of black people in the American democracy and that it must go. Thousands of good men on both sides prepared with near religious fervor to fight. Winston Churchill, in his *History of the English Speaking Peoples* described the irreconcilability of their conflict as "the noblest and least avoidable of all the great mass conflicts of which till then there was record."[8]

Though in his late seventies, Mayor Mayo gave Richmond, now a wartime capital, the imaginative forceful leadership it needed.
Virginia State Library

RICHMOND IN WARTIME 1861–1865

MAP 2

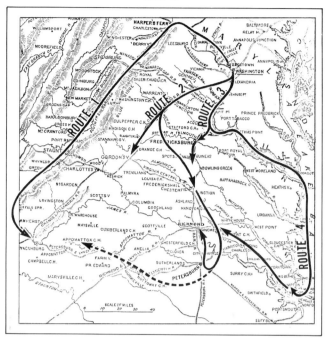

Union Approaches to Richmond, 1861–1865.

Route 1: The Valley Route.
Route 2: The Piedmont Route.
Route 3: The Potomac-Acquia Creek Route.
Route 4: The Potomac-Chesapeake Route.
The dotted line shows Grant's pursuit of Lee to Appomattox.

Virginia State Library

Fighting Comes Close—1862

Although the first three months of 1862 found Richmond plagued by concerns, there were a few lighter moments, one involving the Mayor himself. To play a prank on a friend, His Honor crept up behind him on a dark street, threw a cord around his neck and pretended to strangle him. The younger victim, alert to the realities of the city, turned the tables. Before Mayor Mayo could identify himself he was thrown and somewhat beaten.

The city was just not its pleasant, easygoing self. Now every blow or adverse incident anywhere in the Confederacy reverberated in the new capital. Optimists who had counted on a short war turned gloomy, arguing that the South had squandered its opportunity for decisive victory by not marching directly into Washington after the Manassas success of the past summer. On February 22 many of the citizenry gathered on the Capitol grounds during a downpour to see Mr. Davis formally inaugurated as President. No one could criticize the President's dignity, sincerity and eloquence. Most seemed to feel that the country was lucky to have such a man at the helm, a former soldier, planter and U.S. Senator.

By mid-March all attention was riveted on the war news. People were elated by the sparkling triumph of the ironclad *Virginia* over the Federal fleet in Hampton Roads; then hopes were dashed when this valuable warship had to be destroyed with the evacuation of Norfolk. Spirits sank deeper at news of the loss of Fort Donelson in the west, and plummeted again a month later after the defeat at Shiloh. The Yankees had really lost the battle at Shiloh the first day, holding only a final line. But they came back the next day and won—a disturbing development to those who "knew" the Northerners couldn't fight. March also witnessed the movement by water of an immense Federal army of 150,000 men down the Potomac to Hampton Roads. The ships unloaded safely under the guns of Fortress Monroe. Everyone knew this army would march on Richmond as soon as the roads dried.

April opened with a delightful surprise. Their own army, which had been withdrawn from Manassas, suddenly appeared in full strength on a balmy Sunday morning, marching gloriously down Richmond's streets. Moving to block General McClellan's army, now near Yorktown, solid ranks of gray clad infantrymen passed east on Main Street, while the cavalry and artillery, thousands of horses and men, filed down Franklin Street, a block to the north. For a fleeting moment families were reunited with sons, husbands and brothers. With the army nearby, for a day or two there was a surge of social life—walks along the river, balls, teas and even some weddings.

After the army moved toward Yorktown, trouble returned. To control the ever-climbing food prices, General John H. Winder, the Provost Marshal, established price ceilings and enforced them by sending his detectives among the merchants to threaten them into compliance. Farmers reacted by withholding their produce

The Army of the Potomac sailed down the Potomac River and Chesapeake Bay into the James River. After unloading at Hampton Roads, they began their march on Yorktown, the first step in the attack on Richmond.

Library of Congress

Near Fair Oaks, the Federals shift their reserves across the Chickahominy Swamp, using the ingenious bridge their Engineers built.
Virginia State Library

from the markets. Larders became empty. Quickly a committee called upon the General. Winder gave up; food appeared again in the markets, but inflation accelerated.

Without warning, word arrived that New Orleans, the very pearl of the South, had fallen to a sudden naval assault. This city, which was believed to be secure and safe behind its two strong forts guarding the Mississippi approaches, had fallen victim to a surprise attack. The Federal fleet, led by a Virginian no less, had plowed up the river in darkness, bypassed the forts, and appeared with leveled guns before the helpless city the next day. Citizens of Richmond promptly thought about their own navigable James River, and many shuddered from the fear that Union gunboats also were preparing to attack their city once the spring freshets had raised the river level. Work on the fort at Drewry's Bluff, eight miles below the city at a turn in the river, was given the highest priority.

May found the situation worsening, and the gloom was general. The Union troops had pushed the defenders out of Yorktown, then Williamsburg; they slowly drew closer on muddy roads, dragging along a train of heavy siege guns to batter Richmond to pieces. Some were certain the city would fall after stragglers, sick and wounded men from their own army, entered the city wan, ragged and exhausted. What had happened to the splendid army so recently in their streets? It was, in fact, retreating through the rains to Richmond; there could be a siege or a battle in the streets. Many concerned residents left town. The President sent his wife and children off by train to Raleigh, North Carolina, but Davis himself stayed, declaring martial law within a ten mile radius of the city limits. The Secretary of War carted up his archives and had them hauled to a depot. It remained for General Winder, as usual, to do the unpopular things. He required everyone to carry passports, banned all liquor sales, and began some arbitrary arrests—an odious development for such an individualistic community.

Even the weather seemed to be against the Confederacy. During May it had rained every day, but once the Union army had arrived at Richmond's doorstep, not seven miles away, the sun came out. The people called it "Yankee weather."

Time ran out in midmonth. Weighing anchor, the Federal ironclads, by any standard ugly, lethal-looking warships, nosed their way slowly up the muddy James, carefully avoiding sandbars, sunken ships, torpedoes and other manmade obstacles. Among them was the famous *Monitor*, that had fought to a draw with the *Virginia*. If this fleet hammered its way past Drewry's Bluff, there was nothing left to stop them. It would be New Orleans all over again. The city would have to surrender, or those naval guns would pound Richmond to kindling wood.

On May 15 the Union fleet anchored below Drewry's Bluff. Then began a methodical shelling of the fort with their heavy guns. The four large cannons of the fort replied from its high ground. The *Monitor* could not elevate her one cannon high enough to hit the fort. With the sound of the gunfire Richmond realized that the awaited crisis had arrived. People were calm; apparently the faint-hearted had already left the city. After several hours the cannonading stopped as suddenly as it had begun. The silence was awesome. Either the fleet had broken through and all was lost, or it was repulsed and the city was safe. Suddenly, joyful shouts swept up and down Richmond's streets; there were tears of thanksgiving too. The little, four-gun fort not only had stopped the enemy ships, but had done them severe damage. They were steering slowly, sullenly back down the James. Morale lifted. They had had a whopping success! This was no New Orleans! Crowds gathered at the Capitol grounds to cheer Mayor Mayo as he told them the city would be held to the last!

At the end of May the opposing two armies collided at Seven Pines, about six miles east of the city on the Williamsburg Road. In spite of powerful attacks, the Confederates were unable to budge the Unionists. To make matters worse, the Southern commander, General Joseph E. Johnston, was severely wounded. That same night the President named a new commander, the Virginian Robert E. Lee.

As the early days of a warm June passed, the citizens asked soldiers visiting the city about the new commander. What was he like? After all, his ability as a battlefield commander was untested. Some of the answers did not reassure. Many of the men were disappointed; all General Lee wanted them to do, they said, was dig trenches. Many called him "the King of Spades."[9]

The new general went quietly about his plans, preparing to resume the fighting. To understand the enemy's dispositions better, he sent his cavalry leader, General Stuart, on a raid entirely around the Union army. Stuart returned to tell Lee what he already suspected—that the Union right flank north of the Chickahominy River was not strong enough. Lee secretly began shifting the bulk of his army to attack this vulnerable flank, meanwhile keeping a screen of men in the new trenches that now protected Richmond.

Both sides suffered losses in battles. Near Richmond, soldiers pick up the wounded, bury the dead and burn the horses in the darkness of night after the fighting has ceased.
Virginia State Library

General Jeb Stuart, Commanding General of the Confederate Cavalry Corps, Army of Northern Virginia. *Virginia State Library*

Lee's army attacked the afternoon of June 26 about five miles northeast of Richmond. The noise was deafening. One lady remembered, "It was so near that the first guns sent our hearts to our mouths—like a sudden loud knocking at one's door at night."[10] People rushed to the roofs of the hotels, the Capitol and other high buildings to see what they could of the battle. Many gathered on Shockoe Hill near the President's home, already called the White House of the Confederacy. Everything was shrouded in billows of smoke with here and there an orange flash of cannon fire. One biblically-minded observer wrote, "The noise of thousands of muskets was like the rushing, mighty wind of Pentacost with furious showers of hail in between."[11] Floating serene above the carnage were the Union balloons, as many as three at a time—the first use of aircraft in active battle. In the late afternoon sun they looked like oranges floating in the sky. Crowds remained at their vantage points long after darkness fell, as the battle became a gigantic fireworks display, "beautiful yet awful."[12]

News arrived the next day, brought mostly by a multitude of wounded men. It had the sweet sound of success. Lee had turned out to be a fighter and was

General Stuart's horsemen as they looked early in the war. These men, the pride of the South, rode entirely around McClellan's army in June 1862, bringing back the information Lee needed before taking the offensive. *Library of Congress*

RICHMOND IN WARTIME 1861-1865

MAP 3

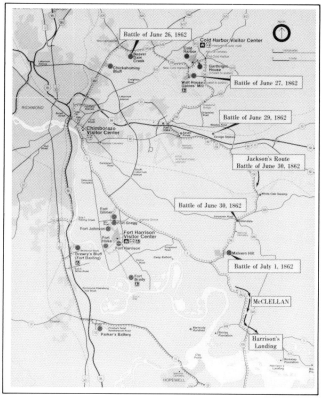

Seven Days Battles, June 26–July 1, 1862. The dotted lines are National Park Service routes to the battlefields. *National Park Service*

driving the Yankees away from the city. Before long, guards brought columns of captured Union soldiers into town, who verified that their side had had the worst of it. For the next six days, General Lee continued his violent offensive, hitting the Federals every time they paused and attempted to rally—at Gaine's Mill, White Oak Swamp, Savage Station, Glendale and Malvern Hill. These names suddenly took on the greatest significance, for the people saw them as the symbols of Richmond's deliverance, and also as places their countrymen had proved themselves invincible in the face of a stronger and better equipped adversary.

By early July the fighting around Richmond was over, except for distant skirmishing. A mauled Union army lay entrenched at Harrison's Landing some 20 miles southeast of the capital, sheltered under the guns of the Union fleet. The price of saving Richmond had been staggering: 20,000 men killed, wounded and missing. Nothing like this had ever happened in North America before. The numbers were too large for people to grasp, but the sights, sounds and smells of the Richmond hospitals brought the enormity of the losses home. Churches, warehouses, stores and tent camps overflowed with sick and wounded men. Perhaps the lucky ones were those killed on the field, for they were spared suffering in hospitals with insufficient medical supplies. Strangers poured into the city, living in odd corners and looking for missing family members. Most often those missing were the men who had been killed, gone forever in hurriedly dug, shallow graves. Occasionally one of them was found in a hospital, and often a relative stayed on to nurse him.

For much of July, the victorious army was camped near the city; the people could see their heroes every day. Even Stonewall Jackson appeared on a Sunday morning at the Second Presbyterian Church on 5th Street. General Lee, the greatest hero of the victory, was seen occasionally near his Franklin Street home or at the War Department on 9th Street, but he stayed mostly at his field headquarters. This quiet, bold man was about to seize the initiative and carry the war north, leaving his broken and stranded enemy behind entrenchments at Harrison's Landing.

Late in the month the bulk of Lee's army marched north, much of it passing through the city. The citizenry watched them go by. The heavily tanned and very lean soldiers seemed so young. They were shabby to the extreme in butternut or faded gray. Most wore bits and pieces of captured Union equipment and clothing. Battered felt hats were preferred; toothbrushes dangled from buttonholes, and folded blankets draped over left shoulders. Musket barrels had frying pans sticking out of the muzzles, and most bayonets were fixed so that the scabbards could be thrown away. Some men were barefoot, but generally they were shod with captured Yankee shoes. They walked with a long stride that seemed to eat up the ground. Elated to be in Richmond, they grinned and called to bystanders, especially the girls.

So the army passed from view, and the rest of the year rang with news of its victories. In Richmond its prowess was becoming legendary. One incredible victory followed another that summer. People heard of places like Cedar Mountain, Thoroughfare Gap, Second Manassas, Chantilly and Harpers Ferry. After a setback at Sharpsburg, there was still another smashing triumph in the last month of the year at Fredericksburg. Citizens took heart from these great events; perhaps victory and independence were in sight. By the fall, parties and gaiety had returned to Richmond's hotels, restaurants and private homes—an antidote to the strain and privation of early summer.

A war torn city seems to bring out the best and the worst among its people; this was certainly true of Richmond. Many used the emergency shortages and dislocations in their own self-interest; others, with crisis and emergency all around them, remained uninvolved. But a substantial portion of the citizens became firmly committed to some kind of service during the stark days of early summer. Like the young but now experienced army, they were becoming veterans too. The

Citizens gathered in the streets to assist wounded men arriving from the nearby fighting after the battle of Fair Oaks and Seven Pines, May 31, 1863.
Virginia State Library

problems were so acute, the suffering so widespread that both ordinary and privileged people accomplished near miracles, creating a kind of esprit, an ideal of devotion and service that came to characterize Richmond during the war. Other cities and towns had time to recuperate between emergencies. This was rarely true of Richmond; its people were nearly always in the forefront of the conflict.

High Tide—1863

The new year of 1863 brought a smallpox epidemic, signalled by white flags flying from the doors of the victims. Concerned by the virulence of the strain, the army provided a separate smallpox hospital to isolate the infected. Shortages of nourishing food and crowded housing contributed to the epidemic's severity. Poorer families were now truly hungry. Even the rats were so famished that people said "They were as tame as kittens."[13] Boarding houses and some hotels, no longer able to purchase food without losing money, began to close dining rooms, leaving boarders to pool their resources and prepare meals in their rooms. Each boarder was expected to contribute his fair share or withdraw.

It was a time to improvise, especially for refugees. Ladies developed unexpected skills. Some made and sold soap. One built a business making pickles and catsup for the restaurants. Another well-born but needy lady concocted a delicious gooseberry wine that sparkled like champagne. Since hats cost $500 apiece, girls plaited new ones from rye straw or cut up old clothes to create fashionable new hats—hats that could pass inspection at the President's home. Even the First Lady, Mrs. Davis, was observed from time to time sitting on her front steps visiting with friends and making straw hats for her family.

Women rediscovered the uses of roots, barks, berries, sodas and other alkalies for dying cloth. Spinning wheels and looms from colonial days came down from attics and went back into service. But these expedients were not enough for most families as prices continued to climb. Some refugees and Richmond citizens became so pressed that they were compelled to send servants from door to door selling family plates, jewelry, books and other possessions. Refugees continued to arrive, crowding their relatives' homes or finding accommodations in expensive rented rooms where conditions were much worse. When asked why they came to Richmond of all places, they always replied, "Why, it's the safest place of all!"[14] Few understood that the capital city lay at the center of the storm.

On the morning of April 2, there was unexpected violence. Some 500 women and boys from poorer families gathered at Capitol Square to protest food prices. Half starved, they walked down 9th Street to Main and Cary Streets where they began plundering food and other stores. The city militia was called out. The crowd dispersed only after a speech from President Davis himself. The authorities were alarmed, and that afternoon artillery was brought into the city and positioned to fire down the main streets. From this time on, some food was always provided the poorest families from government stores, an arrangement which neglected equally needy refugees and middle class families.

Warfare came again suddenly in early May. Strong Union calvary troops under General Stoneman penetrated as far as the intermediate defense lines, within three miles of the city itself. About 900 of the city militia rushed out to meet them, but they had forgotten gunpowder and friction primers for their cannon. Troops were hurried up from Petersburg, but for a time the city was defenseless. Had they been aware of the helpless condition of Richmond, the raiders could have taken it. Instead, they skirmished and maneuvered for a time, then slipped northeast around the defenses, passing over the Chickahominy and Pamunkey Rivers into Prince William County. Little damage was done, but panic gripped everyone. People destroyed papers, hid their valuables and packed trunks—much as they had done before the Federal naval attack on Drewry's Bluff the previous year. The crisis ended quickly, leaving people debilitated from the excitement and fright.

Those same days saw eyes fixed to the north, for the Federal army in great strength was poised to make yet another attempt to take Richmond. What followed at Chancellorsville was perhaps General Lee's most brilliant victory. The Yankees were thrown back across the Rappahannock River, but with fearful losses for both armies; even Stonewall Jackson was wounded though he appeared to be recovering. Train after train carried the wounded into the city. Thousands of Union prisoners were marched through the streets to Belle Isle and Libby Prisons. Longstreet's corps, for several months in position west of Norfolk, passed through the city on its way north to rejoin Lee. Citizens watched, not realizing that within the month these men would be invading Pennsylvania.

On May 10 the people of the city reacted with shock to the news that the paladin of the South, Stonewall Jackson, had died of his wounds at Guinea's Station. Jackson's funeral at the Capitol on May 12 was a momentous event. People came in great crowds to the funeral and the parade which preceded it and, sadly filed by the casket to view his remains. There could not be another Jackson, and one woman wrote, "I feel more disheartened . . . than ever before. It seems to me that it (the war) is to be interminable."[15]

News of Lee's invasion of Maryland and Pennsylvania electrified the city during June. Wounded cavalrymen arrived from the field of Brandy Station and the mountain passes along the Blue Ridge. Names like Upperville and Middleburg were talked about, places where the Blue cavalry had been held back from Lee's infantry columns as they passed north through the Valley of Virginia. Everything was going splendidly; hopes were high that one final push north of the Potomac would end the war.

On July 4 came the first of two great shocks. Vicksburg fell that day, together with its 23,000-man garrison including 11 generals. The whole line of the

From the bed of a wagon on the corner of 15th and Main Streets, President Davis calls on the food rioters to disperse and go home, the morning of April 2, 1863. *Henry Holt & Co., Inc.*

Mississippi was gone; the Confederacy was cut in two. A few days later, newspapers arriving through Northern lines were read in Richmond. Under black headlines were reports that General Lee had been defeated at Gettysburg and was in retreat through wretched weather toward the Potomac River. Everyone said that the Yankee newspapers lied, but the arrival of the first trains of wounded confirmed the essential facts.

The impact of both defeats was profound. European intervention for the South could now be written off, and Richmond would be lost. Croakers spoke openly, "The Confederacy was about gone up!"[16] In lieu of the victorious peace once hoped for, the government and most of the citizens now became determined to prolong the war, hoping to make it so costly to the Yankees that they would despair of their goal to subjugate the South. Thus, they pinned their faith, more than ever, on the army and General Lee.

With the army fighting so far north during the summer months, the city was vulnerable to cavalry attacks, raids and probes from the Federal base at Yorktown. Mostly in New Kent County, these sudden attacks jangled people's nerves and caused alarm. The tocsin in Capitol Square rang unexpectedly during the day and at night. The militia would assemble in Capitol Square or along Broad and 9th Streets, then march away for Bottom's Bridge, Baltimore Cross Roads or some other remote, threatened point. These were not seasoned troops. The City Battalion was manned mostly by older men and halfgrown boys. There was also a Clerks Battalion, consisting of office workers from various departments. Added to these was the Tredegar Battalion, employees from the iron works and an Ordnance Battalion of laborers from the Arsenal. When possible a battalion of convalescents from the hospitals was included in the force. After a few days occupying trenches or marching about, the militia would return, sunburned, caked with mud, exhausted and hungry—only to be called out again as the marauding Bluecoats struck at some other location. Eventually morale of the troops suffered; but of greater concern, the business of government and support for the war was falling behind. Colonel Gorgas, Chief of Ordnance, complained that when his men were away defending the city, his ammunition shipments to General Lee were interrupted.

As the capital and the country absorbed the consequences of the two defeats of the summer, difficulties and conflicts simmering throughout the Confederacy tended to come to a head in Richmond. Problems, bearable with victory in sight, now seemed intolerable. Criticism against the President greatly increased; somehow he became the cause of the calamities that had befallen the country. So severe was the ordeal, he is said to have withdrawn into his circle of friends while still pursuing his purposes with undiminished zeal. Disagreement between the states and Confederate government sharpened, for the Confederate Constitution had reserved so much power to the states that the central government was handicapped in making war against the comparatively more centralized Union. The Congress of the Confederacy grew more obstinate, quarrelsome and divided. One legislator, Henry Stuart Foote, nearly brought legislative matters to a halt. This obstructionist later tried to desert to the North. When caught at Fredericksburg, he boldly announced that affairs had reached such a state he had commissioned himself to negotiate a peace with Washington. The Conscription Law, full of loopholes, worked unfairly and met growing resistance throughout the country. In some of the armies desertions had reached a level that alarmed the War Department.

The old problem of food prices and shortages worsened during the fall. A soldier from Lee's army wrote the Secretary of War that his mother in Richmond was in danger of starving with flour at $100 a barrel. If the

President and Mrs. Davis receiving guests at one of their evening levees in the Confederate White House. General Lee's son, Custis, is seen directly between the President and his wife.

Valentine Museum

government couldn't help, "he and his comrades would throw down their arms."[17]

Lee's army also endured severe shortages. Lee himself wrote letter after letter to the War Department pleading for fodder for his underfed, exhausted horses and food, clothing and shoes for his men. Rifle supplies were so low that he urged the militia forces be disarmed so that his regular forces could have the weapons. With necessities unavailable at home and at the front, it was becoming clearer that an agricultural society like the South faced the gravest disadvantages in fighting an industrialized, wealthy, more populous North. With the blockade of all the southern ports becoming more effective and with large parts of the country occupied, people had become embittered against what now seemed an implacable enemy.

By this time hardships also were the lot of families at the top of the social scale. As one response to so many scarcities, Hetty Cary, her cousins and other belles invented "starvation" parties. Those invited would meet at different homes each week, the hostess providing water only. The guests, mostly military men on leave, provided the dance music. Because some of the young ladies were uneasy about the propriety of dancing in such troubled times, a committee of the prettiest girls called on General Lee during one of his quick trips from his army to the War Department. "If you say no, General, we won't dance a single step!" Their idol smiled and relaxed, for he enjoyed the presence of lovely young women. To their immense relief he responded, "Why of course . . . my boys need to be heartened up when they get their furloughs. Go, look your prettiest . . . !"[18]

The year ended with dangers multiplying throughout the Confederacy. The lands stretching north from Richmond were now so devastated it took a visiting foreigner five days to travel less than 70 miles. Inside Richmond an economic and social revolution was in progress; one in which the old, established families were losing ground to new people who knew how to profit from the war. Almost every square in the older business sections had its auction houses to expedite the transfer of property. The middle class was descending into poverty. "After the war is over," it was said, "the parvenues . . . will roll by in their splendid carriages, and throw the dust of their insolence in the faces of the old aristocrats."[19]

Those who remembered prewar Richmond, a proper family town, were distressed by the increase in gambling places and houses of prostitution. Moreover, something was happening to the old patriotism. Able-bodied, young men appeared on the streets in civilian clothes, and everyone knew they were draft dodgers. Those who wanted to excuse them called them divinity students.

MAP 4

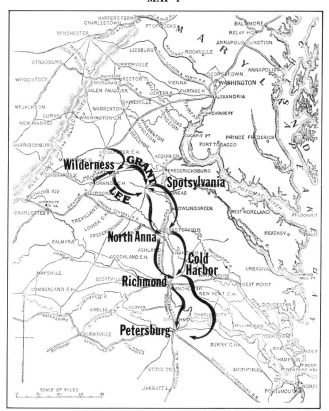

General Grant's Campaign Against Richmond, May–June 1864. Advancing from the Culpeper area and driving toward Richmond, General Grant fought repeated battles with General Lee. Each time Grant was checked, he moved by his left flank, but was always intercepted by Lee.
Virginia State Library

The Onslaught—1864

Parts of Richmond in January 1864 appeared deceptively prosperous to the casual observer. Shops were adequately stocked; hotels, restaurants and barrooms teemed with customers; evenings were still occupied with receptions, balls, *tableaux vivants* and other social events. Yet behind the gaiety dwelt the realization that setbacks were likely to continue. During the past year many thousands of men had been killed, wounded or captured, and they were not being replaced in adequate numbers. Aware of the problem, the new Union commander, General Grant, decided to cease prisoner exchanges to further limit Southern manpower. Everyone realized that the spring would bring the full weight of the Federal army against the city. Mary Chestnut wrote in her diary, "Hope and fear are both gone, and it is distraction or death with us."[20]

Perhaps in response to the seriousness of their situation, the Southern people experienced a religious revival that winter. Even in Richmond which was thought to have become wicked, all the churches were crowded at services. While much of this religious fervor origi-

Confederate Major General William "Extra-Billy" Smith became Virginia's governor on January 1, 1864 and served until the fall of the state to Federal troops April 2, 1865. From time to time he was obliged to issue proclamations like this one. *Virginia State Library*

Call to Arms issued by Governor Smith. *Virginia State Library*

nated among the Baptist and Methodist congregations, other denominations also became immersed in a wave of piety and preaching. The crusade spread to the winter camps of Lee's army south of the Rapidan and Rappahannock Rivers where open fields were the settings for well-attended services. Here the soldiers soberly contemplated their waning chances of survival.

The weather became frigid, and people began begging for food in the streets. Conditions at Belle Isle Prison deteriorated severely from lack of food and the bitter cold. "Everywhere," a citizen wrote, "I meet the rough board coffins of the wretched prisoners."[21] In the winter light, Richmond seemed dilapidated. "Few of the buildings had been brightened by a fresh application of paint since the commencement of hostilities, and where a plank fell off, or a screw got loose, or a gate fell from its hinges, or a bolt gave way, or a lock was broken, it was most likely to remain for a time unrepaired; for the majority of . . . mechanics were in the field and those left in the city were generally in the employment of the government."[22] Newspapers were reduced to half their usual size.

During the remainder of the cold weather the Confederate government prepared Lee's army and Richmond for the coming fighting. The city was combed for able-bodied men. One captain, on being ordered to give up his staff duties and rejoin Lee, turned pale and admitted he would rather go into the crater of a volcano. To escape conscription many ruses were employed. Doctor McClure, a Richmond mortician, was arrested for secreting evaders of conscription in his coffins out of the city. Since masses of wounded were expected to arrive once the fighting started, the large camp hospitals near Richmond were emptied of chronic patients, and hundreds of new beds were prepared. Some of the "chronic" patients had recovered from their wounds but were reluctant to return to the front. It took ingenuity to get them going. At Winder Hospital, a nurse happened to have been given several pairs of General Lee's old, much-darned socks. The socks became well known in the wards, for the nurses hit upon the scheme of putting them on the feet of malingering soldiers. The embarrassed recipient, amid the laughter of his comrades, would slowly rise, dress and shoulder his gear, then head back to his regiment.

A special effort was made to remove everyone not

essential to its defense or the war effort from the city, especially women and children. At Lee's request the preceding fall, thousands of prisoners in the city were moved farther south, mostly into the Carolinas and Georgia. The need to free Richmond from its dangerous burden of prisoners was highlighted by the escape of 109 Federal officers from Libby Prison in early February. As the weather improved and the ordeal drew closer, the factories, arsenals and supply services of Richmond forwarded large quantities of ammunition, food and equipment via the Virginia Central Railroad to Lee's headquarters at Orange Court House.

The first push against Richmond came without warning. During a few wintry days in early March two coordinated cavalry formations struck at Richmond. General Judson Kilpatrick rode in from the north, dismounted 3,000 troopers and attacked down the Brook Road toward the city. Meanwhile, Colonel Ulric Dahlgren and a small party of 300 men attempted to penetrate the city from the southwest under the cover of Kilpatrick's attack. Their purpose was to free Union prisoners at Libby and Belle Isle prisons. Both attacks failed, and during the retreat Colonel Dahlgren was ambushed and killed. On his body was found an order to his men, as yet undelivered, which directed them, with the help of the freed prisoners, to burn Richmond and kill the Confederate leaders. Aghast, the citizens had to conclude that the order was not a forgery; total war had come to Richmond.

General Hugh Judson Kilpatrick, leader of the first raid on Richmond in early March 1864. Later General Sherman asked General Grant to send Kilpatrick west. "I know," Sherman said, "that Kilpatrick is a hell of a damned fool, but I want just that sort of man to command my cavalry . . . *Virginia State Library*

Some of Kilpatrick's riders on the way to raid Richmond. *Library of Congress*

General Grant, the victor at Vicksburg, was given command of the Union armies in March. He joined the Army of the Potomac at Culpeper. Under this stubborn and determined man, this often beaten army would retreat no longer. It would attack and keep attacking in the direction of Richmond. General Grant arranged that two other Union armies, General Butler's and General Sigel's, would also drive at Richmond, one from the south and the other from the west via the Valley of Virginia.

It was almost a relief when the long awaited attacks began in early May. Events then moved so fast and the confusion became so pervasive that the papers could not keep the public informed. Before the end of the month, both Sigel and Butler had been repulsed. But

General Grant at Cold Harbor in early June 1864. Although Grant lost that battle, Lincoln knew he had found the general he needed.
National Archives

attention remained on General Grant's army of 120,000 men which kept striking at Lee's smaller army, drawing closer to Richmond. The two armies collided in the Wilderness (May 5–7), engaged in more heavy fighting at Spotsylvania Court House (May 8–18), fought again along the North Anna River (May 23–25), and by the end of the month eventually arrived close to the city near Cold Harbor. Three days later (June 3), General Grant attempted a knockout blow—an all-out attack against Lee's trenches to break through and smash his way into the city. He was heavily repulsed, losing over 5,000 men in 30 minutes.

Even Richmond had never heard such sounds of war. Throughout the city could be heard an overwhelming, deafening, endless roar of rifle and cannon fire. This time there were few sightseers on Richmond's hills, for the citizenry had had enough of war. Some thought that General Grant would retreat now; he had surely suffered badly. The month's fighting had cost him 45,000 killed, wounded and missing Bluecoats.

Even before General Lee could fully define his purpose, Grant attacked Petersburg, an essential railroad center for Richmond. When he was stopped at the last moment by Lee's veterans, both exhausted armies dug in for a siege.

The residents of the beleaguered city needed a chance to catch their collective breath and take stock of what had happened. Their splendid, laughing cavalry leader, Jeb Stuart, had been mortally wounded at Yellow Tavern, just north of the city. In unprecedented numbers, wounded and sick men were being brought into the city, many in a state of total exhaustion from the incessant marching and fighting.

The soldiers arrived almost always at night, sometimes so many and so fast it was difficult to clean them up and dress their wounds adequately. Upon the floors of the receiving wards, long low sheds, "the ghastly burdens were placed in rows, covered with dirt and blood, stiff with mud and gravel. Nurses moved among them with pails of toddy or milk, giving each man a drink to prepare him for his ordeal with the surgeons, while others with water and sponges wet the stiff bandages."[23] There were not enough nurses; patrols were sent into the streets looking for any servants they could impress into service.

The normal services of the city were disrupted frequently. One lady's letter advised a friend that it was impossible to write for a while, for no mails were going out of Richmond. "The post office clerks are in the trenches."[24] There were good times too, even in an overall deteriorating situation; their own army was close. As conditions permitted, droves of veterans came into Richmond on pass or furlough. Those known to the city were well received and treated to rounds of social events or were simply accepted back into their

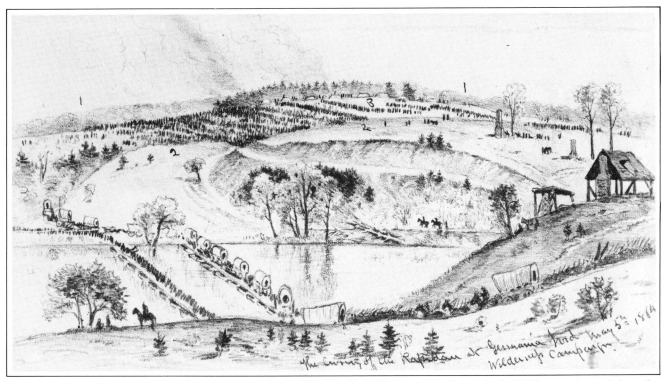

Grant moves south. The Army of the Potomac crosses the Rapidan, May 5, 1864, to attack Lee's army in the Wilderness. A month later they had fought their way to the outskirts of Richmond, but Lee's army stood betweem them and the city. *Library of Congress*

families for a needed rest. What little food people had they shared with the veterans.

By this time Richmond was well known for its beautiful women. Ardent "rebels" who had come as refugees from northern Virginia and Maryland swelled the city's numbers of lovely girls. Courting resumed; there were calls at homes, walks along the James, and as the months went by, numerous weddings. Life eased briefly as food prices fell, for the close proximity of the Federals and their constant raiding forced farmers to bring in their produce "lest the Bluebellies get it."

Midsummer brought a brief time of victory. People exulted over the exploits of General Jubal Early and his men who won a series of lightning victories in the Valley of Virginia and in Maryland. One lady wrote a friend, "Early and his force frightened all Yankeedom out of its wits, threatened Washington . . . and are now back before Lincoln, Seward and Co. have quite opened their eyes. . . ."[25] Relief was short, however, for early September brought another catastrophe. Atlanta, not only the rail center of much of the South, but also with irreplaceable machine shops and foundries, had fallen to General Sherman's army. He was now free to ravage all of Georgia, the largest "breadbasket" that remained to the Confederacy.

With this loss and other conquests to the west and south, Richmond was more than ever the hub of the shrinking Confederacy. Its streets were filled with straining mule teams, guns and caissons, and marching columns of men shifting to new locations in the miles of defense works. One day Wade Hampton's cavalry brigades passed through the city going north, each trooper laughing and joking on horseback—and eating watermelon.

Late September saw a very heavy attack against Fort Harrison, the vital anchor to the whole defense system on the northside of the James River, about eight miles south of Richmond. Fort Harrison fell, and it looked like this time the city was gone. Strong counter strokes, personally directed by Lee, failed. While he eventually avoided the loss of Richmond by building a new defense line west of Fort Harrison, Richmond had undergone another intense period of strain. Patrols swept the streets again, arresting all white males between the ages of 17 and 65 for duty in the trenches. Thousands were herded to the arsenal or taken inside Capitol Square, issued weapons and marched under guard to the front. Among those caught in the dragnet were two Confederate cabinet ministers, the Postmaster General and the Attorney General. As soon as identified, they were released.

This was the year's final burst of heavy fighting; it finished quietly with the besieging army encircling Richmond and Petersburg. A lady's diary contains a passage which encapsulated the city's travail. "Every Sunday Mr. Minnegerode (the pastor) cries aloud in anguish his litany, from 'pestilence and famine, battle, murder and sudden death' and we wail (back) on our

A drawing of a Union forward base at Point of Rocks in 1864 showing supply ships, mule-teamed wagons and a pontoon bridge. Tonnages of supplies, food and ammunition were shipped directly from northeast ports and Washington and then transported to bases of the Army of the James for its attack against Richmond.
Library of Congress

The siege of Richmond during the summer of 1864. Miles of rifle pits (trenches) with shelter halfs (canvas) stretched across to protect the men from the sun.
Library of Congress

knees, 'Good Lord deliver us,' and on Monday, and all the week long, we go on as before, hearing nothing but battle, murder and sudden death, which are daily events."[26]

Admiral Semmes, the former captain of the Confederate cruiser *Alabama*, was shocked when he returned to Richmond in late 1864, his first visit since 1861. He realized that the Confederacy was now very close to defeat. After talking to the leaders, he saw that President Davis refused to accept the truth, but that General Lee understood. With a heavy heart he assumed command of the James River Squadron, the last fleet of the Confederacy, and prepared for a final stand in the spring.

The Unthinkable Happens— 1865

The last winter of the war "rushed by with lightning speed," wrote one of Richmond's belles.[27] Well she might think so, for she was part of the frenetic gaiety that occupied the evenings of the young people in the upper levels of society. One social event followed another. Such "partying" struck many elders like dancing on the edge of the grave. Nevertheless General Lee had given his approval to social events attended by his men. Military men came in nightly from General Longstreet's nearby front, the trenches on the northside of James River, and some rode back through the early morning darkness to face wounds or death.

Though few would admit it openly, many sensed the end was very close. Now there was no point in worrying about tomorrow; life was reduced to daily survival. People spent Confederate currency as fast as it came into their hands, the money becoming more worthless with each passing hour. One barrel of flour cost $1,000, if one could find it to buy. "Robberies were fearfully on the increase."[28] Some devout parishioners stayed home from Sunday services in order to guard diminishing stores of food, firewood and coal. All but a few of the very well-to-do organized small family or mess groups just to get by. The city as a social organism was in its last spasm.

Bereft of reasonable hope, some clung with blind faith to the belief that General Lee and the army would somehow save them. It still stood unbeaten in the miles of frozen trenches that surrounded Richmond and Petersburg, but the severe shortages of food, shoes and clothing, as well as the constant attrition of trench warfare, were wasting its combat power and mobility. Desertions had greatly increased. Each night some of the men crept over to the Yankee trenches and surrendered, but most stayed to see the matter through to the end.

Richmond became the only major city left to the Confederacy. Savannah was now gone; General Sherman had presented it to President Lincoln as a Christmas present. Charleston, birthplace of secession, had been abandoned as Sherman's army moved north. As winter stretched on, the Confederacy shrank to a smaller and smaller circle around Richmond. Fort Fisher and Wilmington fell, closing the South's last open port; soon afterwards Wilmington became a Federal base for raids into the interior towards Raleigh. Eastern Tennessee and the western Old Dominion were savaged by raiding Union cavalry. Having burned out the Valley of Virginia, General Sheridan, the hardest hitting of Grant's generals, turned his forces east to

Union fleet sailing from the Chesapeake Bay into the stormy Atlantic, bound for an attack on Fort Fisher. The fort fell on January 15, 1865, closing Wilmington, N.C., the last Confederate port.
Library of Congress

tighten the circle around Richmond. Near the end of the winter General Sherman's army paused in central North Carolina. Richmond, once the capital of a country, was now no more than a city state.

To those within the city, there were other signs that the end was near. As was her custom, Mrs. Lee sent her husband a bag of socks she, her family and friends had knitted for the soldiers. The General's note back from his Petersburg headquarters advised her, "You will have to send down your offerings as soon as you can and bring your work to a close, for I think General Grant will move against us soon. . . . No man can tell what may be the result."[29]

During March, the government began preparing to abandon Richmond, though by now there was almost no place left for it to go. Government files, machinery from the arsenal, stores of one kind or another which were not immediately needed were taken to the depots. The public heard with some alarm that if the city were to fall, the military planned to burn the tobacco warehouses and military storehouses to prevent their capture. When Congress adjourned the month before, legislators told friends they never expected to return. Private citizens packed up and departed with their families for some safer location. By the end of March, Mrs. Davis and her family quietly took the Danville train, leaving the doomed city, and placing some belongings and mementos to be sold in several Main Street stores.

General Lee was described as looking "dispirited and wretched." No doubt he was gravely worried about the condition of his men. In March he wrote the pastors of the city, asking that they and their parishioners go into the countryside to search for food for the army. He told them there were less than ten days rations left. Another worry concerned the condition of the horses and mules. Their forage had been so lean, he believed they could no longer haul the wagons and guns in active campaigning. Nevertheless, the General made a major attack that month at Hare's Hill near Petersburg, a final effort to break out of the encircling Federal lines. After initial success and the temporary capture of Fort Steadman, Lee's men were driven back to their trenches. The initiative now lay with General Grant; the stage was set for the final moves.

During the last days of March, General Grant marshalled two army corps under General Sheridan against Lee's overextended right flank south of Petersburg near the muddy crossroads of Five Forks, and heavy fighting began. Surprisingly, back in Richmond people remained unaware of a crisis. The papers, too, were ignorant of events. Against all reason, the public was optimistic. For once there seemed to be no rumors of trouble. People reassured one another that with good weather coming, General Johnston's army in North Carolina would soon join General Lee at Richmond. Together, they would attack General Grant and reverse the precarious situation.

Late on Saturday, the first of April, General Sheridan, attacking in rain and miserable weather, broke through the defenders at Five Forks. The Confederates fell back in disorder; large numbers were captured. With Lee's flank destroyed, General Grant ordered a general attack early the next morning against the lines of Petersburg itself. In the dawn of April 2, the Federal army overran the Petersburg lines in three locations. The damage could not be restored. Now began the two most terrifying days in Richmond's history.

Evacuation Day April 2, 1865

After such a rainy March, Sunday, April 2, dawned beautifully in Richmond. The sky was cloudless, the air balmy and the sun warming for the first time that year. Such a glorious day brought people into the streets and to their churches. At St. Paul's the President, slender, erect and austere, sat in his pew on the main aisle. During the service, an usher passed him a message. Mr. Davis got up quietly and left the church, and an "ominous fear fell upon all hearts."[30] The services were hastened to a close, and the emerging people joined others on street corners where they learned that Lee's lines had been broken, and Richmond would be evacuated that day! The news was verified; General Longstreet, whose corps was positioned closest to the city, had received marching orders. Unbelievably, their de-

Federal infantry in the trenches of the Richmond-Petersburg lines in early 1865.

As the siege wore on, elaborate trench systems surrounded Richmond and Petersburg.

National Archives

fenders were about to leave them. It was difficult to accept, but slowly the conviction settled "upon the stricken people that the four year struggle was nearing its end."[31]

The sabbath quiet vanished. With both the government and the army departing that day, the authorities had to do everything at once. Quartermaster wagons, known as "Jeff Davis's musical boxes" because of the uproar they made in the streets, careened by at a gallop, bearing freight, archives and even the gold reserves to the Richmond and Danville Depot, the last rail line open to the outside world. Clerks carried files into the streets and set fire to the papers. Taking their wagons and some artillery, the military marched away from the city during the afternoon. The first units passed in good order; then the men became less orderly; finally there were only stragglers and looters left. Since the last trains were reserved for government officials and essential freight, ordinary people escaped in their own buggies, drays and wagons. Many left on foot to the west, carrying bundles on the canal towpath.

In the afternoon the banks opened so that owners of valuables could retrieve them before the Yankees arrived. People didn't bother with the Confederate money and bonds; the streets near the banks were littered with them. Instead, worried people took jewelry, hoards of Federal currency, deeds, household plate and stock certificates and buried their valuables in boxes under bushes or in basements, hid them in furniture or stuffed them into secret places in their clothing. This allowed some to emerge from the general economic wreckage with a stake for the future.

Pandemonium continued throughout the day and during the night. Those choosing to remain in Richmond spent the night watching the disorder from their windows. Once the troops left all public order vanished. The authorities had tried to destroy liquor supplies, breaking the casks open in the streets and letting the liquor run off through the gutters. However, people gathered immediately; some scooped up what they could in buckets while others simply drank from the gutters. Soon hundreds were drunk. A roaring mob roamed the dark streets downtown, plundering warehouses, commissaries, private shops, stores and offices throughout the commercial district.

In the early hours of the morning a more ominous element was added to this turmoil—fire. Either the military or looters had fired several tobacco warehouses south of Cary Street. A breeze from the southeast fanned the flames to nearby buildings; soon the fire was out of control and spreading through the business district. The citizens watched helplessly, for with the disappearance of all authority nobody was available to put it out, and someone had sabotaged the firefighting equipment by cutting the hoses.

Just before daylight a large powder magazine on the northern slopes of Shockoe Hill was detonated. An enormous blast shook the city, shattering windows, rocking buldings and knocking people in the streets to the pavement. By this time there was only the mob in the streets; prudent citizens were behind locked doors at home. But all were wide awake, terrified by the events of the night and the possibilities of the next day.

Early in the morning of April 3, General Grant, in pursuit of General Lee, sent a wire to General Weitzel, the commander of forces left behind near Chafin's Bluff, about nine miles directly south of Richmond, ordering him to occupy Richmond, establish guards and preserve order.

In the early morning hours General Weitzel's troops were awake and excited. They had heard a series of shattering explosions as the big ironclads of the James River Squadron had been blown up by the Confederates near Chafin's Bluff to prevent their capture. All could see the reflections of fires in the sky above Richmond and hear the sounds of occasional detonations. Just after daylight, the Bluecoats moved safely past Lee's Outer Defense Line, around and through the abandoned fortifications. The infantry, about 12,000 officers and men, were formed into two columns, moving north on Richmond primarily by the Osborn and New Market Roads. Ahead of the main body a small

Union troopers from the 4th Massachusettes Cavalry ride into Capitol Square somewhat after 7:00 A.M. April 3, 1865.
Virginia Historical Society

detachment of horsemen from the 4th Massachusetts Cavalry moved as advance guard. With them rode one of Weitzel's staff officers, Major A. H. Stevens.

Moving at a fast trot, the advance guard arrived near the junction of the Osborn and New Market Roads, about three miles from the city. At about 6:30 A.M. they encountered Mayor Mayo and a few of the city officials in an old carriage. The mayor dismounted and handed Major Stevens a brief note. It read:

"To the General commanding the United States Army in front of Richmond.

General,

The Army of the Confederate Government having abandoned the City of Richmond, I respectfully request that you will take possession of it with an organized force, to preserve order and protect women and children and property.

Richmond, April 3, 1865

    Respectfully,

    Joseph Mayo, Mayor"[32]

Major General Godfrey Weitzel—Bavarian immigrant, West Point graduate and Ohio citizen—who led the Union forces that occupied Richmond the morning of April 3, 1865.
Virginia Historical Society

Major Stevens accepted the surrender, then continued on with the Blue cavalry into the city, riding west on Main Street. The riders turned north into Governor Street, then dismounted at their destination, Capitol Square, the unmistakable symbol of the Confederacy. As their first official act a soldier or two climbed up on the Capitol roof and pulled down the "Stars and Bars." Having no Federal flag with them, they ran up two of their cavalry guidons. It was not much after 7:00 A.M.

The masses of the Union infantry had been held on the southern outskirts of Richmond near Chimborazo Hill until about this time to keep the troops in order. Now they too entered the city, mostly using the same route as the advance guard. The citizens would never forget their first sight of the Federals as they reached the center of the city on Main, Franklin and Broad Streets. "(They) gaped in wonder at the splendidly equipped army . . . the beautiful sunlight flashed everywhere from Yankee bayonets."[33] Crowds of blacks pushed into the streets, sometimes falling on their knees, hailing the soldiers, many of whom were black themselves, as their deliverers, at times almost halting their columns.

For those devoted to the South it was indeed a moment which reached beyond sadness. Watching from her window in agony, one woman asked herself, "Was it to this end that we had fought and starved and gone naked and cold, to this end that our homes were in ruins, our state devastated?"[34]

On the Union side the triumph was nearly spoiled for lack of time to enjoy it. When General Weitzel arrived at the Capitol, about 8:15 A.M., he quickly received Mayor Mayo's second surrender, then devoted his whole attention to putting out the fire. By this time the city "was wrapped in a cloud of the densest smoke through which great tongues of flames leaped in madness to the skies. A few houses on the higher hills, a spire here and there half smothered in smoke . . . were the only buildings that could be seen. . . ." Thousands of shells were bursting with an enormous roar in the burning arsenal or arching over the city and falling on helpless homes. "Fanned by a southeast breeze . . . the fire shot up in great pyramids, and curled up and nestled down on roofs."[35] The business district was gone, and the advancing flames were but a block from the Square itself. It looked like the whole city must burn.

The lead Federal infantry brigade swung into Capitol Square shortly after General Weitzel arrived, and after stacking arms, was committed immediately against the fire, supported by an engineer company. Once the trace of a proper firebreak was determined, the troops, reinforced by more men as they arrived, began to pull down walls and dynamite houses. Mean-

Lt. Livingston De Peyster, an aide to General Weitzel, hoisted a U.S. flag that had flown over occupied New Orleans over the Capitol—the first national flag to fly in Richmond in four years.
Virginia Historical Society

while, citizens made homeless by the fire crowded together on the open space of the Square. Soldiers assisted in guarding their bundles of belongings.

About midafternoon the fire was under control. It had been close, but the wind died, and the firebreaks had succeeded in containing the flames. The embers smoldered on for several days. Once people were able to return to the burned-out area, the devastation was so complete they could not locate their stores or homes; sometimes it was difficult to find traces of their own streets. About 700 buildings had burned, leaving a black ruin from Main Street to the James River. The banks, the best shops, all the newspaper offices, stores, warehouses, most of the government storage depots, offices and industrial buildings—all were gone with the exception of the Confederate Treasury building, the Tredegar Iron Works and the Spottswood Hotel. One citizen saw a good side to the fire. It had destroyed the buildings of "the principal speculators and extortioners." To him it was "like a decree from above."[36]

The next day dawned on a strange city—occupied Richmond. Those who ventured out found the Yankees in the streets and at their headquarters at City Hall well behaved. Ladies who were obliged to approach them for food, for many families were destitute, were met with politeness: "What do you wish, Madam?" But their courtesy rankled, the Southern ladies would almost have preferred rudeness.

With the arrival of the Union camp followers the

streets presented unbelievable sights. One woman paraded about, dressed wholly in U.S. flags. Sutlers immediately opened business in tents or rented stores mostly along Broad Street, since Main Street had been gutted. The currency was greenbacks only. Enjoying their new freedom, hundreds of blacks were in the streets. Northern newsmen, war artists, photographers like Mathew Brady, even sightseers had tagged along with the victors. Less visible were some Confederate ladies who, for one reason or other, had to go out. Heavily veiled, dressed in black but curious too, one lady expressed her feelings to a friend, "I've nearly broken my back holding such a high head. . . ."[37]

On lawns and porches of many of the homes on Franklin and other streets were Union sentries furnishing protection to those who requested it. Other than guards, provost marshal troops and officers with business in the city, the Bluecoats were gone. All other units had moved into former Confederate camps outside the city, generally along the Inner Defense Line at such places as Church Hill, Camp Lee, Monrovia and Manchester, which was garrisoned in strength to block a possible Confederate return from the southwest.

About midmorning a tall, angular figure wearing a top hat walked up Main Street. President Lincoln, anxious to see the rebel capital, had made the dangerous passage by ship, the *Malvern*, passing safely through the sandbars and among the mines and obstacle-infested currents, past the now silent forts at Drewry's and Chafin's Bluffs and past the wreckage of the Confederate ironclads. Nearing the city, the *Malvern* ran aground, and Mr. Lincoln finished the trip in a naval barge rowed by a crew of sailors. Undefended except for this crew, he landed at Rocketts, then walked up Main Street towards Capitol Square. Holding his son, Tad, by the hand he paused occasionally and mopped his forehead with a handkerchief. Somewhere near the Square the President was recognized by a startled cavalryman, who galloped off to tell his commander.

Mr. Lincoln was then taken by carriage to the Confederate White House to meet General Weitzel who was occupying the place as temporary living quarters. After lunch and a brief meeting with two former Confederate officials, the President toured the city with General Weitzel. Among other places, they stopped at Libby Prison. Late in the afternoon Mr. Lincoln returned to the *Malvern*, and the next day the ship and the President were gone, nine days before his assassination.

The next afternoon, April 9, the townspeople heard cannon firing salutes from the star forts outside Manchester. Someone asked a sentry what had happened. He told them that General Lee had surrendered his army at Appomattox. Gloom and despondency settled upon the city. Five days later, on April 14, the day President Lincoln was shot, General Lee and a small group of his officers rode into Richmond across the Federal bridge from Manchester. In the midst of a spring downpour, people gathered to watch him. For Richmond, and General Lee too, the great and terrible years were finished.

Occupied Richmond—a Federal soldier wanders about the ruins.

National Archives

How to Use this Guide

Richmond is growing and changing fast, but a number of its important and fine buildings from the years of the War Between the States are still to be seen. Where many have vanished due to time and new construction, the sites where they once stood often are still identified.

With this Guide, these buildings and sites are easy to find. Turn to the map on the following pages. The Tour and its directions are marked by an arrow. Along this tour route are circled numbers, each marking the location of an old building or site where something special or interesting happened.

The system is simple. For example, choose a circled number on the map, then turn directly to the same number in the text. These numbers are not difficult to find; they appear in heavy print and run consecutively. You can also find the same number on the left hand side of the Table of Contents. Here you receive a page reference.

It is suggested that you read the book first and select the areas which most interest you. Then, rather than attempt the entire tour at one time which can be fatiguing, begin with a segment or two of the tour of your choice. Drive these areas slowly, taking enough time to absorb and discuss what you see as you go along. Reading before you go will add greatly to your enjoyment.

Since the Tour is arranged geographically, the stories which enliven and explain each location are not in chronological order. For this reason a Chronology of Events occurring inside and outside wartime Richmond is included in the Appendix.

GENERAL LEE'S CITY

MAP 5

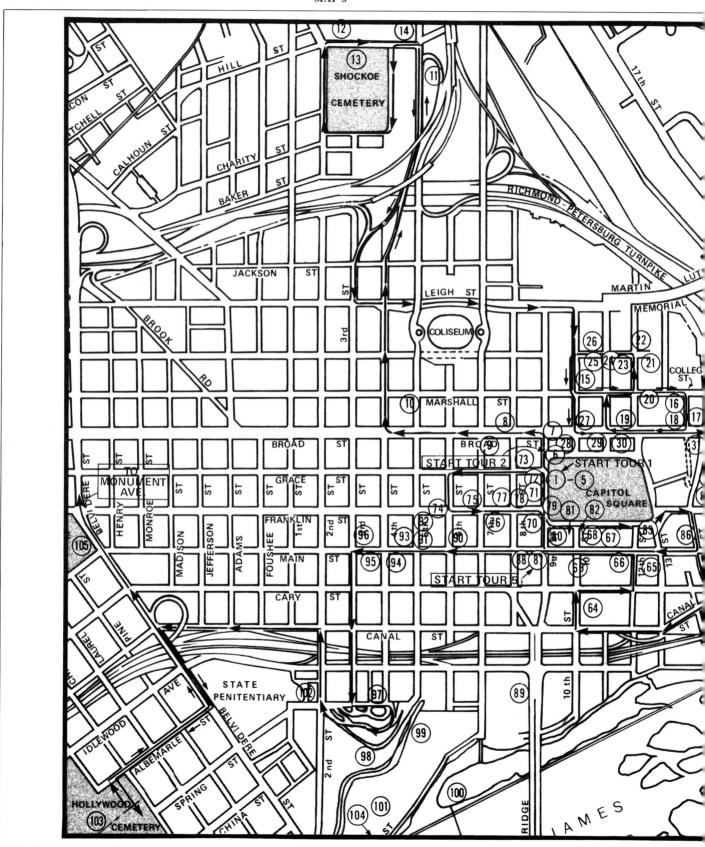

Current Map of Richmond with Complete Tour. Routes for all five tours showing all numbered sites; the start of each tour is indicated. Some retracing of direction is necessary due to one-way streets in the city.

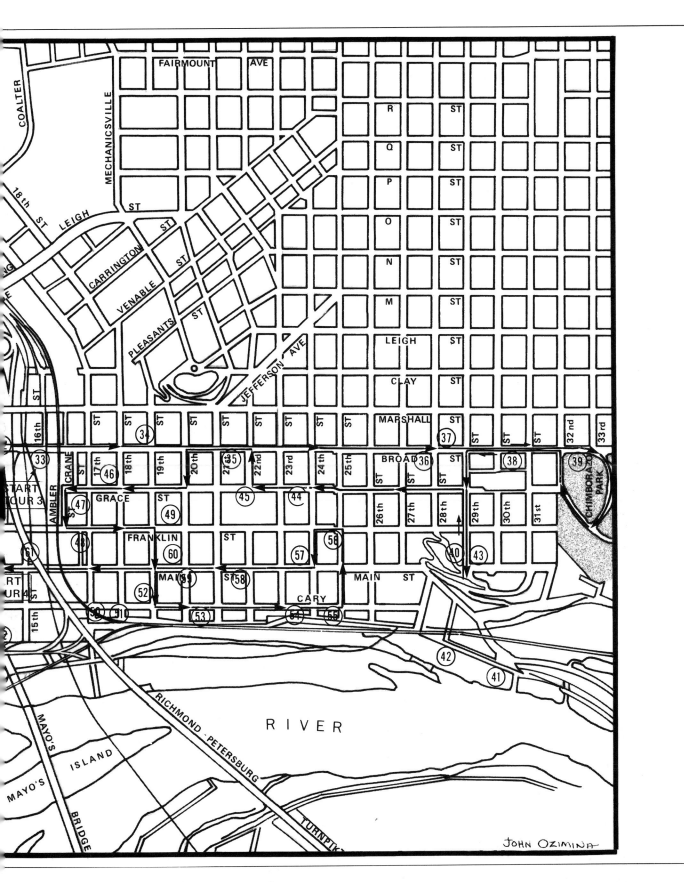

Traffic Engineering, City of Richmond

FIRST TOUR

Capitol Square

To see Capitol Square properly, take the time to walk its tree-lined paths and visit the historic buildings if they are open, especially the Capitol. Since you cannot park inside the square, leave your car at a nearby parking lot. If you plan to pick up the second segment of the tour after your visit to Capitol Square, one of the lots in nearby Franklin Street would be a convenient location.

Capitol Square is the only part of the tour where you walk; the remaining four segments will be done by car.

GENERAL LEE'S CITY

MAP 6

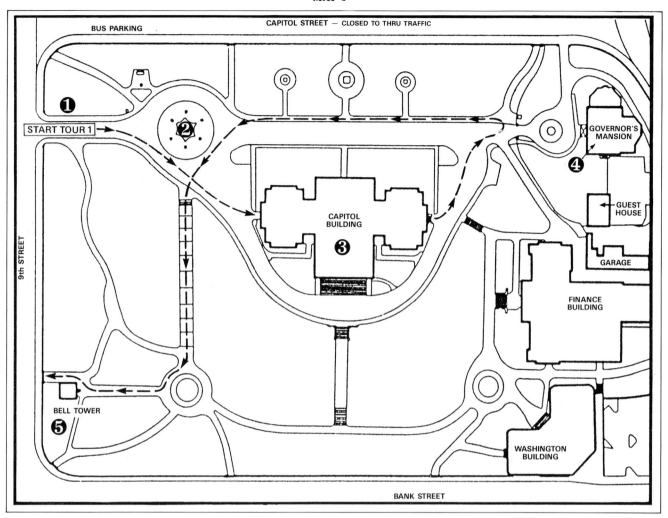

First Tour—Capitol Square.

1.
Capitol Square

Capitol Square dates from the late 18th century and is a striking park of vivid green lawns under an umbrella of tall old trees. The entry to the symbolic heart of the Confederacy is at 9th and Grace Streets. Ahead stands one of Thomas Jefferson's architectural masterpieces, the Capitol of Virginia—modeled after a Roman temple found in France, the Maison Carrée. Closer stands a statue of George Washington flanked by figures of other famous Virginians. To the south of the entrance is the historic Bell Tower and on the eastern side of the Square is the early 19th-century Governor's Mansion.

With the arrival of pleasant weather in mid-April 1861, the customary band concerts at the Square had begun. But some old friends were not speaking to one another on their daily strolls in the Square, for the Union was breaking up. Later in the spring, Richmond found herself the capital of the new Confederacy, and soon its Congress began meeting at Jefferson's old Capitol. On April 17, 1861, the "Stars and Stripes" fluttered to the ground and was replaced by the "Stars and Bars."

By early June a flood of new regiments had arrived, filling the quiet old city with a new and fierce excitement. Nearly all of them, at one time or another, paraded proudly through Capitol Square, which to them symbolized the essence of their new country. They were strange young men from faraway places: wealthy ones from South Carolina with their own body servants; Louisiana Zouaves in red, floppy trousers; Texans in buckskin, and many more, each one intensely proud of his own state heritage and consumed by dedication to the new cause. President Davis had arrived in late May from Montgomery, Alabama, and by fall it was customary to see his slender, erect figure walking briskly through the Square on his way to and from his office on Bank Street.

Less than a year later Richmond lay under siege. Over 125,000 Union soldiers were gathered for an attack on the city, a little over seven miles to the east. Fighting had been steady all spring, and Capitol Square echoed daily to the strains of "Saul's Dead March" as the remains of fallen officers and men passed down 9th Street on their way to Hollywood Cemetery. Day and night, ambulances and wagons bore the wounded past the green lawns to tobacco warehouses and other makeshift hospitals. Then came the Seven Days Battles, with heavy cannon and rifle fire echoing loudly through the sylvan spaces of the Square. The Governor of Virginia and his friends watched the fighting from the Capitol's flat roof; although they could see very little except the drifting smoke and flashes of exploding shells. Yet it was the coolest spot in the city by far.

By June 1863, the war was taking its toll. Mrs. Mary Chestnut and a friend sat on the great steps of the Capitol, deep in grief over the death of Frank Hampton, a close family friend who had been killed at Brandy Station. They had just been inside the Capitol to view his remains which lay in state, and now after the escort had taken the body for burial, they talked of the

Mary Boykin Chestnut (1833–1886) kept a detailed diary during the war, much of it about her life in Richmond. *Valentine Museum*

This picture taken from an upper floor of the Spottswood Hotel shows the center of Richmond shortly after the Evacuation Fire. At 9th Street, Bank Street divides the burned buildings from the lawns and trees of Capitol Square. *Valentine Museum*

After the news of victory at Manassas, July 21, 1861, Richmonders gathered at Capitol Square to join in a celebration marked by a salute of 100 rounds from artillery positioned on the Square.
Virginia State Library

old, happy days. But death was everywhere now, and their world had been "knocked to pieces."[38]

One year later, scenes at the Square reflected the ever deepening crisis. On a warm day in March, several hundred exchanged prisoners were feted in Capitol Square. The President presided; the people brought baskets of food, and a large crowd cheered, "Hurrah for the Graybacks!" But as one lady who stood close, looking straight into the prisoners' faces, wrote: ". . . so forlorn, they were so dried up and shrunken, with such a strange look in . . . their eyes; others so restless and wild looking; others again placidly vacant. . . ."[39] The signs were unmistakable; the strain was becoming too great.

When the end of the war came on April 3, 1865, Capitol Square was again the center of events. Richmond lay open at last. Citizens who had come to the Square that morning were incredulous as a Blue cavalry patrol galloped into the Square from Capitol Street and then slowly raised their flag up the flagpole on the Capitol roof. Shortly there was no time to ponder anything but personal survival. A great fire, started the night before, was advancing to the very edge of the Square. When all seemed lost, Union infantrymen stacked their arms in the Square and began to battle the advancing wall of flame. The courthouse on the southeast portion of the Square went up in flames, and people saw the Confederate War Department on 9th Street "send up jets of flame as it crumbled amid a swirl of papers."[40] On the lawns thousands of people, driven from their homes by the flames, huddled together, paying little attention to the Union troops all around them. The air in the Square was like a furnace—a brisk wind blowing the smoke and sparks into the crowds of refugees.

Eventually, the Union troops were successful in creating a firebreak. Once there was assurance that the Square and everything in it was not doomed, Union sutlers (peddlers who followed the armies and sold their goods to the soldiers) set up their tents on the lawns to display their wares. People crowded around, but few had Federal currency. As it had been the heart of the Confederacy, the Square became the hub of the military occupation of the city.

2.
The George Washington Statue

This imposing statue can be found a few yards directly east of the Grace Street entrance to Capitol Square.

"It's no use, the horses can't pull it up Main Street Hill!"[41] The crowd looked in frustration at the heavy, crated statue of the first President, recently arrived at Rocketts from England. Someone called out, "Let's pull it to Capitol Hill ourselves!" Since long ropes were easily available in this seaport town, several thousand men and boys, working in relays, pulled and pushed the statue up Main, then north up 9th Street. After removing a section of the iron fence at the Grace Street entrance to Capitol Square and chopping down several trees, the crowd finally pushed the statue to its appointed place just west of the Capitol building. People felt that they had participated in a special event in Richmond's history. Several months later, on February 22, 1858, the statue of Washington on horseback was dedicated commemorating the day of his birth.

The sculptor of the Washington statue was Thomas Crawford, an Englishman who did the work in London. People declared that the finest horse in Queen Victoria's stables was used as a model for the President's horse, and that the face of the great man looked exactly like that of the Houdon statue on display within the nearby Capitol. Some have observed that the equestrian statue verged on the overdramatic with George Washington's outstretched arm pointing south and his face apparently convulsed with anger. During the war an irate Confederate senator, addressing his colleagues in the Senate chamber about alleged wrongdoing by some of them, referred to the statue outside and declared it should be a warning—for the father of his country was pointing directly at the State Penitentiary.

FIRST TOUR—CAPITOL SQUARE

The George Washington Monument from the east in 1866. The Capitol building did not have its present two wings. *Virginia State Library*

A Mathew Brady photograph of the Virginia Capitol as the building appeared in April 1865, spared from the Evacuation Fire. General Weitzel stands on the platform beneath the pillars as he receives Mayor Mayo's surrender, directs his troops to put out the fire and assumes control of the city.

National Archives

3.
The Virginia State Capitol

Thomas Jefferson planned the Capitol, whose cornerstone was laid in 1785 as the centerpiece of the Square, placing it on high ground in the north central portion. Its white columns and walls offer a pleasing contrast to the verdant bushes, lawns and fine trees surrounding it. More than any other building in the South it symbolized the very heart of the Confederacy; it was the meeting place of the Confederate Congress throughout the war.

On April 22, 1861, Governor Lecher of Virginia and Alexander Stephens, the new Vice President of the Confederacy, formally escorted Colonel Robert E. Lee into the House of Delegates Chamber. The assembled House rose to its feet to do him honor, for he came with the highest reputation as a soldier and also was the scion of one of Virginia's most important families. Where his statue now stands, Colonel Lee accepted the rank of major general and the command of the military and naval forces of Virginia.

February 22, 1862, George Washington's birthday, marked the inauguration of the first and only Confederate president, Jefferson Davis. It was a dismal, rainy day. One of Richmond's loveliest belles watched the proceedings from an upper window of the Capitol. She saw the Square beneath her as a sea of umbrellas with the ceremonies on a platform just east of the Washington Monument. At the appointed moment, Jefferson Davis took the oath of office and kissed the Bible. Few in the crowd were close enough to hear the inaugural address above the pelting rain, but they admired the calm, dignified bearing of the President. "God bless our President," was heard as Davis accepted, "under God, a great trust of our struggling nation."[42]

Slightly more than a year passed, and again the Capitol became the center of a momentous event. On May 12, 1863, crowds gathered in the square to mourn the passing of General Lee's "strong right arm," Stonewall Jackson. He had died of wounds suffered at Chancellorsville. Truly, "a wail went up from every Southern heart . . . with the crushing news."[43] Following a profoundly sad and impressive funeral parade down Main Street, the coffin was borne up the Capitol steps and into the House of Delegates Chamber. Here it rested on an altar of white linen in front of the Speaker's chair. After the funeral and for the rest of the day, thousands of people passed through the hall to pay their final respects. The General lay wrapped in the new white banner of the Confederacy with its cross of stars upon his breast.

Of the many other events that occurred at the Capitol, none was more moving than the fall of Richmond on April 3, 1865. Suddenly the Bluecoats were there in the South's "Holy of Holies." As soon as General Godfrey Weitzel, commanding the Union 25th Corps, entered the city, he rode directly to the Capitol. For a time he established his command post on the platform of the Capitol, at the entrance above the steps. From here he directed his forces fighting the advancing fire. As soon as the Capitol building was safe, he established the headquarters of the occupation at the Hall of Delegates.

The next day President Lincoln arrived in Richmond after a hazardous trip up the James River past numerous obstacles and torpedoes. He visited the Hall of Delegates among other places but left no record of what he saw. One of his companions, Admiral Porter, remembered . . . "only dreadful disorder in the room with Confederate script and . . . documents lying on the floor."[44]

This statue of General Lee stands at the spot in the old Hall of the Virginia General Assembly where Lee accepted command of the military forces of Virginia. Although shown in full uniform, he was wearing civilian clothes at the time. *Virginia State Library*

GENERAL LEE'S CITY

4.
The Governor's Mansion

Situated on the northeast portion of Capitol Square near the corner of Governor and Capitol Streets, this mansion, a replacement for a more modest frame house for Virginia governors, has housed the state's chief executives since 1814. The two Confederate governors to occupy it between 1861 and 1865 were John Lecher and William "Extra-Billy" Smith. The latter acquired his nickname when he was a contractor for the delivery of the U.S. mail; he was endlessly asking the authorities for extra awards of money.

The Governor's Mansion was the setting for many official events during the war, yet many Richmonders of that time remembered it best as the place where Stonewall Jackson's body lay his last night in Richmond. The body of the hero arrived from Guinea's Station at the depot at Broad and 8th Streets about 5:00 P.M. on May 11, 1863. Businesses had closed, and the casket was carried past mourning throngs to the Reception Hall of the Governor's Mansion where it lay that night awaiting the ceremonial funeral at the Capitol the next day. Although the Mansion was closed to the public, a few prominent Richmond ladies did gain entrance to view the body. Among them, Constance Cary came late in the evening. She left a record of what she saw: "Two sentries paced to and fro in the moonlight streaming through the . . . windows. . . . A lamp burned dimly at one end of the hall, but we saw distinctly the regular white outline of the quiet face in its dreamless slumber."[45]

Mathew Brady took this picture of the Governor's Mansion in April 1865, probably a few days after Governor "Extra-Billy" Smith fled on horseback along the towpath to the west.

National Archives

FIRST TOUR—CAPITOL SQUARE

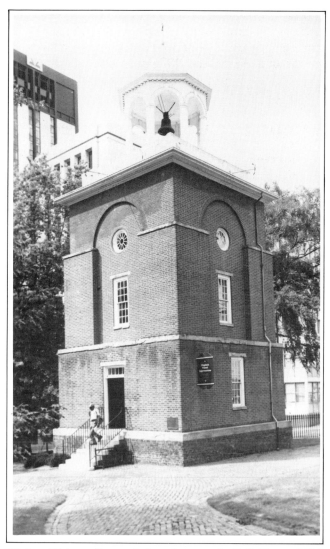

Vital to Richmond even before the war, the Bell Tower (1824) served as a fire alarm, marked the hours and announced both happy and sad occasions. During the war, its most feared sound—three short strokes, a pause, then three more—was an emergency call to war in the dead of night. The militia, volunteers and reserves rushed from their beds to form ranks in the Square.

Virginia Historic Landmarks

5.
The Bell Tower

The Bell Tower, built in 1824, is located on the western border of Capitol Square facing Franklin Street. Its bell rung by hand, was sounded for all Richmond's main events, which were often fires. During the war it was the alarm signal of the enemy's approach and signaled the mobilization of the city's defense forces. Everyone recognized the tocsin—three quick taps—a brief interval, three more taps, etc.

April 21, 1861 began as a perfect spring Sunday morning. The churches were full. At nearby St. Paul's, Dr. Minnigerode was intoning the first lesson of the Book of Job, "I will remove far from you the Northern Army, and will drive them into a land bare and desolate. . . ."[46] Suddenly the dreaded tocsin sounded. Everyone rushed into the streets—the U.S. warship *Pawnee* was reported steaming up the James toward the city's port of Rocketts. From there her four guns could destroy the city at leisure. After initial panic the local militia and citizens too hurried the mile or more eastward down Main Street to Rocketts. Here they occupied Church and Chimborazo Hills preparing such weapons as they had. It all proved a false alarm; the *Pawnee* never came. The occasion is remembered as "Pawnee Sunday."

Sustained Union pressure against Richmond caused everyone to listen with half an ear for the Tower's alarm bell, and as hostilities continued they heard it more and more frequently. On a day in May 1863, Mrs. Mary Chestnut heard its clamor, and shortly thereafter the sound of cannonfire. It proved to be Union General George Stoneman and a division of cavalry raiders probing the fortifications along the Brooke Turnpike. A woman of noted equanimity, she lost her head this time and burned part of her diary. Her maid, Molly, equally frightened, had pleaded for her to burn up everything so her writings wouldn't end up in the newspaper.

By the spring of 1864 the alarm bell became a daily fact of life. General Grant's army was pounding ceaselessly at Lee's smaller forces in battles that ranged from the Wilderness (west of Fredericksburg) to the city's defenses. At this time the local reserves consisted of a clerk's battalion from the government offices, a battalion or two of armorers and artificers from the Tredegar and other ironworks and arsenals, some convalescent soldiers from the hospitals and volunteer units of patriotic civilians. These men were generally used to shore up some weak sector of defense until Lee's regular forces had time to arrive and take over. Theirs was a cold, dirty and exhausting business, and always in the back of their minds was the fear that once they returned to Richmond, they would simply be called out again with little opportunity to clean up or rest.

At the time of surrender on April 3, 1865, it was the Union side that rang the Tower bell. When the Federals arrived in Richmond, they were confronted by a raging fire that threatened to destroy the entire city. A Union Provost Marshal and one of the first to arrive, quickly learned the signal and rang the tocsin. Five city firemen responded, reporting that all the firehoses had been cut. He committed the arriving Union brigades to fight the fire, avoiding total destruction.

SECOND TOUR

Broad Street, Shockoe Hill and Court End

Pick up your car from the parking lot and drive north up 9th Street past the entrance to Capitol Square. Just past the iron railings marking the northern limits of the Square, you will see a broad, paved walkway. This is former Capitol Street, and you are in position to begin this part of the tour.

MAP 7

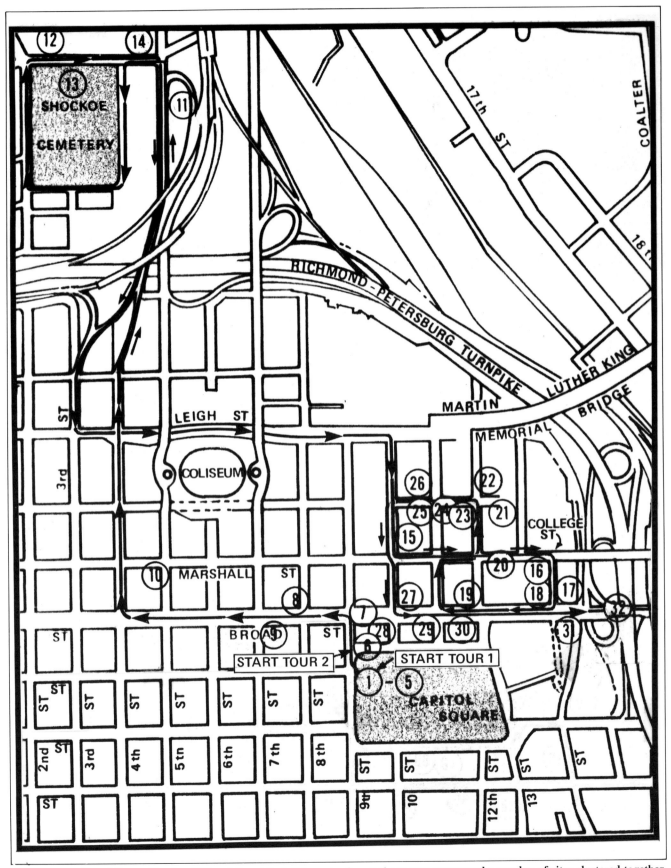

Second Tour—Broad Street, Shockoe Hill and Court End. Take note of several one-way streets and a number of sites clustered together.

SECOND TOUR—BROAD STREET, SHOCKOE HILL AND COURT END

6.
Confederate Government Stables

At the corner of 9th and Capitol Streets, look to the right. Between 9th and 10th, Capitol Street was used as a Government Stable for over 100 riding horses and some additional ambulance horses, all under the control of the Military Department of Richmond. The horses were frequently used by staff officers and government officials in the Richmond area.

It was the morning of April 2, 1865, the day Confederate troops evacuated Richmond. Mrs. Ella Snyder was busy at her household chores when her crying children ran in with the dreadful news that a soldier had just taken George, the family carriage horse, from his stable. George was a noble animal with a glossy black coat, the best horse in the well-to-do neighborhood of 4th Street and Gamble's Hill.

Mrs. Snyder promptly put on her bonnet and set out for the corner of 6th and Franklin Streets, the location of the Headquarters of the Military Department of Richmond. She found the commander, Lt. General Richard Ewell, hard-pressed with arrangements for withdrawing his forces from the city that night. Busy as he was, he took the time to see her. Surprisingly, in view of the army's urgent need for horses, he agreed she should have her horse back, wrote her a note to that effect, and sent an orderly along to help her. They confronted the officer in charge of the Stables with her demand for George. The note succeeded where she alone surely would have failed, and miraculously George was still there on a picket line, most pleased to see his mistress in these strange surroundings. She returned home in triumph to Gamble's Hill with George in tow, a heroine to her overjoyed children.

7.
Broad Street

From 9th Street turn left into Broad Street, going west. Broad Street, the widest street in wartime Richmond, was just starting its transition from a residential to a commercial street. As the main street leading to the west and north, it was of strategic importance; along its length were two of the city's main rail depots, the Virginia Central and the Richmond, Fredericksburg and Potomac. In 1861, the tracks of the latter ran down the middle of Broad Street from the west as far as 8th Street.

On fine spring afternoons in the first year of the war, it was fashionable for Richmond's ladies to drive by carriage on Broad Street to Camp Lee, which lay about a mile to the west of the city. They enjoyed watching the troops drill, engage in sham battle, and sometimes attended parades and receptions. On one such afternoon, Mrs. Chestnut and Mrs. Stannard were on their way out Broad Street when a fine looking officer rode his horse up beside them and conversed for a spell. He sat his horse gracefully and when introduced seemed to know Mrs. Chestnut. But she did not catch his name and couldn't identify the man. After the officer had bowed and ridden on ahead, she asked Mrs. Stannard who he was. "You ought to know" she responded, "why it is Robert E. Lee."

In late summer of 1862, Garnett Wolsely, an English officer visiting the South at the time, saw the captured saddle of Yankee General John Pope displayed in a

Lt. General Richard S. Ewell ("Old Bald Head"), exhausted from the exertions of field command, was transferred by Lee to command the Military Department of Richmond in early June 1864. After serving for nearly a year, he led his men in the evacuation of the city on April 2, 1865 and was captured at Sayler's Creek.
Virginia State Library

shop window on Broad Street. He and all Richmond were vastly amused by this significant capture, because everyone knew that Pope, recently defeated by General Lee's forces in the Battle of Second Manassas, liked to date his orders to his troops from his "headquarters in the saddle." Word had drifted through the lines that President Lincoln had remarked that "he hoped General Pope's headquarters were not where his hindquarters ought to be."[47]

8.
The Richmond, Fredericksburg and Potomac Railway Depot

Look to your right at the northwest corner of Broad and 8th Streets. During the war the depot stood here and the tracks ran down the center of Broad Street to the west, then north. Both the depot and tracks have long disappeared from this site. This important railroad ran about 50 miles directly north to the area of Fredericksburg, where several of the largest and most important battles of the war were fought.

The people of Richmond became accustomed to seeing large numbers of troops, many of them leaving loved ones, entrain here for the fighting zones. One man wrote of these mostly sad and anxious moments: Once the cars were loaded with men, "the wood burning locomotive hissed and snorted, belching clouds of resinous smoke and a shower of sparks. A clank and clatter of link and pin couplings ran down the line of cars. The driving wheels spun for a moment, then bit into the sanded rails; the train pulled slowly away into the darkness."[48] Sometimes, the troops serenaded the ladies as they drew away, singing some tuneful song popular at the time—such as "Lorena" or "Kathleen Mavourneen."

On the evening of December 13, 1862 many people lingered at the depot. They had heard the steady, distant cannon firing all that day coming from Fredericksburg, ominous and distinct above the buzz and clamor of the city. Crowds stood for hours in Broad Street as hospital trains brought in the wounded from the great battle. They watched hundreds of half-frozen, wretched men, filthy and covered with bandages, being unloaded from the cars under the flickering light of pine torches. Some noticed the sheeted bodies of Generals Gregg and Cobb borne out and taken to the Capitol to lie in state. All the city's ambulances, hacks and omnibuses had been requisitioned to distribute the men to the various hospitals. Although a great victory

Broad Street Depot in 1865. Opposite, a train waits in the middle of Broad Street. Trains from this station departed north towards Fredericksburg.
Virginia State Library

=== SECOND TOUR—BROAD STREET, SHOCKOE HILL AND COURT END ===

The Richmond Theater, opened to the public on February 9, 1863, was an active center for plays and refined entertainment for Richmonders during the war.
Virginia State Library

had been won—the Federals were said to have left 10,000 dead on the field—exaltation mixed with grief and despair as people realized that the Union army had escaped once again.

9.
The Richmond Theater

On your left, located on the southeast corner of Broad and 7th Streets is the site of the long since demolished Richmond Theater. Its predecessor, the Marshall Theater, had burned down in January 1862, but was quickly replaced by a "new and gorgeous temple of Thespis," which opened to the public February 9, 1863.

The facade of the new Richmond Theater was "pleasing and impressive." A row of classical pilasters began at the second story and went almost to the top of the building. "A lobby entered by several doors from Broad Street led . . . to the orchestra and to the parquet. There were two or three galeries . . . , the first and dress circle seeming to lead almost under the ceiling. On each side of the stage were tiers of boxes, three on a side."[49]

One evening shortly after the theater had reopened with a play in progress, the audience was interrupted by the clatter of hoofs outside and the shouting of commands. Soon gray clad cavalrymen came noisily down the aisles, sabres clanking. In a few moments they had located some soldiers, arrested them and taken them outside.

Two days later the city heard the rest of the story. General Jeb Stuart's Cavalry Corps was camped near the city. He had discovered that some of his troops were visiting the city without leave, especially the theater. He sent a patrol to rectify a disciplinary problem, but there were repercussions! General Winder, Provost Marshal in charge of the city, was not about to let Stuart use force in his territory. In a brusque note to Stuart, he threatened Stuart's arrest if he repeated his raids into the city. Stuart promptly replied that he would patrol the streets that very evening with 30 horsemen in search of his absent men, and that "Winder might arrest him if he could."[50] The sound of hoofs and jingling spurs was loud in the empty streets of Richmond that night, but General Winder's men were not to be seen.

St. James Church, shown here in the late 19th century, was at the southwest corner of Marshall and 5th Streets. When the congregation moved to West Franklin Street in the early 20th century, the church was demolished. *Virginia State Library*

10.
St. James Episcopal Church

Continue west on Broad Street and turn right on 4th Street. As you pass Marshall Street, be aware that on the southwest corner of 5th and Marshall, one block east, is the site where St. James Episcopal Church once stood. The church was similar to a small Roman temple; its parishioners thought it an appealing and intimate place to worship.

There were many soldiers' funerals at St. James. Surely the most famous, and perhaps the one with the largest impact on the city, was the funeral of the South's cavalier, Major General Jeb Stuart on May 14, 1864. He was mortally wounded three days before at nearby Yellow Tavern, seeking to block an attack by the Union General Sheridan, who, with a force of 13,000 veteran cavalrymen, was trying to break into Richmond. Stuart's stalwart defense had probably saved Richmond for the moment, but at the cost of his life.

Jefferson Davis and the principal officers of the government attended the funeral as did large crowds of citizens, most of whom were obliged to stand outside. Later Stuart's remains were borne by a hearse pulled by four plumed white horses through rain-drenched streets to Hollywood Cemetery. Onlookers noticed that the customary military band and infantry escort were absent. People understood that no one could be spared, since every available soldier was in the trenches as Sheridan continued to probe for weaknesses in Richmond's defense lines. At one point he had broken through the outer line near the Brooke Turnpike, but he was held on the intermediate line. Everyone realized that if this aggressive Bluecoat found a gap, he could stable his horses in Richmond that night.

11.
The Powder Magazine

Several blocks north of Marhsall Street, 4th Street swings right and becomes 5th Street. About 30 yards this side of the intersection of 5th and Hospital Streets to your right and perhaps 50 yards off the road is the site of the city Powder Magazine. Road construction has altered the appearance of the site which used to be located in a ravine. The Confederate Ordnance Department used this repository outside the city to store large quantitites of gunpowder and explosives too dangerous to keep at the Confederate Laboratory (powder loading plant) on Brown's Island near the arsenal. The magazine was a 20 by 30 foot brick building with a low slate roof surrounded by a strong brick wall.

In the blackness just before dawn on April 3, 1865, the retreating Confederates blew up the magazine, a blast "that seemed to startle the very earth."[51] Buildings swayed, people were knocked down in the streets and thousands of window panes were shattered. It was another signal that the end of resistance had come.

A few miles to the south, the Union infantry were marching fast toward the city on the New Market and Osborn Roads. To their commanders, the explosions confirmed that the city was being abandoned—a welcome sign. Passing through Manchester, elements of the Confederate rear guard heard the blast and turned in their saddles to see the pyrotechnics in the sky.

A clerk of the Confederate War Department, John Jones, visited the site of the magazine the next day. He saw the building had been reduced to powder and only a narrow trench remained. The small City Hospital and Poor House was also destroyed by the blast. Eleven residents who had not heeded the request of the authorities to leave were killed.

The City Alms House, built just before the war, was one of the first buildings allocated for a hospital by the Confederate authorities. It served as General Hospital No. 1 until December 1864, when it became the barracks of the VMI cadets. A rare view of wartime Shockoe Cemetery is in the foreground. *Library of Congress*

SECOND TOUR—BROAD STREET, SHOCKOE HILL AND COURT END

12.
City Alms House

From 5th Street turn left into Hospital Street, then left again into 4th Street at the first intersection. The City Hospital and Poor House, mentioned above, was located about 30 yards from Hospital Street on the left side of 4th as you drive south. Keeping the brick wall of Shockoe Cemetery on your right, go around the block, occupied entirely by the cemetery until you are facing east on Hospital Street, the right direction to continue the tour.

On your left in the middle of the block is the City Alms House, a large, four-story, red brick structure built just before the war. Situated outside of the city limits, it was originally intended for use as a poor house but, early in the war the City Council had rented it to the Confederate government as a military hospital. Known as General Hospital No. 1, it was used during the summer of 1861 to house Union prisoners wounded and captured at First Manassas. Through December 1864 it held mostly Confederate wounded and sick men, though some Federal prisoners continued to be treated here.

The winter of 1864 proved a cold one, and during that frigid December the City Council was searching for housing for a very special purpose. The VMI cadets were homeless, since the Federal army under General Hunter had burned the Virginia Military Institute at Lexington to the ground, no doubt in retaliation for the part the cadets had played in the defeat of General Sigel's force at Newmarket the previous May. In that action some 56 cadets and their famous professor, Stonewall Jackson, had been indispensable in the halcyon days of 1861 in training the new Confederate army in the Richmond camps of instruction.

The cadets had been brought to Richmond in May 1864, and were being housed temporarily in tents at Camp Lee. In a special ceremony, President Davis had reviewed them on the Capitol grounds, praised their victory at Newmarket and declared that they were the "seed corn of the Confederacy."[52] Governor Smith then presented the cadets with a new stand of colors; the old ones had been shot full of holes. A band played the Corps to its new quarters at the City Alms House on Shockoe Hill with a lilting Irish quickstep:

> *"There's not a trade that's going,*
> *Worth showing or knowing*
> *Like that from glory growing*
> *For the 'bowld' soldier boy."*[53]

13.
Shockoe Cemetery

After you pass the City Alms House, look for an open gate on the right leading into the Shockoe Cemetery. You can drive in and park if you wish to look around. The attendants can help you locate graves of Richmond citizens like Chief Justice Marshall. From here the tour continues east on Hospital Street.

In 1820 the Richmond City Council purchased four acres of land outside town and high on Shockoe Hill for this cemetery, which contains the remains of some Revolutionary War soldiers and many soldiers of the 1861–65 war. Some of Richmond's notables, such as Joseph Mayo, the city's wartime Mayor, are also buried here. In fact you will see graves that comprise a whole array of important Richmond and Virginia 19th-century families.

South of the entrance gate to the left is a large marker indicating the graves of 577 Union and 220 Confederate soldiers who died directly across the street at the City Alms House (General Hospital No. 1). Hundreds of other soldiers are buried here without any markers at all, those of whose burial no records were kept.

In the center of the oldest part of the cemetery is the grave of one of the most controversial figures of wartime Richmond, Miss Elizabeth Van Lew. Her life and death symbolized the deeply felt tensions and bitterness generated by the war in people on both sides. She was the fearless and vigorous leader of the Union network of spies in Richmond who throughout much of the war sent much valuable information through the lines to Federal commanders. Ostracized from Richmond society for nearly 40 years, she died on August 25, 1900 and went to her grave in Shockoe Cemetery without a single mourner. For a time no stone stood over her neglected grave. Eventually, admirers living in Boston placed a pudding stone over her grave which contains the following inscription:

> *"She risked everything that is dear to man—friends, fortune, comfort, health, life itself—all for the one absorbing desire of her heart, that slavery might be abolished and the Union preserved."*[54]

Miss Elizabeth Van Lew as she looked when she organized and led a Union spy network in Richmond. *Virginia State Library*

=SECOND TOUR—BROAD STREET, SHOCKOE HILL AND COURT END=

The military sections of the Hebrew Cemetery where Jews who served in the Confederate forces are buried. Located across Hospital Street from Shockoe Cemetery, the northern borders of the cemetery provided a view of the fighting near Mechanicsville on June 26, 1862.

Susan C. Lee

14.
Hebrew Cemetery— Shockoe Hill

Continue on Hospital Street to the east. The Hebrew Cemetery, opened in 1816, is on your left as you pass 4th Street. Of special interest is the Confederate Section where lie the remains of Confederates of the Jewish faith. Around it is a beautiful cast-iron fence of crossed sabres and stacked rifles.

After an early dinner at his Clay Street home on June 26, 1862, John Jones, a War Department clerk, decided to watch his first battle. He walked through the warm June afternoon a few blocks north to the bluffs of Shockoe Hill, joining a small crowd just north of the Hebrew Cemetery. They stood on high ground with a fine view to the north and east as they waited for the battle to begin. General Lee's "surprise" attack against the Federal right flank at Mechanicsville was an open secret in Richmond that day.

During the afternoon the crowd could hear distinctly the regimental bands, fifes and drums of General A. P. Hill's Light Division as it took assault positions near the Meadow Bridge, about four miles to the northeast. About 3:00 P.M. they heard Hill's attack begin. The noise of the cannon fire mounted into a loud, continuous roar, and through it could be heard the firing of thousands of rifles, that sounded like "driving hail."[55] Jones remained riveted at the scene as the battle continued into the night, and Richmond's skyline was brilliantly lit by the flash of the guns and the exploding shells. About nine the firing died down and he with many others, wandered the streets trying to find out which side had won.

The Richmond Female Institute, erected in the Italian villa style, was a boarding school for some 250 teenage girls. *Library of Congress*

15.
Richmond Female Institute

At the corner of Hospital and 5th Streets turn right (south) and continue more than a quarter of a mile on this road that becomes 3rd Street to the corner of 3rd Street and Leigh. Turn left, following Leigh under an underpass to 10th Street. Turn right into 10th, go nearly two blocks and look to your left just before you turn left into Marshall Street. About 20 yards north of the intersection on the east side of 10th Street is the site of the Richmond Female Institute. A bronze marker on the wall of the present building identifies the school's location.

During the exciting spring of 1861 it was evident that the girls at Richmond Female Institute were ardent secessionists. On March 14, 1861, the first Confederate flag was flown over Richmond from one of the school's towers. Two South Carolina girls were responsible, and the Institute's president, the Reverend Charles Winston, had it removed promptly. Unrepentant, the young ladies ran it up again the next day—with identical results.

During the winter of 1862–63 classes were suspended when the building was required as a military hospital for wounded junior officers. After the severe fighting at Chancellorsville, the Institute (then called General Hospital No. 4) was crowded with battle casualties. The volume of wounded had exhausted medical supplies in the Richmond area; the Union blockade of southern ports prevented more from getting through. Consequently the primary medicine used was a coarse, simple diet. When visitors commented on the scarcities, the young men invariably responded, "Never mind; this will do. It is indeed very good."[56]

In June of 1864 the hospital was full again, this time a consequence of General Grant's powerful offensive against the city. An epidemic of pyaemia (pus in the blood) struck the wards, "a most malignant disease" in the words of the time, "for which a specific cure has yet to be found. . . . In this disease the virus that should be discharged by suppuration is disseminated through the circulatory system, causing chills, and soon death intervenes."[57] The situation deteriorated so severely that the institute took on the appearance of a charnel house. As a last resort all the patients were removed to the City Alms House (General Hospital No. 1). Here the disease disappeared quickly, although no one knew why. However many of the patients had died—an irreplaceable loss, for these were courageous, young, motivated officers that Lee could not do without.

The Egyptian Building. Built in 1845, this building was a major departure from Richmond's Greek Revival architecture. Still used by the Medical College of Virginia, this building is the oldest medical college edifice in the South. *Virginia Historic Landmarks*

the midst of their medical studies underlines how strongly the people of the North and South were coming to feel about the issues dividing them.

16.
The Egyptian Building

From 10th Street, turn left on Marshall Street and drive a little more than three blocks. To the right on the southwest corner of Marshall and College Streets is the Egyptian Building, which housed the Medical College of Virginia during the war. Designed by Thomas Stewart, the same architect who built St. Paul's Church, it was completed in 1845—a 19th-century attempt to create an Egyptian temple. One historian calls it the finest piece of Egyptian architecture in this country. Notice the unique cast-iron fence that uses replicas of mummy cases as fence posts.

The building served a vital purpose; it was the only medical college in the Confederacy that remained open for the four war years. Some 333 doctors graduated between 1859 and 1865, and these were the men who provided much of the invaluable medical service for the Confederacy.

Shortly after John Brown's raid at Harpers Ferry (October 1859), 144 southern medical students at the University of Pennsylvania's Jefferson School of Medicine, led by Doctor Hunter Holmes McGuire (later chief surgeon of Stonewall Jackson's Corps) transferred to the Medical College of Virginia. Their departure in

17.
The First African Baptist Church

Turn right from Marshall into College Street. On your left at the next intersection, College and Broad Streets, is the site of a wartime church for blacks where both religious and civic events were held. In 1870 the old church was torn down and replaced by the Victorian church you see today.

It was February 7, 1865—an intensely cold day with four inches of snow on the ground. Lee's frozen, starved army huddled in the trenches outside Petersburg and Richmond. The Confederate leadership had called a public meeting at the African Church, which could accommodate sizeable numbers. In desperation the government had sent peace commissioners to talk to President Lincoln on board the *Malvern*, at anchor at Hampton Roads. They had just returned empty-handed. Mr. Lincoln had demanded the Confederate States must lay down their arms and return to the Union before the fighting could stop.

His terms were rejected with scorn at the meeting. One speaker denounced Mr. Lincoln, referring to him as "His Majesty, Abraham the First."[58] President Davis gave perhaps his finest speech in a lifetime of oratory. Even his political enemies said he worked a "strange pity, his worn gray clothes, his stricken, careworn face." Whenever he paused, the crowd chanted, "Go on! go on!" He answered them "with a smile of singular sweetness," and cheering shook the rafters.[59] In spite of his brave words Mr. Davis must have realized the end was near. Fifty-five days later Federal troops were tramping into Richmond.

18.
The Old Monumental Church

Turn right from College into Broad Street. The Old Monumental Church stands on the northwest corner of College and Broad Streets to your right.

Completed in 1814 on the site of a disastrous theater fire where 72 lives were lost, the Monumental Church was designed in the classic style by Robert Mills, for a time architect of the U.S. Capitol in Washington. Its denomination was determined because more Episcopalians bought pews than members of any other Protestant faith. As a boy, Edgar Allan Poe sat in the Allan pew on Sunday, and one parishioner remembered him as "a wistful-eyed lad with chestnut ringlets."[60]

On the evening of April 3, 1865, the day Richmond fell, Miss Constance Cary walked to services at the Old Monumental Church. While the rector was praying for the sick and wounded soldiers, she recalled "there was a sound of weeping all over the church." A hymn, "When Gathering Clouds Around I View," was sung, but there was no organ accompaniment. The voice leading the singing faltered; another took up the lead and then broke down too. Miss Cary stood up and alone sang the hymn to the end. When she reached the passage, "Though Savior see'st the tears I shed," sobs swept the congregation.

Miss Cary later wrote, "I wanted to break down dreadfully, but I held on and carried the hymn to the end." As she left the church, many people came up and squeezed her hand, tried to speak, but could not. Just then, a large Federal band passed by, swinging up Broad Street. She noticed its "fine uniforms and blaring, cheerful music." After the scene in the church, it seemed "a mockery of the shabby congregation" clustered around her on the way to their homes.[61]

The First African Baptist Church was located on the corner of College and Broad Streets. It was large enough to be used for important civic as well as religious purposes.
Virginia State Library

============ SECOND TOUR—BROAD STREET, SHOCKOE HILL AND COURT END ============

Brady photograph of the Old Monumental Church in 1865. Located on Broad Street at College, this historic building survives in a district that has seen a number of old buildings like City Hall torn down.
National Archives

19.
The First Baptist Church

Continue on Broad past 12th Street. On the northwest corner of Broad and 12th Streets rises the First Baptist Church, a severe and beautiful example of the Greek Revival style, built in 1841. Its architect was Thomas U. Walter, who also designed the new dome and wings of the U.S. Capitol in Washington.

A number of Confederate wounded were brought to the church and cared for by the ladies of the congregation after the battle of Seven Pines (May 31, 1862), a few miles east of Richmond on the Williamsburg Road.

Mr. John Thomas, Jr., a parishioner, listened in growing consternation at Sunday services the morning of April 4, 1862, as a resolution was adopted by the church membership which formally offered the church's bronze bell to the Confederate government to be recast into cannon. After some days of conflict between his patriotic and religious convictions, Mr. Thomas called on the Secretary of War. The two soon reached an understanding that if Mr. Thomas provided an agreed upon amount in gold coins, the bell could be retained by the church. He complied, and the bell continued to serve its religious purpose.

In the late 19th century the First Baptist congregation moved to a new church at the corner of Boulevard and Monument Avenues, taking Mr. Thomas's cherished bell along. There it remains in the churchyard with a plaque describing its history.

The First Baptist Church. Although no longer used by its congregation, who relocated in 1938, the church (built in 1841) stands as a severe and beautiful example of the Greek Revival style.
Virginia Historic Landmarks

67

Jefferson Davis, President of the Confederacy. Gifted, stubborn and sometimes wrong-headed, he nevertheless held the Confederacy together for four years. Castigated by many Southerners by the war's end, his ill-treatment in Federal prison at Fortress Monroe restored his popularity throughout the South.

National Archives

SECOND TOUR—BROAD STREET, SHOCKOE HILL AND COURT END

20.
Twelfth Street

Turn right at the corner of 11th and Broad Streets, go one block to Marshall; turn right again retracing one block of Marshall Street, then turn left on 12th and drive one block to Clay Street. (Detour caused by 12th Street being one way to the south between Broad and Marshall Streets.)

Twelfth Street was the route customarily taken by the Davis family between the Confederate White House and Capitol Square. The President normally walked to and from work. Since his office was in the old U.S. Customs House on Bank Street, just to the south of the Square, people became accustomed to seeing him striding along with an erect military posture.

On the morning of his last day in Richmond, Sunday, April 2, 1865, Mr. Davis had breakfast at the White House, read through some reports, then walked down 12th Street toward the Square. After a time of rain and disagreeable weather, a delightful, balmy day suddenly had come to Richmond. Davis graciously exchanged sabbath greetings and lifted his hat to the ladies. Pausing briefly at the War Department to obtain the latest news from the front, he strolled into St. Paul's at 9th and Grace Streets. During services a note was handed to him that the Petersburg lines had been broken, and that General Lee must retreat that night. By midnight Jefferson Davis was a fugitive, leading a government in exile by train to Danville.

21.
The Confederate White House

As you approach the corner of 12th and Clay Streets, look right at the southeast corner, the location of the Confederate White House. Just to its south on the mansion grounds is the Confederate Museum, which displays part of its priceless collection of uniforms, weapons and memorabilia of Confederate leaders.

This fine Greek Revival mansion stands high on the northeastern tip of Shockoe Hill. Designed by Robert Mills of South Carolina for Dr. John Brockenbrough and finished in 1818, it was leased to the Confederate government for the use of President and Mrs. Davis. They lived here throughout the war.

After the Davises moved in during August 1861, levees were normally held every fortnight, a Washington custom. Mr. Davis would generally pass through the parlors, cordially extending his hand to each guest and saying, "I am glad to meet you here tonight." Anyone could come. On one of these evenings, Mr. Davis heard the comment that "every Southerner was equal to three Yankees at least." He responded, ". . . it will be a long war . . . only fools doubted the courage of the Yankees . . . and now we have stung their pride, we have aroused them until they will fight like devils. . . ."[62]

One pleasant spring evening, Mrs. Chestnut went to the President's House and found the family still at supper. She waited outside on the marble front steps and listened to General Elzey "tell us how things stood." At the moment Union General Stoneman's cavalry raid was moving on Richmond, and there were no reserves to check them. After a time Mrs. Davis came out and the two ladies chatted. "It is dreadful," Mrs. Chestnut said, "the enemy is within 40 miles of us—only 40." "Who told you that tale?" asked Varina Davis. "They are within three miles of Richmond!" Mrs. Chestnut dropped to her knees "like a stone."[63]

January 1864 brought some strange occurrences to the first family. On the 9th the President's manservant, Jim, and Mrs. Davis's maid ran away. On the 19th a reception was held, during which an attempt was made to burn the house down. A fire had been kindled in a woodpile in the basement. Smoke led to its discovery in time; meanwhile two more servants escaped to the North, and the mansion was robbed—all in the same night. People were inclined to blame "Yankee plotters"—and with cause, for Miss Van Lew was later known to be involved.

In late March 1865, with the end approaching, President Davis insisted on sending his wife and children to a place of greater safety, fearing Richmond faced the

A photograph by Mathew Brady of the Confederate White House as it looked in 1865. *National Archives*

dangers of a siege. Varina Davis dreaded the idea of separation from her husband. She lamented . . . "selling all the pretty little pieces of china, cabinet glasses, sandlewood boxes, cardracks, little pictures, etc., of which each one is a dear memorial of former happiness. My exquisite silver too must go, and last . . . all of my wardrobe not immediately necessary to me. . . . I am in the agonies of packing and disposing of my earthly treasures here."[64]

A few days later, the evening of April 2, it was the President's turn to go; Richmond would fall the next morning. He instructed the housekeeper to surrender the house to the Federal troop commander who would capture the city. He walked slowly through the rooms for the last time, looking here and there, glancing at the fine furniture and lingering to finger mementos and bric-a-brac Varina had collected. His aide, Burton Harrison, helped him pack a small dressing case and a large valise. At the last moment he slipped into them two small photographs—one of Varina and the other of General Lee. Also included were four pistols and a box of ammunition, for he was determined to continue the struggle. Then he left abruptly for Danville Station.

The next morning, not 12 hours after Mr. Davis had gone, the Union commanding general of the occupation force, Major General Godfrey Weitzel, who started life in the United States as a German immigrant, moved into the mansion. The following day he had an unexpected visitor. A Union trooper, patrolling the streets, gasped as he saw a tall, thin man in black clothes walking up Main Street with a long, careless stride, looking about with an interested air and taking everything in. "Is that Old Abe?"[65] the trooper cried, then wheeled his horse, galloping towards Weitzel's headquarters in the Capitol building. It was indeed, and he had probably walked most of the way from the landing at Rocketts, trailed by a cheering throng of blacks.

Once at the White House, the President rested for a moment at a desk in the drawing room. "This must have been President Davis's chair," he speculated, looking out the window with a strange, reflective gaze. Then he jumped up. "Let's go!" he said in a boyish voice, "Let's look at the house."[66] He did so, then had lunch. That afternoon he went sightseeing around the city in a carriage, visiting among other places the Confederate Capitol and Libby Prison.

Illustration from Frank Leslie's Illustrated Newspaper, April 29, 1865, showing President Lincoln's visit to the Confederate White House.
Virginia State Library

SECOND TOUR—BROAD STREET, SHOCKOE HILL AND COURT END

Photograph of Abraham Lincoln taken by Alexander Gardner in Washington, April 10, 1865, six days after Lincoln visited Richmond and four days before his death. It shows a slightly smiling President—his only known smiling photograph. *National Archives*

GENERAL LEE'S CITY

The corners of 12th and Clay Streets. The photograph, taken near the Executive Mansion, shows the sentry box for the President's military guard, and across 12th Street, the Bruce-Lancaster Home where Senator Semmes of Alabama lived. Some memorable wartime social events occurred here: one evening Jeb Stuart in full uniform acted in a tableaux vivant. *Library of Congress*

22.
Corners of 12th and Clay Streets

After seeing the Confederate White House and the Confederate Museum, take a moment to stop at the intersection of Clay and 12th Streets. Except for the vacant northeast corner, the other quadrants held fine mansions. On the northwest corner was the Bruce Lancaster Home where Senator Semmes of Alabama lived during the war. During 1861–62 Alexander Stevens, Vice President of the Confederacy, rented two rooms in this building. On the southwest corner, directly west of the Executive Mansion, was the Booker Home. The gracious entertaining that went on in these mansions marked the area as one of the social centers of wartime Richmond.

The Bookers and other well-to-do families along Clay Street offered open hospitality to soldiers and young officers, especially during the early part of the war when good food and fine wines were still available. Since their son was a member of the Richmond Howitzers, they were anxious to share their meals with servicemen. Young soldiers from more humble origins remember that the table was always set with snowy damask, elegant china, sparkling glassware and handsome silver, all under a glittering chandelier.

For a time in 1862 Mrs. Chestnut rented one of these fine homes. Her diary contains a story about her entertaining. "Friends came to make taffy and stayed the livelong day," she wrote. "They played cards. One man, a soldier, had only two teeth, one left in the upper front and one in the lower—and they overlapped across each other. On account of the condition of his mouth, he had maintained a dignified sobriety . . . though he told some funny stories. Finally a story was too much for him, and he grinned from ear to ear. (One of the young girls) Maggie gazed, and then called out as the negro fiddlers call out dancing figures, 'Forward two and cross over!' Fancy our faces!"[67]

Some of wartime Richmond's more notable parties, balls and charades were held in the Semmes home. The end of the parlor was turned into a stage, for charades and pantomimes were the rage. At one of these events, Jeb Stuart played a role in full uniform—to the delight of Richmond's belles.

The house where Maury's first experiments took place—in a washtub in his third floor bedroom. A marker commemorating the event can be seen on the front wall at 1105 Clay Street.
Virginia State Library

72

SECOND TOUR—BROAD STREET, SHOCKOE HILL AND COURT END

Matthew Fontaine Maury, one of America's distinguished scientists in the mid-19th century, invented an electrically-detonated, floating mine for the Confederacy.
Virginia Public Library

23.
The Maury House

Driving west on Clay Street, you will find this house on the left side in mid-block at 1105 East Clay Street between 12th and 11th Streets.

During the spring and summer of 1861, one of America's most distinguished scientists, Captain Matthew Fontaine Maury, lived here for a time in the home of his cousin, Robert H. Maury, a Richmond broker. A former U.S. naval officer, Captain Maury made important discoveries concerning the influences of tides and winds on sea navigation. These findings led to changes in shipping routes worldwide, greatly increasing the safety of ships at sea.

As a Southerner devoted to Virginia, Maury offered his services to the Confederacy in the spring of 1861. While waiting to assume the post of "Chief of the River, Harbor and Coast Defenses," he began experiments in the third floor front room of this house with the idea of inventing an electrically fired, submerged torpedo. Miss Belle Maury recalled that the servants hauled tubs of water up to the room. The Tredegar Iron Works provided a water tank, and batteries were loaned by the Richmond Medical College. His first efforts were to explode small charges of gunpowder under water with an electrical current. By early summer, Maury was far enough along for trials on the James River near Rocketts.

In Washington, the U.S. Navy was also experimenting with a submersible, electrically powered torpedo. A trial was held at Washington Navy Yard attended by Gideon Wells, the Secretary of the Navy. The guidance system went awry. One torpedo blew up a nearby schooner riding at anchor; another exploded off-course on a sandbar. The U.S. Navy gave up.

Although Captain Maury did not discover a moving torpedo, he did invent a naval mine that could be detonated by an electric current passing through a wire from the shore. This device proved most valuable for the defense of Richmond and other southern ports. The combination of cannon batteries on shore, Maury's mines and ships sunk in the channel were enough to block the Union fleet in its attempts to steam up the James River to the Confederate capital.

The James Caskie House where Mrs. Robert E. Lee lived for a time after arriving in Richmond in 1862. Hard to recognize because of the store front now superimposed on its facade, the house was built in the early 19th century by Judge John Brockenbrough.
Susan C. Lee

24.
The James Caskie House

As you approach the southeast corner of 11th and Clay Streets, notice the old building on this lot which now bears a store front. It was the James Caskie home. Mrs. Robert E. Lee stayed for a time in this house as a guest of the Caskie family during the first year she spent in wartime Richmond (1862).

We know of Mrs. Lee's travels after hostilities began in May 1861, when she left Arlington House, across the Potomac River from Washington, D.C. Staying with

Major General George B. McClellan, commander of the Army of the Potomac during its 1862 offensive against Richmond.

Virginia State Library

friends or on family properties, she gradually moved south. By early 1862 she was staying at White House, one of the family plantations on the Pamunkey River, and feeling fairly secure from Federal encroachments. However, by mid-spring the very wharves and fields of White House became the main Northern logistics base for General McClellan's attack on Richmond.

Though the courteous Federals offered to protect her with an escort, she did not want "the Bluecoats buzzing around her ears."[68] She decided to leave, but not before posting a note on the front door of White House which read:

> "Northern soldiers who profess to reverence Washington, forbear to desecrate the home of his first married life, the property of his wife, now owned by her descendants."[69]

Moving in an old carriage, she stayed with friends and was forced ever closer by the advancing Federals toward the Confederate lines. Mrs. Lee finally decided to come into Richmond. General Lee, who had recently arrived from duties in Georgia, arranged with General McClellan, the Northern commander, to enable her to pass through the lines.

On the appointed day she arrived at General McClellan's headquarters (Trent House) in her old carriage, where she was received with great courtesy. Some say she had lunch with the Northern commander. Then a cavalry detail escorted her carriage to the Meadow Bridge where she was passed through the lines. Her waiting husband welcomed her, the first time he had seen her in 15 months. It must have been a shock for him. She had aged and was so crippled by arthritis she could barely walk.

In spite of Mrs. Lee's note, White House was burned to the ground after she left it.

25.
The Wickham-Valentine House

On the left at the southwest corner of 11th and Clay Streets, you will see one of the handsomest mansions of wartime Richmond. Probably designed by Robert Mills, the house was built in 1812 for John Wickham, the lawyer who represented Aaron Burr when he was tried and acquitted of treason against the United States. Its owner during the war was James G. Brooks who entertained Confederate congressmen and senators in his home. In the 1880s Mann S. Valentine II bought the mansion, and his collection of books and manuscripts provided the basis for the outstanding Valentine Library and Museum there today. As the collection grew, the three adjoining houses to the west were bought to hold it. The owner's brother, Edward Virginius Valentine, was the gifted sculptor who executed the recumbent statue of General Lee, now resting in the chapel of Washington and Lee College in Lexington. In the back of the home facing the garden is the studio where Mr. Valentine worked and where the final plaster model of this splendid work can be seen.

Mrs. Robert Edward Lee. *Virginia State Library*

In April 1870, the young, cultivated and attractive Richmond sculptor, Mr. E. V. Valentine arrived in Lexington and set up his temporary studio in a vacant store. As General Lee previously had promised, he came to the studio to sit for a bust. By this time he had aged greatly. Though uncomfortable and probably in pain, for he occasionally put his hand over his heart, the sittings were pleasant for them both. The two men liked and understood each other.

In the course of many relaxing conversations, young Valentine told General Lee this story. "An officeseeker," he said, "besought Andrew Jackson to make him minister to England, and when told that post was filled, asked if he might not be secretary of legation. Advised that no vacancy was in prospect, he appealed to be made vice-consul. Jackson gave the same answer. 'Well then, Mr. President,' said the ambitious seeker after fame, 'would you give me a pair of old boots.'" Then Valentine came to his purpose, "That is what I would like to have you do for me, General." Pleased by Valentine's tact and adroitness, Lee brought a pair of his old army boots to him the next day. Apparently the sculptor needed them for his work. Today, the boots are on display in the Museum of the Confederacy at Richmond.[70]

26.
The Grant House

Notice the old building, with other buildings joined on each side, on the right of Clay Street at 1008 East Clay Street near the junction of 10th Street. This Victorian mansion, now used by the Medical College of Virginia, is virtually unchanged despite its conversion into the Sheltering Arms Hospital, which has now moved to modern accommodations. During the war it belonged to Mr. William H. Grant who owned large tobacco warehouses in Richmond, some of which were used as hospitals.

In a letter long after the war, Mrs. Grant recalled how she and family members would climb to the roof in order to see the smoke of battle and, at night, the

The Wickham-Valentine House. One of the finest in the city, this mansion was owned by James C. Brooks in the 1860s. It is said he wined and dined influential Confederate senators and congressmen here during the conflict. *Virginia Public Library*

SECOND TOUR—BROAD STREET, SHOCKOE HILL AND COURT END

A photograph taken in the 1930s shows city mansions on the north side of Clay Street. The Grant House is the third down the block. Built in 1857, it represents a departure from the austere Greek Revival style popular prior to the war. *Virginia State Library*

flashes of the guns. In those days the house was higher than its neighbors and well situated on Shockoe Hill to see to the north and east.

She also recalled how "the children were always wishing for the Yankees to come." The alarm bell on Capitol Square would ring to announce the approach of the enemy, and then the teachers would close the school. "What excitement and how delighted they were!"[71]

27.
The Broad Street Methodist Church

From Clay Street, turn left onto 10th Street. Drive two blocks and turn left into Broad Street driving east. The Broad Street Methodist Church, demolished in 1968, stood on your left on the northeast corner of 10th and Broad Streets. Some distinctive features included a very tall spire and symmetrical rows of arched windows.

The church's wartime pastor here was Dr. James A. Duncan, who was regarded as a spellbinder in his pulpit. General Lee and President Davis, though not Methodists, were both close friends of Dr. Duncan and occasionally attended his services.

On April 2, 1865, President Davis was at St. Paul's when he received word that Richmond would have to be abandoned that night, but his Secretary of War, Major General Breckenridge, was attending Dr. Duncan's service at Broad Street Methodist Church.

That same night, Dr. Duncan was surprised to receive an invitation from President Davis to accompany him by train on his flight to Danville, an indication of his respect and friendship. Torn between a desire to accompany and support his friend, the President, and his responsibilities to his flock at a time of greatest crisis, Dr. Duncan decided to go and accepted one of those greatly prized seats on the last train to leave Richmond. After General Lee surrendered his forces, Dr. Duncan decided that his own course lay with his parish, returned to Richmond and resumed his pastoral duties.

The Broad Street Methodist Church (1858–1859). The church's distinctive features included a very tall spire and symmetrical rows of arched windows. A parking lot now occupies its site.
Virginia State Library

GENERAL LEE'S CITY

A northern view of the frame building that served as headquarters for the city's Provost Marshal. In the background is the George Washington Statue on nearby Capitol Square and the spire of St. Paul's Church. After Federal forces arrived in Richmond, this building was used by the Freedman's Bureau.
Virginia State Library

28.
Provost Marshal's Headquarters in Richmond

On the southwest corner of Broad and 10th Streets stood a frame building which, for most of the war, was the headquarters of the Provost Marshal of Richmond. He was commandant of its prisons, including the compounds for Federal prisoners of war at Libby and Belle Isle camps. The incumbent provost marshal for much of the war was Brigadier General John H. Winder.

Mr. John B. Jones, a War Department clerk, visited this two-storied frame building on March 12, 1862. He wrote of his disgust in his diary, "The office was a filthy one. It was inhabited, for they slept here—that is, the rowdy clerks. And when I stepped to the hydrant for a glass of water, the tumbler repulsed me by the smell of whiskey. There was no towel to wipe my hands with," and in the long basement underneath were "thousands of garments of dead soldiers, taken from the hospitals and the battlefields, exhaling a most disagreeable if not deleterious odor."[72]

General Winder, a man of fierce temper and dominating manner, was generally disliked and feared. He was a West Point classmate of President Davis and came from an old Maryland family. Many residents believed he staffed his force of detectives and police with "puguglies" from the slums of Baltimore. If provoked, they might incarcerate citizens in one of the two military jails on Cary Street, Castle Thunder and Castle Lightning, which were allocated for criminals and suspicious characters.

Early in the war Winder's men operated without

restraint. They commandeered private carriages and personal property. "They are Lords ascendant," the people complained. "They loll and roll in their glory!"[73] But a day of reckoning slowly arrived. Winder had failed to control food prices; the farmers had simply withheld food from the markets. Corruption surrounded his control of passports through the Federal lines. Controversy marked his administration of Union prisoners. Little by little his powers were curtailed, and in early 1864 he was transferred to Goldsboro, North Carolina. He died of apoplexy on February 8, 1865, still in the company of some of his "puguglies" and his favorite sutler, Cashmeyer.

Brigadier General John H. Winder, Provost Marshal in Richmond for much of the war. By the time of his death in early 1865, he was profoundly disliked by both sides for his harsh and arbitrary ways. His death may have saved him from being hanged, as was Capt Henry Wirz, Commandant of Andersonville Prison, for mistreatment of Federal prisoners. *Virginia State Library*

29.
The City Hall

Driving east on Broad Street, look to your right at the site of the wartime City Hall located on the eastern half of the block between 10th and 11th Streets. The columned front faced south toward Capitol Square.

This fine Greek Revival building, designed by Robert Mills and finished in 1815, served as Richmond's City Hall during the War Between the States. It came to an untimely end because of an accident in 1870 in the Supreme Court chamber of the nearby State Capitol. During a notorious trial that contributed to the end of Reconstruction in Virginia, so many people crowded into the chamber that the floor collapsed, killing 63 people and injuring many others. Worried that the old City Hall across the street was also unsafe, the authorities decided to pull it down. When they did, in 1874, they discovered too late that the building was structurally sound. The new City Hall, an elaborate Romanesque building, now occupies the whole block between 10th and 11th Streets.

Historic photograph of City Hall (right) taken from the north side of Capitol Square. In the foreground are Federal infantry troops resting in the shade with their rifles stacked nearby.
Library of Congress

SECOND TOUR—BROAD STREET, SHOCKOE HILL AND COURT END

On the evening of April 2, 1865, Mayor Mayo and his council of important Richmond citizens met in the City Hall. Realizing that Richmond, the symbol of Rebel power to the Yankees, would fall the next morning, they decided that a formal surrender might appease the approaching Unionists. Under the flickering candlelight, a surrender note was drafted which the Mayor signed.

A little after 3:00 A.M., two old and dilapidated carriages drove out from the city in the darkness bearing the city's delegation. About 6:30 A.M., near the junction of the New Market and Osborn Roads (three miles southeast of the city) the delegation ran into a Blue cavalry patrol from the 4th Massachusetts Cavalry Regiment screening the advance of troops from the Federal 24th and 25th Corps.

The Mayor dismounted from the lead carriage and handed the surrender note to Provost Marshal Major Stevens, one of the leaders of the patrol. After reading the note, the Major promised to deliver it to General Weitzel, his commander. The Mayor and his party then returned to Richmond.

As seen from the north border of Capitol Square, the Powhatan House (later Ford's Hotel) occupied the northeast corner of 11th and Capitol Streets. On this site now is the Virginia State Library.
Virginia State Library

30.
The Powhatan House

Continuing east on Broad Street, you will see the Virginia State Library. It takes up the whole block, but during the war one of Richmond's prominent hotels, the Powhatan House, later known as Ford's Hotel, stood here on the southeast corner of 11th and Broad Streets.

Though it appeared in early 1861 as though all of Richmond was celebrating the final steps toward joining the Confederacy, there were those who opposed Virginia's secession. Most numerous among them were legislators from the western, mountainous third of Virginia, where there had long been social and political differences with the lowland east.

Probably the first major steps toward forming the state of West Virginia were taken at the Powhatan House. On the evening of April 20, 1861, some of these legislators met in the room of Sherrad Clemans and decided to return to the trans-Allegheny portion of Virginia and try to form a new state. They reasoned that if Virginia could secede from the Union, western Virginia could secede from Virginia. Behind the shield of Union forces in 1863, this plan became a reality when West Virginia was admitted to the Union.

31.
John Moncure Daniel House

At the southeast corner of 14th and Broad Streets was the wartime home of John Moncure Daniel.

Mr. Daniel was a strange, contentious, ambitious man in his mid-thirties. "Half genius, half misanthrope," he was the vitriolic editor of the *Richmond Examiner* throughout almost all of the war; his was the most acid pen in Richmond, and he used it often against a favorite target—President Davis.

It was an age of unrestrained journalism, and his fiery columns generated conflict and trouble. During the Seven Days Battles in June 1862, Mr. Daniel served briefly as a volunteer aide to General A. P. Hill. Wounded slightly at Gaine's Mill, he returned to Richmond and took up his pen again. His subsequent columns glorified General A. P. Hill, crediting him for "breaking the spirit of the enemy" and also with the overall victory at Frayser's Farm, when in fact, much of the success was due to Hill's superior, Major General James Longstreet. Generally an easygoing man, Longstreet became incensed about the articles, quarreled with Hill and eventually placed him under arrest. A duel barely was avoided. Daniel had generated serious discontent among the Confederate high command, and it took General Lee to solve the problem by trans-

John Moncure Daniel, fiery editor of the Richmond Examiner.
Virginia State Library

The Richmond Examiner building was located on the west side of Governor, halfway between Franklin and Main Streets. The building was destroyed by the Evacuation Fire, although this print suggests it survived.
Virginia State Library

ferring Hill and his light division to Jackson's Corps.

In another column a year later, Daniel reported on the cavalry battle at Brandy Station. Without mentioning General Stuart's name, Daniel stated that the Confederate cavalry had been surprised by the Union horsemen's attack, using phrases like "vain and weakheaded officers . . . surprise . . . more earnestness (needed) on the part of officers. . . ."[74] General Stuart, usually a favorite of the press, was deeply wounded. It had been suggested that Stuart's unusual behavior in the Gettysburg campaign, which deprived General Lee of most of his sorely needed cavalry, was in compensation for Daniel's criticism.

John Moncure Daniel did not outlive the Confederacy he loved yet lashed so harshly. On March 25 he lay dying in his home as Lee made his final attack to break the union line at Hare's Hill on the Petersburg front. "Pneumonia was succeeding where antagonists in three duels had failed."[75] He received the news of Lee's early success, but Mr. Daniel died before receiving word that Union forces had rallied and restored their lines.

SECOND TOUR—BROAD STREET, SHOCKOE HILL AND COURT END

32.
Wartime Railroad Tracks Down Broad Street

Continue east down Broad Street, noticing its steep descent.

Because of the unrestricted private enterprise of the times, it was customary for every railroad entering a city to have its own depot, unconnected by rail to any other. There were five railroads entering Richmond and five depots. Besides the inconvenience for everybody, this arrangement was especially inefficient in wartime, for it was essential that supplies and troops move quickly through Richmond to meet tactical demands. There was neither the manpower, horses, wagons nor time to off-load, shift then reload large quantities of freight at another depot.

In order to cope with this problem, by May 1862 the authorities simply laid down tracks in the middle of Broad Street from 8th to 16th Streets, thus joining the Richmond, Fredericksburg and Potomac Depot with the Virginia Central Depot. The previous year tracks had already been laid joining the RF&P Depot with the Richmond and Petersburg Depot.

Noisy and smoky trains ran through the city streets at all hours. One can scarcely imagine a wood-burning engine pulling loaded cars on Broad Street climbing Shockoe Hill. Yet, this was apparently done regularly. Rolling stock was moved from the Virginia Central and the RF&P tracks in May 1862 using these makeshift tracks to prevent the advancing Federals from capturing valuable cars and engines. After the crisis, the equipment was all moved back to the Virginia Central Station.

A panorama taken by Mathew Brady from the western slopes of Church Hill. In the background Broad Street, with its railroad tracks down the center, climbs steeply up Shockoe Hill.
Virginia State Library

83

THIRD TOUR

Eastern Quarter

This part of the tour takes you through some of Richmond's oldest sections. With a number of old homes, factories and warehouses dating from the war era or earlier, these neighborhoods have changed less than any other part of the city.

GENERAL LEE'S CITY

MAP 8

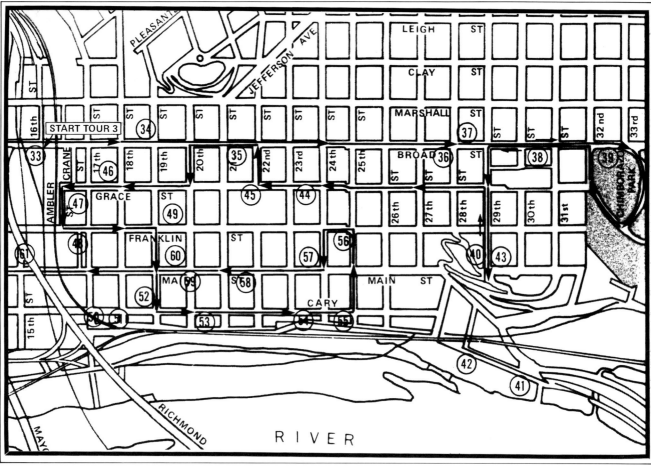

Third Tour—The Eastern Quarter.

Robert E. Lee as shown in the Northern press in late April 1861, about the time he went to Richmond. The photograph from which this likeness was taken was probably made earlier, but was representative nevertheless.   *Virginia State Library*

33.
The Virginia Central Railroad Depot

As you approach the bottom of Shockoe Hill, you will see where the Virginia Central Railroad Depot once stood on the southwest corner of 16th and Broad Streets. This area is now dilapidated, but during the war years momentous events took place here. The station, only a modest wooden shed, was the terminal for this strategic railroad which ran north and west to main battle grounds in the Virginia Piedmont and Valley of Virginia.

On April 22, 1861, a middle-aged man in civilian broadcloth and a silk top hat stood up as the conductor cried, "All out to Richmond!" He didn't realize it, but the safety of this city was to be his "supreme military responsibility" for the next four years. Robert E. Lee was arriving at the Virginia Central Depot to report to

THIRD TOUR—EASTERN QUARTER

Governor Lecher of Virginia, having left his home, Arlington House, that morning for the last time in his life. A fellow traveler described him as "handsome beyond all men I had ever seen."[76] He was 54 years old and five feet eleven inches tall; his hair was full and black with a "sprinkle of gray." He wore a short black mustache, and his face was slightly florid. Above all, people noticed a calmness and self-control.

Three years later, in early March 1864, General Lee boarded a train at this same station. Now the famous leader of the Army of Northern Virginia, he was deep in preparations for the spring campaign against the new Federal leader, General Grant. Unaware of impending danger, he sat quietly as the train passed Frederickshall Station, a few miles up the line. Moments later, Union Colonel Dahlgren and his cavalry raiders seized the station on their way to attack Richmond. Had Lee been captured, one wonders what consequences this might have had for the hard-pressed Confederacy. (Curiously, this same month General Grant also had a narrow escape. Riding north on the Orange and Alexandria Railroad to attend a conference in Washington, his train barely missed interception by a cavalry force under Colonel John Mosby.)

On May 26, 1870, General Lee left Richmond from this depot for the last time. His health impaired by the war's hardships, he spent a brief time in the city, probably seeing a few of his many friends. It is not likely that people came to see him off. "He passed from the central stage of his life's drama as though he had been the humblest actor. . . ."[77] Five months later he died at his home in Lexington.

The war years took their toll on Lee's health and appearance. He left Richmond for the last time in May 1870, five months before his death at age 63.
Virginia State Library

87

GENERAL LEE'S CITY

MAP 9

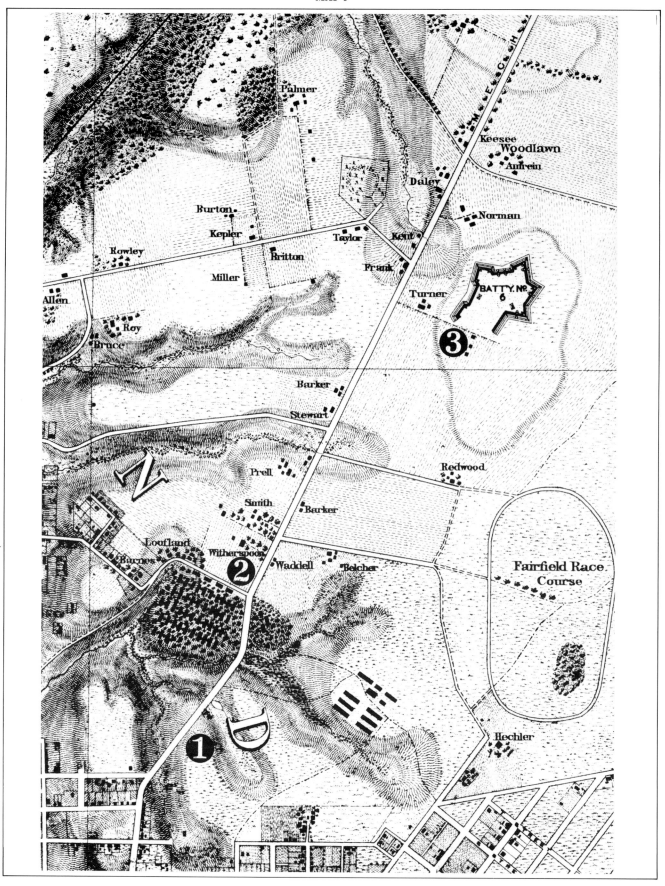

THIRD TOUR—EASTERN QUARTER

34.
Mechanicsville Turnpike

Still driving east on Broad Street, look left (north) as you pass 19th Street. Its northward extension was the wartime entry to the Mechanicsville Turnpike. Famous in the defense of Richmond, this Pike led to the small village of Mechanicsville, some six miles north and east of Richmond. General Lee fought two successful battles near this road—one in June of 1862, and another in June of 1864—to prevent the Federal army from using it to enter the city.

On the warm sunny afternoon of June 26, 1862, Miss Van Lew, a Union spy, and a friend drove by buggy out the Mechanicsville Pike to see as much of the fighting as they could. She watched the Confederate troops forming up on the road for an attack. The scenes were more thrilling "than she could have imagined. The cannonading was heard more loudly as we progressed . . . men riding and leading horses at full speed—their canteens and arms—the rush of the poor beasts into and out of the pond where they were watered—the dust, the commotion—the ambulances—the long lines of infantry awaiting orders. . . ." They asked a guard who stopped them what was going on. His eyes gleamed, "We are whipping the Federals—right, left and center—and have taken many prisoners." The noise of the guns grew louder and louder; Miss Van Lew decided that "no ball could be as exciting as our ride."[78]

About this same time farther out that dangerous road, President Davis and General Lee exchanged strong words. Lee was absorbed in the progress of the battle, concerned about the lack of coordination of his attacking troops, the whereabouts of General Jackson, and the heavy losses in his first major battle. Turning in his saddle he noticed Jefferson Davis and a large group of cabinet heads and politicans sitting on their horses nearby intently watching the battle. The usually tactful Lee rode over to Davis. "Mr. President," he inquired, saluting coldly, "Who is all this army and what is it doing here?" Taken aback, the surprised President squirmed in his saddle. "It is not my army, General," he responded. Lee went on bluntly, "It certainly is not *my* army, Mr. President, and this is no place for it!" Mr. Davis seemed stunned. "Well, General, if I withdraw, perhaps they will follow me."[79] With this, he lifted his hat and rode down the hill toward safer ground near the Chickahominy River. That day a soldier was killed near Davis by a shell explosion, confirming that General Lee had cause to worry about the President's presence on the battlefield.

35.
Church Hill

As you drive east on Broad Street from the valley of Shockoe Creek, your car climbs the substantial slopes of Church Hill. After passing 21st Street you enter this old district.

Church Hill has more antebellum and Victorian homes than any other section of Richmond, and in the war years it was far less crowded than it is now. In 1956 the Historic Richmond Foundation, a nonprofit organization, was founded to preserve old homes and to protect this valuable neighborhood. It selects, buys and restores old houses to the extent funds permit. With its lofty setting above the James and its quiet 19th-century charm, Church Hill has a potential to be as pleasing as the restoration of 18th-century Williamsburg. However, much still remains to be done.

Of interest are certain homes which have architectural and historic value but no significant connection to the 1861–65 period.

1. The Turpin Yarborough House. 2201 East Broad Street. It was built in 1861 and is a charming return to the earlier Greek Revival period.

2. Carrington Row. 2307–11 East Broad Street. Built in 1818 by the Carrington brothers, these examples of early row houses are three of the handsomest houses in Richmond. In the Greek Revival style, they are two-story buildings, and perhaps show what the Confederate White House might have looked like before a third story was added to it in 1851.

3. Carrington Square. The whole block between 23rd and 24th Streets on your right. All the houses were restored by the Historic Rich-

---

Mechanicsville Turnpike, U.S. Corps of Engineers Map, 1865.

(1) The Mechanicsville road northeast toward the battlefields of Beaver Dam Creek, Gaine's Mill and Cold Harbor.
(2) Howard's Grove—training camp (1861); camp hospital (1862–65).
(3) Battery No. 6—one of the Star Forts of the Inner Defense Line. *Library of Congress*

mond Foundation and deserve your attention, for they are beautiful period homes of the 19th century.

4. St. John's Episcopal Church. Between 24th and 25th Streets, the whole block is given over to the church and its cemetery. Patrick Henry gave his celebrated "Give me liberty or give me death" speech at the beginning of the American Revolution at St. John's Church.

The oldest church in Richmond, St. John's Episcopal Church on Church Hill in a photo apparently taken shortly after the war. The steeple seems to have been demolished. A Federal ambulance is in the foreground, and children, some in Confederate uniforms, are nearby.

Virginia State Library

36.
Crenshaw House

Continue east on Broad Street past St. John's Church three blocks. On the southeast corner of Broad and 28th Streets is the site of the Crenshaw House. Not even a photograph, insurance document or drawing remains to tell us how the house looked.

On the darkening evening of May 31, 1862, President Davis and General Lee guided their horses down the Nine Mile Road through the drifting smoke of battle, then pulled up amazed at what they saw approaching them from the direction of Seven Pines. A litter halted near them; on it lay the badly wounded commander of the Confederate army, General Joseph E. Johnston. With wounds of the shoulder and the leg, he was in pain and barely conscious. Meanwhile all around them was the debris of battle—scattered equipment, wounded men and mud-covered infantrymen waiting to be told what to do. This was more than enough to dismay the two leaders, but their concern grew when the Deputy Army Commander reported. He seemed to know little of the situation or what to do about it. Fortunately, the Bluecoats were too badly shaken to counterattack.

They rode the few miles back to Richmond discouraged and silent, expecting the fighting to be renewed on the morrow. Out of the darkness, President Davis's voice interrupted General Lee's thoughts. "General Lee," he said, "I shall assign you to the command of this army as soon as you reach your quarters. I shall send you the order when we get to Richmond."[80]

The wounded Johnston was brought by ambulance to the Crenshaw House on Church Hill, a quiet neighborhood remote from the hustle and noise of downtown Richmond. Here he convalesced stoically. He had often experienced battle wounds. Before choosing the Confederacy he had served in the U.S. Army and gained a reputation as one of its most wounded men from battles with Indians and in Mexico.

Months later, General Johnston was assigned to command the Confederate armies in the west. Before leaving Richmond he was given a ceremonial breakfast by his friends at Old Tom Griffin's Restaurant on Main Street. A bumper of champagne was brought in during the festivities, and his host rose with a toast, "Gentlemen, let us drink to the health of the only man who can save the Confederacy." In response, General Johnston rose to his feet, and replied "Mr. Yancy, the man you describe is now in the field, in the person of General Robert E. Lee. I shall drink to his health."[81]

General Joseph E. Johnston, a skillful military leader greatly admired by his officers and men; however, he could not get along with President Davis at all. *Virginia Public Library*

37.
Oakwood Cemetery

Before you leave the Crenshaw House, look to your left (north) up 28th Street. During the war the road from Church Hill to Oakwood Cemetery led four blocks up 28th Street to M Street, then right on M Street past Star Fort No. 4 to the cemetery. Oakwood holds the remains of more than 17,000 Confederate soldiers who were killed on the nearby battlefields or died in the Richmond hospitals. Many Union soldiers who died in Richmond's prisons or hospitals were also interred here. Oakwood is also the setting for a curious tale of bodysnatching and espionage.

Colonel Ulric Dahlgren, one of President Lincoln's friends, was a youthful, zealous Union cavalry officer. In the first days of March 1864 he was one of the leaders of an unsuccessful raid against Richmond. During the retreat Dahlgren was killed in an ambush, and papers were found on his body which spelled out his intention of killing the Confederate leaders and burning Richmond. Due to the public's outrage, President Davis ordered Dahlgren's body to be buried secretly at Oakwood Cemetery. The unmarked grave lay near the cemetery's entrance, with a sapling planted over it to hide the fact that the place was a fresh grave.

Mr. F.W.E. Lohman, one of Miss Van Lew's circle of Union agents in Richmond, discovered the body's location from Martin Lipscomb, an official in charge of burying Union dead at Oakwood. About 10:00 P.M. on the moonless evening of April 6, Lohman and others drove a wagon to the cemetery. At the entrance they had difficulty quieting the horses because of the stench of hastily buried men. Once all was quiet, Dahlgren's pine coffin was dug up, the grave refilled with dirt and the sapling replanted.

About an hour later Lohman's wagon arrived at William S. Rowlett's house on Chelsea Hill, a half mile or so from the cemetery. Miss Van Lew came in the darkness of early morning to view Colonel Dahlgren's remains. "The comeliness of the young face was gone, yet," she wrote, "the features seemed regular, and there is a wonderful look of firmness or energy stamped upon them."[82]

Around noon the next day, Rowlett drove the body in another wagon out of Richmond by the Brook Road, the casket well hidden beneath young fruit trees. He was bound for the farm of Robert Orrick, a German living near Hungry Station. Halted by a sentry at a check point on the Outer Defense Line, Rowlett waited for the sentry's questions anxiously. "Whose fruit trees are these?" he asked and then went on, "Well, you've got them packed so nicely I hate to disturb them." Rowlett responded, his heart in his mouth. "When I packed them, I did not expect them to be disturbed, but . . . being a citizen, I know a soldier's duty and expect him to do it. So of course you may take them out." The guard stood indecisively a moment, then waved him on. "Your honest face is guarantee enough for me."[83]

As the sun was setting at the Orrick farm, the body was reburied. Again the dirt was shaped in a circular mound, on which was planted one of the fruit trees.

Rumors circulated; the authorities investigated and discovered that the body had been stolen. But the farm held its secret until the day after Richmond's fall. That day the body was exhumed and sent to Washington where it was received with full military honors and lay in state in the city. The following day the casket was taken to Philadelphia by train, where again it lay in state, this time at Independence Hall. Then the late Colonel Dahlgren was buried once again at Philadelphia's Laurel Hill Cemetery.

38.
Richmond Dueling Grounds

As you pass the block between 30th and 31st Streets, the defile of Bloody Run opens to your right. Along its steep banks, between Grace and Franklin Streets was a quiet, wooded area where duels were fought.

An 1846 map of Richmond identifies this area as a "Dueling Grounds." Duels were a custom of Southern society both during and after the war. Men who felt their honor attacked would challenge the offender to a duel. The men would meet in the early morning hours to settle accounts with dueling pistols.

Honor was a most sensitive matter; an affront to a citizen's honor could arise in many ways. Most often it seemed to come from a careless remark, or statement in the press that seemed to or, in fact, did defame one's self or family members. If a lady's name was mentioned—wife, relative or betrothed—the matter had gone beyond apologies. People talked openly about their honor; it was important to them. Confederate congressmen were fond of sounding forth on the floor "that their honor would not tolerate" this or that action.

Newspaper editors especially had to be very careful about what they said or wrote, or they could end up in an early grave. In addition to writing skills, they had to demonstrate exceptional courage and also had to be good shots. John Moncure Daniel survived at least two duels. Another editor, O. Jennings Wise, survived numerous duels only to be killed by the Federals during the fall of Roanoke Island early in 1862. Some editors paid the price; this epitaph was found in Shockoe Cemetery: "X, distinguished editor, died from wounds received in a rencontre with another editor."

39.
Chimborazo Military Hospital

Still driving east on Broad Street, turn right after you pass 32nd Street into Chimborazo Park, a broad plain fronting on a high bluff to the south overlooking the James River. Named after a peak in Ecuador, Chimborazo Hill was used first as an infantry camp of instruction in the spring of 1861. From October of that year to the end of the war, the plain was the setting for perhaps the largest and certainly the most renowned hospital in the Confederacy, far larger than any of the Washington hospitals.

Today, Chimborazo Park provides an impressive setting for the Richmond National Park Service Headquarters and Information Center, the place to start a tour of the battlefields surrounding the city.

Phoebe Yates Pember, one of the hospital's chief matrons, left a remarkable account of her life and adventures there. The following is an account, mostly in her own words of what happened one day in 1864 when she was making her rounds of the wards.

"Kin you writ me a letter?" drawled a voice from a nearby bed. The recumbent speaker was what the soldiers called a "Gouber," an up-country Georgian—lean, attenuated, yellow with wispy strands of hair hanging over high cheekbones and fingernails like claws.

"Why do you not let the nurse cut your nails?" asked Mrs. Pember.

"Because I aint got any spoon, and I use them instead."

"Will you let me have your hair cut. . . ?"

"No, I can't . . . kaus as how I promised my mammy . . . Oh, it's onlucky to cut it!"

"Then, I can't write any letter for you. . . ."

That was plain talking. The Gouber considered, then surrendered; his hair was cut, but the fingernails had to wait for another day. True to her promise, Mrs. Pember sat down by the side of the Georgian's cot as soon as she could find the time, carrying her writing materials. He dictated, "My dear Mammy, I hope this finds you well, as it leaves me well, and I hope that I shall get a furlough Christmas, and come and see you,

The white frame buildings of Chimborazo General Hospital seen from near Bloody Run. This was probably the biggest hospital in both the North and South during the conflict.
Virginia State Library

and I hope that you will keep well, and all the folks be well . . . , as I hopes to be well myself. . . ." The Georgian was going in circles.

Mrs. Pember looked up and began to ask questions about the soldier's home, what he had done in the summer's fighting, where his brigade was located, and how he got sick. She wrote the letter rapidly, using up the four sides of a folded paper, for no soldier would think of sending a letter home that showed unused space.

When she read the letter back to him, his pale face brightened; he sat up and looked around anxiously to see that nobody was listening. "Did you write all that?"

"Yes," said Mrs. Pember.

"Did I say all that?" he went on.

"I think you did," she responded.

"Are you married?" the voice dropped very low.

"I am a widow," she answered.

After a long pause, his thin, feverish face lit up. He sat up straighter, and stretching out a long piece of bone with a talon attached, he gently touched Mrs. Pember's arm. Then he whispered mysteriously, "You wait!"[84]

On the morning of April 2, 1865, Mrs. Pember saw the Federals arrive. Not long after dawn she saw a "single Federal bluejacket rise above the hill, standing transfixed in astonishment at what he saw"—the enormous hospital stretched before him. "Another and another sprang up as if out of the earth, but all remained quiet. About seven o'clock, there fell upon the ear the steady clatter of horses' hoofs and winding around Rocketts, close under Chimborazo Hill, came a small and compact body of Federal cavalrymen, on horses in splendid condition, riding closely and steadily along. They were well mounted, well accoutered, well fed—a rare sight in Southern streets. . . ."[85]

40.
Libby Hill Park and the Confederate Soldiers and Sailors Monument

Circle Chimborazo Park back to Broad Street, then drive west two blocks to 29th Street. Turn left and go three blocks which will bring you to the park and monument.

When this quiet, wooded park was begun in 1851, it was called Eastern Square, a name now almost forgotten. Because of the nearness of Mr. Luther Libby's home and the notoriety of Libby Prison, it became known as Libby Hill Park. During the summer of 1865, the park was the site of a camp of black U.S. soldiers who were part of the occupation force of the city. Today, numerous 19th-century houses, some of them in the process of restoration, surround the park on three sides.

Near the southern rim of the park at the edge of a steep bluff providing a fine view of the James River is the Confederate Soldiers and Sailors Monument. Completed in 1894, the tall column is a copy of Pompey's Pillar in Egypt. The bronze figure of a Confederate soldier at the top is the work of Richmond sculptor William R. Sheppard. Contributions from all over the South and much effort by the people of Richmond made its construction possible. The growth of Richmond to the west and north has left this tribute to the ordinary soldier and sailor sadly isolated from the statues of their leaders, Lee, Stuart and others, on Monument Avenue.

Confederate Soldiers and Sailors Monument on Libby Hill.
Virginia State Library

THIRD TOUR—EASTERN QUARTER

MAP 10

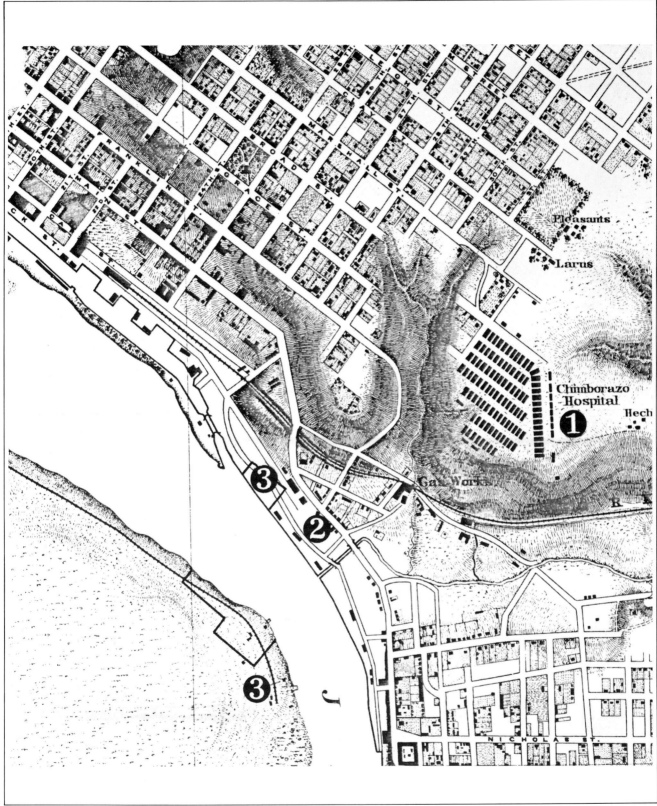

Chimborazo Hospital Area, U.S. Corps of Engineers Map, 1865.

Library of Congress

(1) Chimborazo Hospital.
(2) Rocketts Landing.
(3) Confederate Navy Yards.

41. Rocketts Landing

After you have looked at the Soldiers and Sailors Monument, walk over to the edge of the bluff. Look down and slightly to your left—just to the right of Gillies Creek. Except when the leaves are very full, you can see the site of Rocketts Landing. The map on the adjoining page will assist you. Today, Richmond's port facilities and some warehouses occupy the area, a much quieter scene than in the war years. Rocketts Landing was then outside the city. Since it was at the head of navigation for ocean shipping on the James, the landing was often busy. Troops and supplies moved from here to locations on the lower James. Prisoner-of-war exchange vessels put in here, and people would meet them, hoping that friends or relatives were aboard. The steamer Shultz *left Rocketts Landing daily at 3:00 P.M., sailing down river about seven miles as far as Drewry's Bluff.*

Early on April 4, 1865, a small flotilla of three Union vessels, *Malvern, Bat* and *River Queen* were struggling up the James from City Point. On the first was President Lincoln and his son, Tad. Richmond had fallen to the Union the day before. "Thank God I have lived to see this," Lincoln said. "It seems to me that I have been dreaming a horrid dream for four years, and now the nightmare is gone. I want to see Richmond."[86]

Bat and *River Queen* ran aground trying to avoid the formidable array of sunken ships and mines left by the Confederate navy. When *Malvern* also grounded not far from Rocketts, the Lincoln party transferred to a naval barge and finished the trip by oar. Accompanied by a small group of sailors, Lincoln stepped down on Rocketts Landing. A Boston reporter named Coffin, who happened to be there, recognized Mr. Lincoln and said to an old black man working nearby: "Would you like to see the man who gave you your freedom—Abraham Lincoln?" "Is that Massa Lincoln, sure enough?" "That is he." The man rushed toward Mr. Lincoln, shouting, "Bless the Lord! The Great Messiah!

Brady photograph of Rocketts Landing, April 1865, taken from Libby Hill. The open air sheds to the far side of the large brick building identify the Landing itself. The Confederate Navy Yard on the Manchester shore is clearly visible as are the Union war vessels anchored downstream.

National Archives

A photograph of Federal vessels unloading railroad freight cars at the Confederate Navy Yard across the James from Rocketts, about April 1865. By her sleek lines, the large sidewheeler in the right foreground must be a captured Confederate blockade runner. *National Archives*

I knowed him as soon as I seen him . . . come to free his children from bondage. Glory Hallelujah!" The old man fell on his knees and tried to kiss the President's feet. Mr. Lincoln was ill at ease. "Don't kneel to me," he said. . . . "You must kneel to God only, and thank Him for (your) liberty . . . but you may rest assured that so long as I live no one shall put a shackle on your limbs."[87] For a brief moment the spectacle held the President's party motionless; then the sailors cleared the way. Lincoln started up Main Street, the way the Union soldiers had gone the day before, heading for Capitol Square. People recognized him as he walked along the potentially hostile and still smouldering street. He strolled ahead unharmed, looking around curiously, a tall, awkward figure holding Tad by the hand.

42.
The Confederate Navy Yard Sites and the James River Squadron

*Directly below to the right of Rocketts Landing is the site of one of two navy yards. The other is directly across the James River and a little downstream from Rocketts Landing. See Map No. 10. These yards were the headquarters and base of the James River Squadron, and three heavy, armored warships were built here—*Virginia II, Fredericksburg *and* Richmond. *Positioned about seven miles down James River near Drewry's Bluff was the James River Squadron.*

Before dawn on the morning of April 3, 1865, the Squadron Commander, Admiral Raphael Semmes, had been obliged to blow up his own finest warships, because the Federal army was about to capture them on their way to Richmond. With 500 naval cadets and seamen, he withdrew up the James River in five small wooden gunboats, passing his own flaming Navy Yards (which he had ordered burned) and steaming as far as Mayo's Bridge. After the drawbridge opened, his small flotilla proceeded until just beyond the bridge, where the rocks and fall line of the river blocked further progress west, and he steered for the Manchester shore. By now it must have been close to 8:00 A.M., and looking back, the sailors could see Union patrols already moving about on Church and Chimborazo Hills.

On shore Admiral Seemes ordered the gunboats to be set on fire, and they drifted downstream burning, then exploding. Semmes ordered his men to search the nearby Manchester Depot in hopes of finding an engine and some cars. The sailors found an old engine, chased some tramps from three or four dilapidated cars, then tore up some fencing for firewood. By coupling the cars to the engine by hand, they had a train. The train moved out of the station and puffed mightily to a halt about 200 yards away on the first slight incline. The situation appeared hopeless, for even the Confederate army's rear guard by now had disappeared over Manchester's hills.

The Admiral ordered another search for an engine. Amazingly, a sailor, poking behind some partitions in an old building, found one carefully hidden away in good condition. Again they shifted cars by hand to the new engine, and using what was left of their wood fired up the engine and drew out of the station cheering, with a sailor at the throttle.

Admiral Raphael Semmes, who commanded the Confederate commerce raider Alabama and was the last commander of the James River Squadron. Semmes was the only Confederate officer to hold the rank of both admiral and general. *Virginia State Library*

Frantic for firewood, they came upon a heaven-sent woodpile six miles down the track. From there on it was "clear sailing." They got through just before the Federal cavalry cut the line, stopping along the way to pick up refugees. The sailors steamed on to Danville and safety, the last train from Richmond. Not for them the foot slogging, the hunger, the losses, fatigue and surrender of the last retreat. Semmes and his sailors joined Jefferson Davis in Danville.

43.
Luther Libby House

Just to the east of Libby Hill Park you will see Mr. Luther Libby's house on the northeast corner, 1 North 29th Street.

Mr. Luther Libby was a Richmond businessman whose warehouse at 20th and Cary Streets was appropriated by General Winder for use as a prison for "live Yankees"—the name Richmonders gave to captured Bluecoats. The General's haste did not allow Mr. Libby time to remove his sign. This sign "L. Libby and Son, Ship Chandlers" remaining on the warehouse ensured its notoriety all over the North as Libby Prison.

Later during a Federal raid south of Richmond, the Libby family was unlucky enough to be in the vicinity and was captured. All were thrown into prison at Fortress Monroe, commanded by Major General "Beast" Butler (as he was known in the South). From here Mr. Libby was moved to Fort Warren in Boston Harbor. In this damp and sometimes frigid climate, he contracted tuberculosis, from which he eventually died in 1871. Ironically, Mr. Libby was a Yankee himself, originally from Scarborough, Maine, who was in business in Richmond. Even his son, the younger Luther Libby, felt the odium of his name so keenly that he felt obliged to flee Richmond after the war. However, the family returned to the city in due course.

The Luther Libby House (1850). Here lived the unlucky man whose warehouse became a notorious prison for Union officers—making Libby infamous throughout the North. *Susan C. Lee*

The Van Lew Mansion where Richmonders believed Miss Van Lew hid escaped Union prisoners of war in a secret room before smuggling them to safety. Some say the people of Richmond took their revenge on Miss Van Lew after her death by refusing to stop the demolition of her home in 1911, thus destroying one of Richmond's most beautiful houses.
Virginia State Library

44.
The Van Lew Mansion

Go north on 29th Street two blocks and turn left onto Grace Street. Drive five blocks and on the left, halfway between 24th and 23rd Streets you will see Belle Vue School. Built in 1911, it occupies the site of the Van Lew mansion. The Van Lew mansion was one of the finest in Richmond, occupying a city block; its rear gardens descended from Church Hill to Franklin Street. John Van Lew, the owner, was a prosperous Richmond hardware merchant.

John Van Lew's daughter, Miss Elizabeth Van Lew, was one of the most remarkable women of the war. To most of Richmond she was known as "Miss Lizzie" or "Crazy Bet," but highlights of her life reveal a woman of courage and conviction.

She became an abolitionist while in school in Philadelphia; on her father's death in 1860, she freed the family slaves.

Never hiding her Union sympathies, she carried special foods to Federal prisoners at Libby Prison, a custom which aroused hostility against her in the city. The authorities kept her under surveillance.

During General McClellan's 1862 campaign against Richmond, she and her mother prepared a "charming room" in her home for his use after he took the city. The two called it the "McClellan room."

On days of fasting decreed by President Davis, the two Van Lew ladies dined in abundant style.

Miss Van Lew opened secret correspondence with Union forces at Fortress Monroe, passing military information on Richmond via secret couriers.

She was the leader throughout the war of the small, well organized Union underground in the city, a group of spies and sympathizers.

She succeeded in placing at least one and probably more black servants as spies in the Confederate White House and is credited with responsibility for the arson attempt on the mansion in the winter of 1864.

She is believed to have assisted the escape of 109 Union officers from Libby Prison on February 9, 1864.

She did visit a leader of the escape, Colonel Streight, at Howard's Grove, all at great danger to herself.

In early April 1864, she organized the theft of the body of Colonel Dahlgren from Oakwood Cemetery; she then had it secretly reburied to await the end of the war.

On evacuation night escaped Union prisoners hid in secret passages in her home.

She was considered so important to the Union that

Miss Elizabeth Van Lew seated in her garden at the rear of her house. The photograph was made sometime after the war.

Valentine Museum

General Grant sent a member of his staff, Colonel Parke, to protect Miss Van Lew and her property when Federal forces entered Richmond.

As President, General Grant showed his gratitude to Miss Van Lew by making her postmistress of Richmond. She served throughout his two terms.

By the 1880s Miss Van Lew was old, ailing and poverty stricken. Never forgiven by the people of Richmond and socially ostracized, she kept 40 cats as companions. When she died in 1900 nobody came to her funeral, and no stone was raised over her grave in Shockoe Cemetery. Later some people from Boston placed a stone there.

45.
The Wilkins Home

Between 23rd and 22nd Street on Grace, notice the Mount Marie Convent on your left whose grounds share the whole of a large double block with Taylors Hill Park. Built into the center facade of the convent is the Wilkins House at 2209 Grace. Easily recognizable and intact, it is the survivor of two large homes in this block during the conflict.

Benjamin Wilkins, long after the war, wrote a book of recollections of what wartime Richmond was like to a boy in his early teens. It is titled *War Boy*. His father, a wealthy Mississippi planter brought the family and servants to Richmond just before hostilities began. Anxious to have his children educated in the city, he kept his family there throughout the war.

With the "war boy" in tow, Mrs. Wilkins visited the wartime hospitals from time to time, on the lookout for some needy relative. Occasionally she found one, brought him home and took care of him. On one such visit, a "bearded, begrimed" soldier looked up from his cot as she passed by. "Howdy, Coz Margrit," he said. True enough, a first cousin he was, but totally disguised by blood, mud and bandages. She took him right home.[88]

With a household of about 20, consisting of her own large family, slaves and convalescent relatives, Mrs. Wilkins was hard pressed to feed them all in a Richmond noted for high prices and scarcities of nutritious foods. As the war dragged on, she began buying four or five barrels of rice and black-eyed peas at a time; her extended family ate them for every meal—in soup, boiled, steamed, fried and baked. Meat was a luxury; one day in 1864 she brought home a five-pound ham which had cost $500.

During much of the war Mr. Wilkins served as a

The Wilkins House at 2209 Grace Street was the "War Boy's" home. In 1866 it was purchased from Mr. Wilkins and incorporated into the facade of Mount Marie Convent and thus survives.
Susan C. Lee

colonel of the local defense forces. In 1863 the regular Confederate troops were withdrawn from Richmond to join Lee's army, and it fell to the local forces to block the frequent Union raids into the nearby countryside. More and more, Colonel Wilkins had to take to the field with his often reluctant troops. He was rarely home, and by the end of the war he was a totally exhausted, dispirited man.

Meanwhile, throughout the war Benjamin, the "war boy," roamed about the city, recording its excitements and spectacles in his mind. A favorite vantage point was a nearby cupola, possibly that of St. John's Church or perhaps Trinity Methodist Church on Broad Street. From here he remembered seeing seven spies hanging from a scaffold high on Shockoe Hill. Whenever the Federal army drew close to the city, he and his cronies repaired to the cupola where they could see the smoke of battle and the flashes of the cannon.

Seabrook's Warehouse (General Hospital No. 9). *Valentine Museum*

46.
Seabrook's Warehouse (General Hospital No. 9)

Turn right on 22nd Street and go one block to Broad Street. Turn left on Broad and go two blocks to 20th and turn left again. Proceed one block and turn right. You are now back on Grace Street. Further along Grace Street, Seabrook's Warehouse occupied the entire north side between 18th and 17th Streets.

Seabrook's Warehouse was converted to hospital use in early June of 1862 to house some of the wounded and sick men coming in from the Fair Oaks and Seven Pines battlefields. Because of its proximity to the Virginia Central Railroad Depot, it was also used as a receiving and distributing center for wounded men entering the city. From time to time it included among its patients disabled Union prisoners. With room for 900 patients, it was large for a city hospital. Its reports for July, August and September 1864, show how active it was. Of some 10,000 patients received, 9,663 were transferred in due course to other Richmond hospitals, 96 men died of wounds or illness, and 344 were on hand as the period ended. Seabrook's was also called "the billboard of Richmond," because its exterior wall space was invariably plastered with advertisements and notices. It was torn down in 1910.

Mrs. Jennie Harrold remembered that as a girl her mother sent her to the city's hospitals every weekday in the summer of 1862 "with what delicacies she could provide" for the unfortunate men. After giving the men the food, Jennie's duty was to fan some of them, for the heat was oppressive. Once while at Seabrook's, she recalled hospital attendants coming in to take two dying soldiers to the "death house." Every hospital had this somber place where the dying were sometimes taken because their last moments were so distressing to those less sick. The two men lay side by side, each minus a leg and dying of infection. Jennie was fanning them at the time. One of the suffering men asked, "What are you going to do with us?" The attendant responded, "We want to make room for those coming in." The soldier came back, "Can't you wait until we are dead?" The attendant answered, "No."[89]

Superb Brady photograph (April 1865) from Church Hill showing the intersection of Grace and 21st Streets (foreground) and Richmond's churches and Capitol on Shockoe Hill (background). Notice the Union supply wagons grouped around the entrance of Seabrook's Warehouse (General Hospital No.9) some four blocks down Grace Street. *National Archives*

THIRD TOUR—EASTERN QUARTER

47.
The Oldest Part of Richmond

Drive a short block past 17th Street to Crane Street, then turn left and go one block to Franklin Street. You are now in the oldest part of Richmond. The town was laid out in 1737 by William Byrd II. Incorporated in 1741, the village grew slowly at first. In 1779, when it was chosen as Virginia's capital, it had fewer than 700 people. Less than two years later, a British force under Benedict Arnold occupied and burned Richmond. Upon its ruins the modern city was begun.

By the time of the War Between the States the prosperous business and residential sections of Richmond were west of Shockoe Creek, and this oldest section already had a rundown appearance. A wartime visitor walking east of Shockoe Creek would encounter tobacco factories, warehouses, livery stables, small struggling businesses and slave markets as well as other kinds of auction houses.

A slave market looked like any other auction house with a red flag flying from a window or the roof. Typically, a slave would be walking slowly in front of the building, ringing a bell and carrying a red flag. He periodically shouted out the nature of the establishment and the particulars of the auction. Inside, the appearance and atmosphere was that of a livery stable with sales being conducted in a relaxed workaday manner. People from the north and abroad were curious about these places. During his stay in Richmond not long before the war, Charles Dickens, the English novelist, witnessed one of the slave auctions. It deeply troubled him, and he thought the sight "gloomy" and "shadowed by slavery's curse."[90] His contemporary William Thackeray, also one of Richmond's prewar visitors, thought otherwise—to him the blacks seemed "happy" and "healthy."[91]

MAP 11

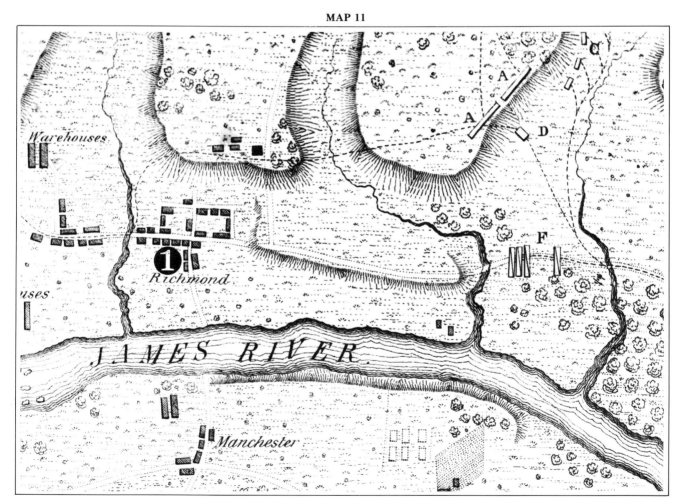

Richmond in the Late 18th Century.

(1) **The approximate location of the Old First Market, Watch House and Public Hall. (To the left is Shockoe Creek and toward the top of the map is Church Hill.)**

Virginia State Library

The First Market as it looked during the war.

Virginia State Library

THIRD TOUR—EASTERN QUARTER

48.
The First Market, Watch House and Public Hall

On your right after you turn left into Franklin Street from Crane is the oldest of the city markets, known generally as the First Market. It originated with the founding of the city, and in its early days it was an open space stretching from 17th Street west to Shockoe Creek. After a succession of wooden sheds, the first brick market was built in 1794, and above it on the second story was erected a hall. In 1854 a new and more commodious brick market was built on this same site, again including a large hall above the market stalls. Used for militia drills and public meetings, this hall was the decorative setting, on April 16, 1861, for a patriotic Southern Flag Ball. Still another market building was erected on the site in 1913, and in more recent years it was replaced by the present metal building. The market is in the process of revitalization.

When hostilities began in 1861, the market had long been famous for its bountiful supplies of all kinds of foods at modest prices, especially meats, fish, shellfish and many kinds of fowl. By the spring of 1863 food was still plentiful, but an ample basket of food, which two years earlier cost $6.55, now cost 11 times that price. In another two years, food was nearly gone from the stalls. Very little but "greens" could be had at any price. Richmond's famous dish, "bacon and greens" now lacked the bacon. Corn was selling for $100 a peck; a barrel of flour brought $1,000. Everyone was saying, "You carried your money in your market basket, and brought your provisions home in your purse."[92] Starvation was rampant in the city.

Richmonders shopping at market. The time must be the Occupation, after April 1865, for a Union officer is seen in the left foreground with a shopping basket under his arm. *Virginia State Library*

The Grant Tobacco Factory (1853) was first used as a barracks for Confederate soldiers in 1861, then became a military hospital (General Hospital No. 12), and finally a barracks again for Union soldiers of the Occupation force. *Virginia State Library*

49.
The William H. Grant Tobacco Factory (General Hospital No. 12)

As you cross 18th Street, proceeding east on Franklin, notice in mid block to your right the white Mason's Hall. It survives from the 18th century, the oldest Masonic Lodge in continuous use in this country. During the war the building was used by a number of Richmond Lodges, and it had many visits from out-of-town Masons serving in the Confederate army.

Before turning right into 19th Street, look at the northeast corner of 19th and Franklin. Here stands the handsome, brick Grant Tobacco Factory which served as an army hospital from December 1861 through the remainder of the war. This general hospital could hold approximately 100 patients.

Especially in the earlier months of the war, a young, handsome patient could sometimes receive much, if not too much care. This often-repeated story which in one account occurred at Grant Hospital, could as easily have happened at any Richmond hospital.

During the Seven Days Battles near Richmond in late June 1862, the hospital was crowded with wounded and sick men. In their eagerness to help the sufferers, the ladies of Richmond rushed to provide nursing care and any aid they could. One tender-hearted girl approached a young patient's cot. "Can't I do something for you, Sir?" "No, thank you, ma'am." "Can't I wash your face for you?" "Well, if you insist, ma'am, but 14 ladies have washed it already today."

Grant Hospital was also known as Wayside Hospital

because of a necessary and popular purpose it served after August 1863. Periodically, this notice would appear in the Richmond press or on military billboards:

> "Sick and disabled soldiers on furlough or honorably discharged from the service, who are temporarily detained in Richmond, Va., will be comfortably provided with food, quarters and attention at the Wayside Hospital, corner of Franklin and 19th."[93]

After the war ended, the U.S. military authorities took over Grant's Factory and used it as a barracks for occupation troops.

50.
The Federal Pontoon Bridge

Drive two blocks on 19th Street south to Cary Street, turn left and park your car on Cary. Two short blocks west is the place where 17th Street intersects the James River.

On April 3, 1865, the day of Richmond's fall, General Weitzel's Federal Engineers began a pontoon bridge across the river. Working around the clock, they completed it in two days. An essential task it was, too,

Pontoon Bridge, called "the Pontoon" by Richmonders, from the foot of 17th Street. Built April 3–4, 1865, it was really two bridges, one each way.
National Archives

A Northerner's drawing of units of the Army of the Potomac moving across the Pontoon Bridge from Manchester to Richmond during May 1865. These troops are on their way to Washington for the Victory Parade.
Virginia State Library

for all of Richmond's bridges had been burned; the city was cut off from the south.

Like all such military bridges, it was constructed from a line of anchored wooden boats stretched across the river. Across the boats were laid heavy wooden timbers to bear the traffic. Only a few feet above the water, the bridge undulated up and down as heavy loads crossed. General Lee used this bridge when he entered Richmond after Appomattox, riding up 17th Street and turning into Main Street.

The entire Union field army, General Sherman's western army and General Meade's Army of the Potomac crossed over this "Pontoon," as the townspeople called it, on their way to Washington. The city's weary inhabitants looked at this immense blue-coated legion as it traversed Richmond in April and May of 1865, and wondered out loud to one another how they could have resisted so long.

On the night of May 10, Sherman's 14th army corps was camped on Buck Hill, just outside of Manchester. Very early the next morning Colonel J. T. Holmes, commanding officer of a Wisconsin infantry regiment, put his horse at the front of his men as the thousands of Bluecoats formed into a long, winding column, then headed toward the pontoon bridge. The Colonel noted how the many flags and bayonets sparkled in the early morning light. As they moved across the bridge, the men were cautioned not to march in step or the rhythm would break it. Once the men passed over Mayo Island they were close enough to the city to stare at the burned commercial district and the outlines of Libby Prison.

The column skirted the burned buildings along Main Street, then passed up Governor Street, turning left into Capitol Street. The men gaped at Jefferson's columned Capitol, the center of the Confederacy, its classic beauty unharmed but blighted by ruined buildings on three sides. Turning west into Franklin Street, they passed General Lee's home on their left. Every soldier looked respectfully, for General Lee was bigger than life to these Northern boys too. Colonel Holmes could see no one outside except a Union sentry, but somehow everyone knew the great man was inside. The column then turned north, taking the Brook Turnpike out of town. As they trudged past the three defense lines, the men contemplated those terrible and formidable trenches that had held back the Federals for so long.

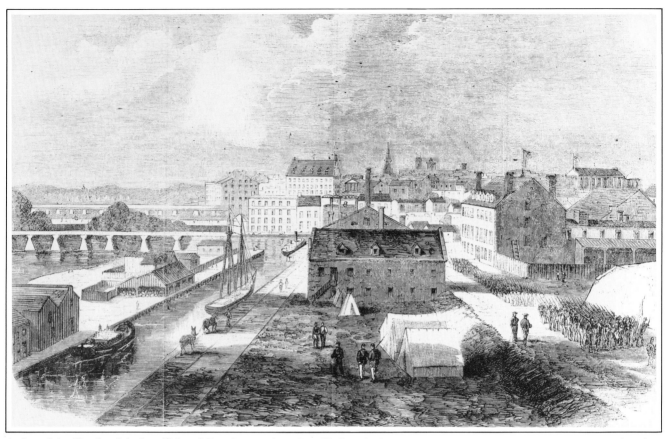

A view of the City Canal dock at 17th and Cary Streets where the "silk dress balloon" was inflated prior to her land and sea excursions into battle, June 1862.

Virginia State Library

51.
The City Gas Storage Tanks and the Confederate War Balloon

As you stand here, imagine seeing the inflated Confederate "silk dress balloon" as it was being hauled east by wagon or later sailing past on board Teaser *through the City Canal before proceeding down James River for an appointment with destiny near Malvern Hill.*

Just east of the corner of 17th and Cary Streets was the dock of the City Canal and nearby were the city gas storage tanks. On this site on the morning of June 27, 1862, Confederate Major E.P. Alexander inflated his "silk dress balloon." He was about to be the first Southerner to go into air combat in this exotic weapon which was constructed from silk dresses contributed by many Southern ladies. After being filled with 7,500 cubic feet of gas, for which the gas company charged $22.50, the balloon was hauled by wagon down Cary Street to the York River Railway Depot, about six blocks east. The Major tied the balloon to an engine, climbed aboard a flat car with his crew, and the small train puffed out of Rocketts.

After the train halted on a good elevation, Alexander climbed into the gondola. The crew cranked the balloon about 500 feet into the air, and the Major began watching the battle at Gaine's Mill to his north. He stayed for hours, observing enemy movements and signaling matters of interest down to the ground. It was he who first saw and reported the move of General Slocum's Blue Corps across the Chickahominy River to support the hard-pressed Union troops under General Fitzjohn Porter. Thereafter the balloon was used almost daily, taking different positions along the York River Rail Line as the battles shifted to the east and south. Both sides used balloons during the Seven Days Battles near Richmond. Both also did their best to knock down each other's balloons with cannon fire (the first attempt at antiaircraft fire). But even though the gunners tried to elevate the muzzles of their cannon, the balloons remained undamaged by cannon or rifle fire.

THIRD TOUR—EASTERN QUARTER

52.
Castle Thunder and Castle Lightning

Look now at both sides of Cary Street between 18th and 19th Streets. On the north side of the block was located Castle Thunder and on the James River side was Castle Lightning. Both were large brick factory buildings used as prisons throughout the war. They held citizens of doubtful loyalty, those who had committed serious crimes, spies and deserters. Occasionally executions were performed here, although more were done at Camp Lee and on Shockoe Hill.

On an autumn day in 1862, a strikingly handsome young Confederate lieutenant slightly over five feet tall, Lt. Buford by name, was clapped into a prison cell in Castle Thunder. One of General Winder's "lynx-eyed detectives" had found something suspicious about the young man; however, in due course it was discovered that the young man was not suspicious at all—just a young woman in disguise.

She was born Loreta Janeta Valesquez in Havana, Cuba, and was 24 years old. In 1856 she had married a planter named Roach in St. James Parish, Louisiana. After Roach's death for the Confederate cause, Loreta was compelled to act. Seeing herself as a 19th-century "Joan of Arc," she disguised herself in a Confederate officer's uniform, raised a company of infantry (the Arkansas Grays) and led it to Virginia. Here, she commanded the Grays through the First Battle of Manassas.

Major Alexander, the prison commandant, although shocked by her insistence on wearing male attire, was sympathetic to Loreta's plight. He enlisted his wife's support to try to obtain her release. They urged her to resume female attire, but she remained adamant. Nonetheless, the Major decided to put her case directly to General Winder, the provost marshal, who was also nonplussed by her insistence on wearing a uniform. However, the General agreed to her release, and she was taken into the Confederate "Secret Corps," and given dispatches to carry to General Van Dorn in the west. She served the Confederacy with courage, wounded twice while fighting under General Polk.

Later, Castle Thunder hosted two other male impersonators: sisters Mary and Molly Bell, who had served together in the army in Virginia for two years and had risen to the ranks of sergeant and corporal before being detected. They were released and sent back to their home in southeast Virginia.

A Northern drawing of crowded Libby Prison. There was no separate arrangement of cells. The officers slept on the floor at night.
Virginia State Library

53.
Libby Prison

Drive one block to 20th and Cary Streets. On the south side of Cary between 20th and 21st Streets is the site of Libby Prison. After the Seven Days Battles in late June 1862, the city found itself swamped with thousands of "live Yankees," as prisoners of war were called by the citizens. To house them, the Libby Warehouse, among other places, was hastily commandeered. It was a dirty, three-story, rectangular building in the midst of a commercial district. The prisoners were confined en masse to the open floors of the top two stories.

The winter of 1863–64 was life-threatening to the Federal prisoners at Libby. Food was scarce, and prisoners of war came last in line. As the winter grew

No photograph of the "silk dress balloon" has been found. However, the Federal balloon Intrepid, shown here in a photograph taken at Fair Oaks in May 1862, was probably similar. Inflated by field gas generators, Federal balloons enabled observers to see much of the Confederate capital and its surrounding military camps.
National Archives

frigid, Colonel William Irvine wrote from Libby, "Our men . . . are suffering and dying from exposure for want of necessary clothing." Another inmate, General Niel Doe, wrote, "The entire (daily) ration is a piece of hoecake . . . one small sweet potato and water."[94] Furthermore the prison was overcrowded; that winter over a thousand men were kept in the prison, when earlier it was thought full with 600. And, of course, there was no heat.

The prisoners believed they must escape or die, and some eventually did escape. One officer had discovered access to the basement floor by sliding down the inside of a chimney. The prisoners' leader, Colonel Thomas Rose, organized an escape team, and each night a small group dug under the eastern wall of the prison, using only a knife, auger, chisel and wooden spittoon to carry dirt. With extreme caution and secrecy they dug a 60-foot tunnel under the building. The night of February 9, 1864, 109 officers crawled through the tunnel, escaping into the darkness. Breaking into small parties, the groups headed east, trying to reach the Union lines at Williamsburg. One group went to Miss Van Lew's home for help, but she was not at home, and they disappeared back into the night.

About half of the officers escaped; the remainder, starved and nearly frozen, were rounded up over the next few days and were herded back into Libby Prison. The Bluecoats who reached the North carried the terrible tale of suffering at Libby and Belle Isle prisons that angered the North.

Retribution came quickly. Within a month of the escape, a large body of Union cavalry under General Kilpatrick descended on the city in an all-out effort to free the prisoners. The effort failed, but caused the city to take drastic action. Guards in Libby Prison's basement marched around a six-foot square mound of fresh dirt. Beneath the dirt was enough powder to blow the prisoners and the prison to eternity if the Blue cavalry approached.

Some 14 months later, the day after Richmond fell, President Lincoln paused on his walk into Richmond to look at Libby Prison. A group of blacks who were following called, "We'll pull it down!" "No," the President replied, "Leave it as a monument."[95]

Later that day, Mr. Lincoln, riding this time in a carriage with General Weitzel, paused again to look at the prison. The General used the opportunity to ask the President how to treat the captured people of Richmond. "I don't want to give you any orders on that, General," Mr. Lincoln replied, "but if I were in your place, I'd let 'em up easy."[96]

Libby Prison was not kept as a monument as Mr.

Looking down 20th Street at Libby Prison just after the fall of the city. The City Canal and the James River can be seen just behind the building.

National Archives

THIRD TOUR—EASTERN QUARTER

Lincoln suggested. After the war it remained idle for a while. Then, for a time, the brooding old place became a fertilizer factory. In 1889, it was sold to a Doctor Brambler of Cincinnati for $11,000. He had it dismantled, shipped to the Chicago World's Fair (1892–93), and rebuilt as an exhibition. When the fair closed, the building was again demolished. It is said that some of its bricks are in the walls of the Chicago Coliseum. The remaining bricks, floors and rafters were used to build a large barn in Hamlet, Indiana. Reportedly, some of the prisoners' names carved into the wood can still be seen.

54.
The York River Railroad Depot

Drive three blocks on Cary Street crossing 23rd Street. On your right, between 23rd and 24th Streets, and a few yards south on Canal Street, is the site of the York River Railway Depot. The depot sat close to the City Canal, and the tracks ran east for about three blocks along the quayside. This railroad was so badly damaged that it was the only one of Richmond's five railroads that did not resume operations after the war.

Shortly after noon on March 6, 1864, Lt. Christian, Co. H, 9th Virginia Cavalry, arrived at the York River Depot with half a dozen of his troopers guarding a baggage car containing the body of Colonel Ulric Dahlgren, the leader of a Union cavalry column raiding Richmond. Dahlgren had been ambushed and killed the day before in the swampy countryside of King and Queen County. On his body had been found an order to his troops instructing them to free the thousands of prisoners of war at Libby and Belle Isle prisons. Together with his raiders, the freed prisoners were to burn Richmond and kill the leaders of the Confederate government. This, if the order was genuine, was indeed total war. The people of the city were shocked.

The next day a crowd of curious and angry citizens arrived at the station, and filed by the open white pine box in which the Colonel's body lay. Among them was the Union spy, Miss Van Lew. John Jones, a War Department clerk, one of those who came, described the remains. "Its appearance," he wrote, "was good, dressed in a clean, coarse white shirt, blue pants, enveloped in a dark military blanket." The late Colonel was about five feet ten inches tall and around 30 years old.

Colonel Ulric Dahlgren, leader of a small column of Federal cavalry that, on March 5, 1864, attempted a surprise attack on Richmond. Dahlgren was killed in an ambush while trying to escape back to Union lines. *Virginia State Library*

His right leg was missing, having been amputated after Colonel Dahlgren was wounded at Gettysburg. The severed leg had been interred in the wall of a new foundry being built at the Navy Yard in Washington commanded by Admiral John Dahlgren, the Colonel's father.

About 2:00 P.M. a file of soldiers carried off the young Colonel's remains and buried them secretly at Oakwood Cemetery. Miss Van Lew and her Unionist friends, however, had other plans for the body.

55.
General Lee's Railroad Gun

Pause briefly at the corner of 25th and Cary Streets before turning left on 25th Street.

The small York River Railroad, whose terminal is described above, remained in operation fewer than five years and played a role in the history of warfare. As mentioned earlier, the first balloon used by the Confederates was moved to the battlefield by this rail line. Another first also occurred here.

At his headquarters on June 5, 1862, General Robert E. Lee, new commander of the Army of Northern Virginia, penned a note to the Confederate Chief of Ordnance, Colonel Josiah Gorgas:

> *"Is there a possibility," he wrote, "of constructing an iron plated battery, mounting a heavy gun, on trucks, the whole covered with iron, to move along the York River Railroad? Please see what can be done. See the Navy Department & officers. If a proper one can be got up at once it will be of immense advantage to us."*[97]

General Lee realized that his opponent, General McClellan, needed to move his heavy siege guns forward to blast his way into Richmond. With the roads made impassable to such heavy loads by the spring rains, Lee knew that McClellan would have to move the guns on the York River Railroad. If an armored gun could be built in time, he could move it to the front on the same railroad and shoot up the enemy's trains—thus keeping their heavy cannon too far back to do any damage.

The heavy gun with its armor plating was prepared quickly at the Confederate Navy Yard near Rocketts Landing. The gun and different segments of its armor were probably floated in separate loads by barge from the Navy Yard up the City Canal to a landing near the depot. Then the gun and its armor were off-loaded directly onto a railroad flatcar and securely bolted in place. During the Battle of Savage Station, June 30, 1862, the armored gun, pushed by an engine, moved east on the York River Railroad to a good firing position near the lines and went into action—the first railway gun in the history of warfare.

Lee's new invention probably did not affect the outcome of the campaign, for by this date the Federals were in hasty retreat towards Harrison's Landing. They were frantically trying to pull their supplies, siege guns and other heavy baggage back to safety.

Apparently no picture of General Lee's armored railroad gun was made, but this photograph shows a Federal heavy mortar mounted on a small flatcar which served as a firing platform.
National Archives

56.
The Second Alabama Hospital and Mrs. "Judge" Hopkins

Turn left into 25th Street; drive two blocks to Franklin Street and again turn left. On the southwest corner of 25th and Franklin Streets stands the old Yarborough and Turpin Tobacco Factory (now Pohlig's Paper Box Factory), which in wartime was the Second Alabama Hospital. It was customary for sick and wounded men from each state to be hospitalized together, sometimes in a hospital bearing their state's name, or at least to be placed in a ward or wards together in one of the large camp hospitals.

Colonel (later Brigadier General) Josiah Gorgas, chief of the Confederate Ordnance Department, was the best man the Confederacy had in the area of supply and logistics. *Virginia State Library*

On a day in May 1862, young Mrs. "Judge" Hopkins of Mobile, Alabama, strode into Soldiers Rest Hospital on Clay Street, announcing she had come for Mrs. Beers. The latter declared that she was happy working where she was. Mrs. Hopkins stood firm. "A large number of wounded Alabamians will arrive this morning . . . Come now with me; I have no time to lose!" Fannie Beers succumbed. They drove by carriage through the city, then hurried into dusty Yarborough and Turpin Warehouse, which Mrs. Hopkins had just secured from the army. About 50 Alabama soldiers had just arrived and were sitting and lying about on the rough floor "in every conceivable position . . . of feebleness, extreme illness . . . utter exhaustion."[98]

Workmen began to unpack large boxes sent from Alabama containing pillows, sheets, medical supplies and even wine and clothing. As the hospital took shape, the worst cases were handled first. By nightfall all the men were in cots between clean sheets. But four men died that night, the first deaths Mrs. Beers had seen. She fought for needed control since Mrs. Hopkins had made her the matron of the hospital.

Mrs. Hopkins never waivered in her commitment to the care of the men from her state. She gave her whole fortune of $200,000, received from her late husband, Judge Hopkins, to the Second Alabama Hospital and even put her own life at stake. When she heard of the wretched conditions among the wounded at one of the nearby battlefields, she drove out from the city into the battle itself. She moved about the field, improvising ways to move the wounded to the Richmond hospitals. Fighting raged all around her, and she was wounded twice. One leg wound caused her to limp the rest of her life. General Johnston, the field commander, allowed "that the Second Alabama Hospital was more useful to his army than a new brigade."

Now Pohlig's Paper Box Factory, the Yarborough and Turpin Tobacco Factory (1853) occupied this building at the beginning of the war, which looks much the same today as it did in the 1860s. It later became the Second Alabama Hospital where Mrs. "Judge" Hopkins tended to the wounded.

Virginia Historic Landmarks

57.
Richmond's Horsecars

Drive one block west on Franklin Street, and turn left on 24th Street. Go one block and turn right into Main Street going west.

In 1860 the Virginia Legislature chartered a street railway for the city. On September 4, 1861, the *Richmond Whig* reported that a spacious car drawn by two horses "is now making regular trips daily between the corner of Main and 9th and the head of Rocketts Street,"[99] about one and a quarter miles at a cost of five cents. Soon service was extended from Rocketts as far as Brook Road.

Less than a year later, the tracks were taken up and the service discontinued. The steel rails were needed by the navy to make armor plate for an ironclad warship being built at the Richmond Navy Yard. When completed it would strengthen the defense of the James River, now dependent on the fort at Drewry's Bluff. Richmond's streetcar tracks had gone to war.

58.
Trooper Boykin Retreats Down Main Street

Go west on Main Street. At the intersection of 22nd Street on the southwest corner are two late 19th-century buildings which make up the Henrico County Court House. They replaced the wartime courthouse which was damaged by fire during the Evacuation (April 2, 1865). Imagine a few hundred horsemen, dressed in ragged gray and heavily armed, trotting past this site at dawn on April 3, 1865. They were the rear guard of the Army of Northern Virginia leaving Richmond.

Trooper Boykin was tired; everyone was tired— horses and men—as they rode west along Main Street, for they had eaten little and been riding most of the night. He didn't realize it, but the only world this young veteran knew, horse soldiers, camp life and defiance of the Union, was about to end. He had watched the infantry and artillery retreat off the Richmond lines the night before, leaving only several hundred troopers from his own outfit (Gary's South Carolina Cavalry Brigade), to cover them. After midnight the Brigade too had silently departed, broken into groups to cover all the roads into Richmond from the south and east, for a great flood of "Blue Bellies" would be using them as soon as they discovered that the way was clear. Gary's South Carolina boys dropped off small parties to hold key road junctions briefly, then mounted up and galloped back to their comrades. Boykin could see that Richmond was on fire and he could hear occasional large explosions.

By 7:30 A.M. the whole brigade was trotting through Rocketts and into Main Street. Trooper Boykin was riding the rear party, glancing occasionally over his shoulder; some of Union General Kautz's horsemen were not far behind. At 21st Street a wall of flame blocked them, but the column detoured around this pocket of fire back into Main. The troopers fought to control their horses, maddened by the flames and by the rising pandemonium in the city streets. Even the veteran Boykin was startled by the howling mob of looters swirling around them after they crossed over Shockoe Creek. Added to the confusion was an inferno of flame and smoke up ahead, the pounding of shells exploding at the Arsenal and the gnawing certainty that the Blue cavalry were gaining at their backs. Yet Boykin was still able to see the sad, silent faces of women peering out of the windows who knew they were seeing the last of that "beloved army."

Reaching 14th Street, the rear guard turned left into the approaches of Mayo's Bridge, the only James River bridge left. Boykin felt the intense heat of the nearby fire, a cliff of flame and smoke. The mob was thicker

East Main Street at 19th looking west toward Shockoe Creek. The Union Hotel is in the left foreground. The last of the Confederate army left Richmond by this route. Gary's South Carolina Cavalry Brigade, with the Yankees behind them, were the last to cross Mayo's Bridge before it burst into flames. *Library of Congress*

THIRD TOUR—EASTERN QUARTER

Henrico County Courthouse, on the southwest corner of Main and 22nd Streets, as it looked during the war. Damaged by the Evacuation Fire, the original building was replaced in 1896 by one of Romanesque design.
Virginia State Library

than ever here, for this was the district of the food commissaries and warehouses. Gary's men had to brandish their weapons and shoulder their horses through; the noise was too great for voices to be heard. Finding the small bridge over the City Canal aflame from end to end, the troopers hunted desperately for another. They found one, and soon they were all across. The horsemen clambered up onto Mayo's Bridge. They reformed their ranks and trotted slowly over the timbers, vastly relieved. It must have been about eight o'clock. Behind them, they noticed gray-clad soldiers torching bundles of wood spaced along the dry timbers of the bridge. They rode toward Manchester alone, with the bridge behind them in flames.

As they went, few onlookers in the traumatized city remembered that it was a South Carolina regiment that was the first out-of-state contingent to arrive in Richmond in the spring of 1861. Now, a South Carolina brigade was the last to leave.

59.
The Travail of Rebecca Jane Allen

As you continue on Main Street to 20th Street, take note that the small home of Rebecca Jane Allen once sat on one of the south corners of the intersection.

She was neither rich nor famous; only her name and a few lines about her remain. With her four small children, a husband away fighting with Lee, food nearly impossible to come by and her money worth less every day, she struggled courageously to get by. She had heard that the Yankees would enter the city on the early morning of April 3, 1865, and looking east she might have glimpsed their lead patrols advancing on the slopes of Church Hill.

But Rebecca Jane Allen had more pressing problems. The city was on fire all around her house. From the direction of the business district to the west, she could see billowing smoke and high tongues of flames. Another fire burned fiercely from the Canal, sweeping over 21st Street, a block away. Sometime after seven that morning, she led her brood of four to a vacant lot just across Main Street, seated them on a pile of boards and instructed them to stay there. The children watched their mother make numerous trips back and forth, carrying her possessions which she stacked near the boards. Finally she too sat on the boards, hugged her children close and guarded her belongings from looters.

Although she left no record of what she saw or felt, she surely had a front seat at the world's most important drama. Past her on Main Street hurried the watchful soldiers of both sides, including Trooper Boykin; Mayor Mayo returned wearily from his surrender; escaped criminals and the city poor looked for loot. There were freed Union prisoners from Libby Prison, just a block away, seeking food and help; convalescent soldiers trying to rejoin Lee or at least escape a Union prison camp; families like her own milling about; and later on the Bluecoats digging, dynamiting and pulling down walls on both sides of her to create firebreaks.

By midafternoon she knew her house was spared. Thankfully, she and the children returned with their possessions. That night they ate Union army rations—salt fish, hardtack and "glory-be!"—sugar and real coffee. They were survivors.

60.
The Old Stone House

On your right after you pass 20th Street, you will see the Old Stone House built in the 18th century. It is near curbside and easy to recognize because of its stone construction, unusual for Richmond. It is the oldest dwelling in the city.

After Richmond's fall, the headquarters of the Union Provost Marshal, Colonel Manning, was moved almost immediately from City Hall to the Old Stone House. Since the Provost Marshal's task was to restore order, the new location was ideal. The house sat in the oldest part of Richmond where gambling, crime and vice were endemic during the war. Near it were two buildings, Libby Prison and Castle Thunder, that the Provost Marshal had taken over and filled to overflowing with looters, criminals, deserters and other undesirables seized in a dragnet.

To establish order at the earliest moment, he was authorized to offer paroles to all Confederate soldiers who would apply. Thousands of them roamed the streets, hungry and uncertain about what to do next. The parole paper, when signed, constituted a promise not to bear arms against the Union. Suspicious of such a commitment and filled with doubts, the Southern soldiers looked for help from their old commander, General Lee. He had returned to the city but seemed inaccessible to the rank and file in his Franklin Street home with a Federal guard in the front yard.

During these trying days after his surrender, General Lee found much solace in taking walks in the darkness of the evening, sometimes dropping in on old friends, trying always to avoid any act that could appear provocative to the Union authorities. On one such visit to a friend's home, he was surprised to see standing before him in the candlelight one of the most daring of Colonel Mosby's scouts, Channing Smith. Mosby's men were still together and in the field. They had not surrendered, Smith told him, and Mosby had sent him to ask General Lee whether they should fight on or take

Colonel John Singleton Mosby, dynamic leader of partisan rangers behind Union lines in Northern Virginia. Shortly after Appomattox, Mosby sent his scout, Channing Smith, to General Lee to ask if the rangers should give their paroles. *Virginia State Library*

The Old Stone House, oldest house in Richmond, was probably built in 1737 by Jacob Edge, a German immigrant. For a time in 1865, it was the headquarters of the Federal Provost Marshal.
Virginia State Library

THIRD TOUR—EASTERN QUARTER

their paroles. After a pause, for Lee was under parole himself, the General quietly suggested that Channing and the rest of his boys "go home and help to build up the shattered fortunes of our old state."[100]

Lee's opinion quickly passed through the Confederate grapevine in Richmond and eventually throughout the South. In effect, it assured the soldiers they had done all that honorable men could do; they could now go home and rebuild their lives. Thousands of men again followed their leader, took their paroles and started their long walks home. No doubt the Provost Marshal, Colonel Manning, never realized what the quiet man on Franklin Street had done to bring peace to the city.

61.
The Bread Riots

As you approach the intersection of Main and 15th Streets, you are at the center of the ten square blocks where the Bread Riots occurred.

Since many of the farms near Richmond that produced food for the city had been devastated by the Seven Days Battles, the winter of 1862–63 was a hard one for Richmond. Prices spiraled, food was hoarded and by late winter the poor were in serious want.

On the morning of April 2, 1863, a crowd of 400 to 500 women and boys gathered at Capitol Square. A Richmond lady on her daily walk before breakfast was surprised to see so many people milling about at that hour. She asked a pale young girl, "Is there a celebration?" "There is," she replied. "We celebrate our right to life. We are starving. . . . We are going to the bakeries, and each of us will take a loaf of bread."[101] Soon the crowd left the Square, moving down 9th Street.

When they reached the food shops on Main and Cary Streets, the crowd was out of control, breaking into food and other shops. Their numbers grew as undesirable elements joined them; spreading disorder from Main and Cary Streets all the way to the First Market on 17th Street. The local militia arrived and confronted the rioters at the Market and also at the core of the disorder, the intersection of 15th and Main Streets.

The troops were reluctant to shoot their own neighbors. In the midst of the confusion a wagon arrived. From this vantage point Mayor Mayo and Governor Lecher tried to calm the crowd. The women and their supporters did not budge; the situation grew tense and

One onlooker identified Mrs. Jackson, a painter's wife, as the leader of the Bread Riots. She was said to have been a large woman carrying a bowie knife and a pistol. *Virginia State Library*

ugly. Then Jefferson Davis arrived and addressed the crowd with a conciliatory talk, but ended it with an order. "I will give you five minutes to disperse. Otherwise you will be fired upon!" The troop commander ordered, "Load!"[102] For a time no one moved. Then the mob began to scatter.

The government was alarmed. By evening artillery batteries took positions at this intersection and elsewhere, siting their pieces to sweep the streets. Under official pressure, the press made no mention of the riot, for the government did not wish the Federals to know how desperate the city was for food.

The riots nevertheless had a good effect because they forced the City Council to take steps that probably saved many lives before the war was over. Acting through the Overseers of the Poor, the council established a Board of Supplies to maintain a coordinated search of the countryside for food to be sold at cost. The system worked, and in the next winter about a thousand families a month were fed under this arrangement. As conditions further deteriorated, the council was forced to abandon distinctions between the better off and the poor; food was collected for all. In the final weeks nothing worked; the Federals arrived to find a starving city.

FOURTH TOUR

Area of the Evacuation Fire

Even though burned by the Evacuation Fire and rebuilt in the years since, the business center retains much of its old character. Enough of the 19th-century district survives among the tall modern buildings to let you know what it was like. It still serves, as it did during the war, as the business center of Richmond.

GENERAL LEE'S CITY

MAP 12

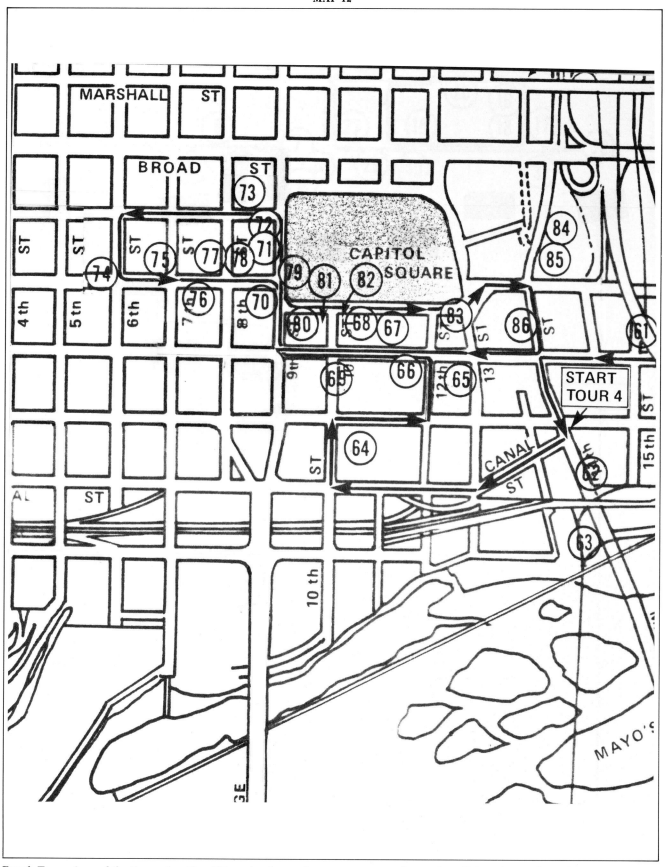

Fourth Tour—Area of the Evacuation Fire. Take note of several one-way streets and a number of sites clustered together. *Library of Congress*

FOURTH TOUR—AREA OF THE EVACUATION FIRE

As Richmond's only bridge for wagons, buggies and pedestrians, Mayo's Bridge was a vital link to Manchester and the south. During 1864 and 1865, troops and supplies moved constantly on it as forces shifted back and forth between the Richmond and Petersburg lines.

Library of Congress

62.
Mayo's Bridge

Mayo's Bridge after 8:00 A.M., April 3, 1865. The fire had destroyed all but its stone abutments. *National Archives*

Turn left from Main Street into 14th Street, drive to Canal Street and stop for a few moments. Stretching across the James River from the foot of 14th Street, the wartime wooden bridge occupied the same site as today's bridge, a location where bridges and ferries have stood since the beginning of Richmond.

Lt. General Ewell posted Colonel Clement Sulivane of Custis Lee's Division at Mayo's Bridge about 4:30 A.M. on April 3, 1865, directing him to burn the bridge when so ordered. Barrels of tar and bundles of kindling had been scattered near the Richmond shore by an Engineer party. Considering the bridge's dry timbers, the preparations were adequate.

It is a lonely job to stay behind and burn a bridge, the Colonel thought. His waiting men watched anxiously as a constant stream of troops, wagons, cannon and refu-

GENERAL LEE'S CITY

gees moved rapidly across. It was light now; the two railroad bridges had been ignited just before dawn and burned brilliantly, and the fire in the city was spectacular. His was now the only bridge left across the James. It must go soon! About 8:00 A.M. he heard horsemen clattering up onto the bridge. It was General M.W. Gary's Brigade of South Carolina Cavalry—a small remnant of veterans who had fought in the defenses of Richmond for nearly a year, now the rear guard of the army.

It was time for somebody to give that order! At that moment, General Joseph Kershaw of Ewell's Command trotted up to Sulivane, pulled in his horse and coolly tipped his hat. "All over," he yelled above the din. "Goodby! Blow her to hell!"[103] Sulivane gave a signal. The Engineers and his own men put their flaming torches to the tar barrels and bundles of wood. Almost instantly the dry timbers caught as the men hurried along toward Manchester. Behind them the bridge became a roaring inferno.

63.
President Davis Leaves Richmond

Before you leave 14th Street near its intersection with Canal Street, look to the right of Mayo's Bridge, and you will see the site of the depot of the Richmond and Danville Railway. It was not more than 75 yards to the right of Mayo's Bridge between the canal and James River.

When President Davis arrived at Danville Station about 7:00 P.M. on the evening of April 2, 1865, a

MAP 13

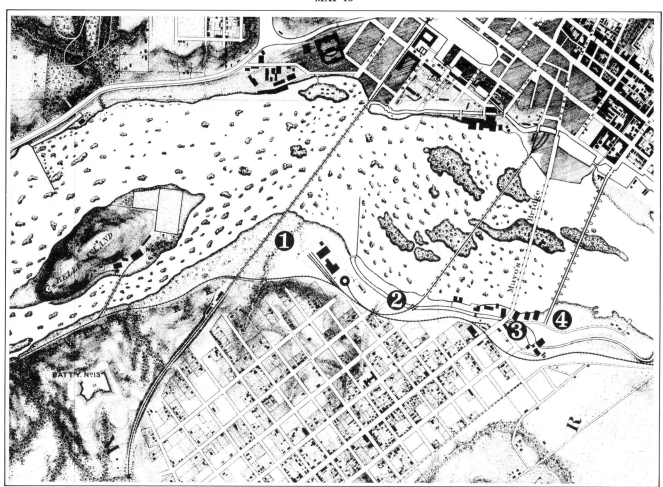

Richmond's Wartime Bridges, U.S. Corps of Engineers Map, 1865.

Library of Congress

(1) The Richmond and Petersburg Railroad Bridge.
(2) The Richmond and Danville Railroad Bridge.
(3) Mayo's Bridge.
(4) The Federal "Pontoon" Bridge (built April 3–4, 1865).

FOURTH TOUR—AREA OF THE EVACUATION FIRE

This portion of an 1851 panoramic print by Bohn shows the Richmond and Danville Depot just to the right of Mayo's Bridge. Its railroad bridge was the only covered bridge across the James River at Richmond.
Virginia State Library

special train with steam up was waiting to carry him and the cabinet to safety at Danville. Some naval cadets saluted him as War Secretary Breckenridge led him to his seat. One coach was reserved for the presidential party of about 30 people. The other cars carried a contingent of 60 naval cadets, escort to the President and guard for the Confederate treasury reserves in gold on board. Also on flat cars were boxes of archives and crated ordnance machinery as well as a few citizens who had begged or bribed their way aboard.

In spite of the mounting danger, Mr. Davis would not allow the train to start. Hour after hour it sat on the tracks as he hoped for news from General Lee that could cause him to cancel his flight. While they waited, the Secretary of State sedately smoked cigars, the Postmaster General and Navy Secretary strolled along the line of cars in the semi-darkness, and the War Secretary rode his horse back and forth along the platform, on the ready for any word from General Lee. No message came; in fact at that moment Lee was being forced from Petersburg, and Richmond lay open. Some of the distinguished passengers wondered if Mr. Davis was waiting too long and whether the galloping Union Cavalry might not have crossed the rail line and would be waiting for them down the track.

Finally Mr. Davis abandoned hope and gave the word to go. It was about 11:00 P.M. when the train slowly chugged out of the station, tooting its whistle as it went. People in the city long remembered that mournful sound. As the train picked up speed, passing through Manchester, another "whistle blast floated back in salute to the doomed city."[104]

64.
Shockoe Warehouse

Drive west on Canal Street, then turn right on 10th Street. Follow 10th one block, then turn right again into Cary Street and drive east to 12th Street. Turn left into 12th Street. Due to construction and one way streets, you have circled the Shockoe Warehouse district. All buildings here at the time of the war were destroyed in the Evacuation Fire.

During the fall of 1864, a plan matured in Lt. General Ewell's Military Department of Richmond for destroying supplies before they could be seized by the Union should the city fall. Mayor Mayo and many citizens strongly opposed the plan, knowing that the only way to destroy bulk quantitites of supplies was by fire. So great was the faith in Lee's army that few believed the city would actually fall, and consequently no final decision was reached. Marked for destruction in the plans were four public warehouses, including Shockoe, which consisted of three buildings containing tobacco, wool and possibly some military supplies.

Then on April 2, 1865, the unthinkable happened. The Yankees would enter Richmond the next morning. About 3:00 A.M. at his home on 12th and Clay Streets, Judge Campbell, Confederate Assistant Secretary of War, was awakened by tremendous explosions down James River. Warships had been blown up to prevent their capture. Buildings had been so shaken that people had taken to the streets. The judge himself walked through the warm night toward his office in the War Department, continuing down 9th Street to the Canal Basin. He noticed twinkling lights resembling lamps in the windows of Shockoe Warehouse and realized the building had been set on fire. Soon it was ablaze from end to end. As he watched, the flames began to spread to the Gallego Flour Mills just west of it and to shops on Cary Street. He could see none of the customary emergency actions taking place. There was no alarm bell from Capitol Hill, no signs of the city fire engines. He turned and walked quietly to his home.[105]

Most historians believe that General Ewell's soldiers started the Evacuation Fire, but General Ewell sought to refute this charge in his report to General Lee shortly after the war. Not his men, he wrote, but the rioters and arsonists had set fire to Shockoe and other warehouses.

was here, high and low centers of entertainment—variety shows, fine restaurants, gambling houses, the better houses of prostitution, scores of saloons. The Confederate government's departments, bureaus and offices were spread out along Bank and Main Streets. Along and south of Cary Street was the largest and most active industrial center of the Confederacy, employing thousands of men and pulsating day and night. Its foci were the Arsenal and the Tredegar Iron Works, and around them were crowded satellite shops and businesses involved in making the tools of war. Anything one wanted or needed in Richmond could be found in this area, but by 1865 anything of consequence cost a fortune in Confederate script.

In the midst of the Evacuation Fire, John Leyburn, a businessman, was trying to save some papers in one of the district's commercial buildings. "I cast a farewell look up Main Street. The *Dispatch* and *Enquirer* newspaper offices were all in a blaze; the banks and the American Hotel were just catching, and from the doors and windows of some of the fashionable stores volumes of flame were bursting."[106]

Inside the American Hotel, an aged guest, Isaac Davenport, had simply refused to leave. After repeatedly urging the old gentleman to go, the hotel employees were obliged to leave him or lose their own lives. Perhaps he had chosen to die, and if so, he quickly got his wish among the tumbling, flaming walls.

After the Fire residents found the incineration so complete that, in poking through the ruins, they had difficulty identifying their own streets.

65.
The Business District

Drive north one block up 12th Street; turn left on Main Street, driving west.

Even in the last days of the Confederacy, the business district west of Shockoe Creek retained its noisy, crowded character. This was the center of the city's life, much more so than the political center of the Capitol. The good food shops, fine clothing, furniture and luxury stores were here; until very late in the war such goods were reaching the city via blockade runners, putting in at Wilmington. The district also contained the banks, leading business offices and a number of hotels and newspaper offices. Almost all the night life

66.
Kent and Paine Dry Goods Warehouse (General Hospital No. 5)

Proceed west on Main. General Hospital No. 5, burned in the Evacuation Fire, was located on the south side of Main near 11th Street.

On June 25, 1862, Mrs. Sara Rice Prior entered the new hospital at the Kent and Paine Warehouse and asked for work as a nurse. Arriving there the next morning, she found cots on the lower floor of the large, airy building already filling with casualties from the fighting near Richmond. An aisle between the rows of cots stretched to the rear of the building. Broad stairs

FOURTH TOUR—AREA OF THE EVACUATION FIRE

MAP 14

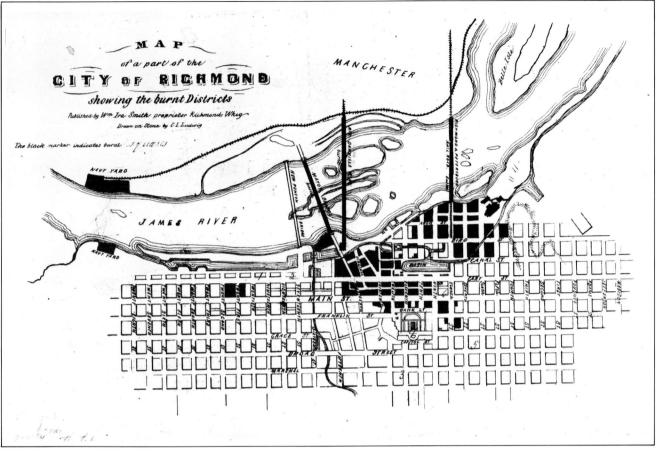

Burned districts after the Evacuation Fire. The Richmond Whig, the only one of Richmond's papers to resume publication after its fall, published this map of the damage to the commercial and industrial districts.
Virginia State Library

led to a second floor where more cots were being laid.

The matron, a beautiful Maryland woman named Mrs. Wilson, regarded her doubtfully, stressing how exacting and sometimes shocking the work was: "The nurses have to do anything and everything." Reluctantly, she agreed to give Mrs. Prior a try. A few moments later, while passing a cot, Mrs. Prior saw a nurse holding a pan for a surgeon. The red, raw stump of an amputated arm was held over it. Mrs. Prior fainted.

"You see, it is as I thought," the matron said bending over her as she regained consciousness, "You are unfit for this work. One of the nurses will conduct you home." But Mrs. Prior was back the next day armed with smelling salts and spirits of camphor. Mrs. Wilson seemed friendlier. "I will give you a place near the door, and you must run out into the air at the first hint of faintness." She went on, "You will get over it. See if you don't."[107]

Mrs. Prior stuck it out and gradually adapted. Her appearance a few days later, accompanied by a man bearing a basket of clean, well-rolled bandages, with promises of more to come, cinched her acceptance. All of Mrs. Prior's sheets, tablecloths, dimity counterpanes, chintz furniture covers, napkins and fine linen underwear had been cut up with the help of a sewing circle at the Spottswood Hotel that was just now finishing the job.

One night after she had become an experienced nurse, Mrs. Prior was awakened with a summons to attend a patient, Colonel Brokenborough. When she reached his bedside, . . . "the end was near. Once, as he stirred," she was to write, "I slipped my hand under his head and put his canteen once more to his lips. After a long time his breathing simply ceased, with no evidence of pain. We waited awhile, and then the young soldier who had been detailed to nurse him rose, crossed the room, and stooping over, kissed me on my forehead, and went out to his duty in the ranks."[108]

Judah Benjamin, former U.S. Senator from Louisiana, became Confederate Attorney General, Secretary of War and finally Secretary of State. Fleeing from Federal authorities in 1865, Mr. Benjamin reached the British West Indies and then took ship for London, where he lived the rest of his life. *Library of Congress*

think it somewhat remarkable that he was not carried off three or four months ago."

Readers in Richmond must have enjoyed the article, for President Davis was very much alive and active. Indeed, he lived on another 28 years. Local editors fulminated against the *Herald*, hurling epithets—"Yankee delusion and unreliability . . . most mendacious journal . . . a record for lying second to none."[109]

67.
Confederate Reading Room

When you reach the intersection of Main and 11th Streets, look north. The Confederate Reading Room was located two doors up on the west side of 11th Street.

On September 19, 1861, the *Richmond Examiner* announced that a reading room for soldiers had opened, offering newspapers, books, magazines and writing materials. A special effort was being made to stock papers from all over the South so that soldiers could read their hometown news; Northern papers were there when available. The entry fee was 10¢.

Late in 1861 the *New York Herald* reported that "Our latest telegraphic advices from Louisville, Washington and Fortress Monroe assure us positively of the death of Jefferson Davis. . . . Considering that his health has been in a very shattered condition for several years, and considering his extraordinary labors, anxieties, and exhausting excitements of the last five months, we . . .

68.
President Davis's Executive Offices

On the right of Main Street, taking up the whole block between 11th and 10th Streets, is the three-story U.S. Post Office, a building of Italianate design. Built in 1858 as the U.S. Customs House, it held the principal offices of the Confederate government throughout the war. On the first floor was the Treasury Department; the second, the Department of State and the cabinet room; the third, President Davis's offices.

Built very solidly of steel and concrete, the old Customs House was a credit to its designer, Albert Hybrock, and its contractors, for it stood in the direct path of the engulfing Evacuation Fire and survived.

Shortly after noon on April 2, 1865, Mr. Davis held his last cabinet meeting in Richmond in the second floor cabinet room. Debonair Secretary of State Judah Benjamin, the President's confidant to the end, was there puffing the usual cigar and holding his slender, goldheaded cane. Also attending were Secretary of War Breckenridge, Postmaster General Reagan, Treasury Secretary Trenholm (though unwell) and Navy Secretary Mallory. Special guests included Mayor Mayo and Governor Smith of Virginia.

The President reviewed the current military situation. He reported that he had wired General Lee to see if Petersburg could hold, but Lee's reply emphasized that the lines could not be restored; retreat was inevitable that evening. The Richmond & Petersburg Line was under fire already, and the last escape route, the Richmond and Danville tracks, would not remain open long. Mr. Davis stressed the importance of the government remaining as a unit functioning elsewhere and announced that they would convene the next morning at Danville. It was the sunset of all their dreams, but the President acted with dignity and style. He adjourned the meeting, then walked up 12th Street to the Confederate White House to begin packing.

FOURTH TOUR—AREA OF THE EVACUATION FIRE

69.
High Jinks at the YMCA Hospital

Continue west on Main to 10th Street. An emergency YMCA hospital was located to your left, down 10th Street between Main and Cary. During the war the YMCA maintained three emergency hospitals: the aforementioned, plus one on Clay Street between 7th and 8th, and a third at a location no longer known.

This small, temporary hospital stood in the midst of Richmond's crowded business district, among the shops, saloons, gambling places, commercial buildings and eating establishments. Directly across 10th Street from the hospital was a house of prostitution.

The girls of this place, sometimes referred to as "Cyprians" by the newspapers, solicited directly from the windows. They would entice young men off the street and patients from the hospital as well, to the dismay of the authorities. Any breaches of discipline at the hospitals were dealt with severely. A favorite "corrective" was to lock unruly patients in the "Dead House" or morgue where they could cool off in the company of their dead comrades.

Although this punishment appeared humorous to some, there was nothing amusing about the fact that many young men, Union and Confederate alike, fell victim to venereal diseases contracted in the brothels.

70.
Mechanic's Hall

Proceed on Main Street to 9th Street and turn right. Go one short block on 9th. The site of Mechanic's Hall is on your left just opposite to the opening of Bank Street.

About 8:15 A.M. on April 3, 1865, when the raging Evacuation Fire failed to demolish the Customs House, it then swirled around the building's east and west sides in two gigantic walls of flame and smoke. The westernmost column of fire ignited Mechanic's Hall which held the War Department more than a block away, and consumed it quickly "sending up great jets of flame

This photograph of Main Street and the Customs House, the office building used by Mr. Davis and other Confederate leaders, was taken after the Evacuation Fire looking east from the Spottswood Hotel at 8th Street, also a survivor because of a fluke in the wind.

National Archives

and smoke."[110] This building had great significance for the Confederacy.

It was here on April 17, 1861, that the Virginia Convention passed an Ordinance of Secession of Virginia from the Union by a vote of 103 to 43. This was in response to President Lincoln's call for 75,000 volunteers to suppress secession in the South which was regarded by Virginians as an act of invasion. After the vote, celebration and pandemonium reigned in Richmond.

With war ahead, the Mechanic's Hall was partitioned into offices for the Confederate War and Navy departments and other offices too. One Sunday evening in March 1862, a Navy clerk at the building received an incoming cable that announced a spectacular victory. The *Virginia*, an ironclad of original design rebuilt from the scuttled *U.S.S. Merrimac* had attacked the Union fleet at Hampton Roads. The *Virginia* had knocked out three of the most powerful Federal warships. The *Cumberland* had sunk; the *Congress* had gone ashore and blown up; and the *Minnesota* had been driven aground. When the clerk got off duty that evening, he rushed to his boarding house. Though it was after eleven, he began knocking on doors, waking the sleeping people to tell them the glorious news. "It was too much to endure alone."[111]

By September 29, 1864, the news was not as good. In a surprise attack, Grant captured Fort Harrison, the very anchor of the strongest part of Richmond's defenses on the James River. Richmond must surely fall! John Jones, a war office clerk, felt the anxiety and climbed to the War Department roof. Before his eyes stretched vast, "rising clouds of white smoke and dust which obscured everything, spreading gradually over the distant tree line, floating along the horizon . . . and down the trench of James River."[112] The sounds were terrifying, especially the heavy pounding of siege guns and the incessant roar of field artillery. Over the next two days General Lee, moving forces from Petersburg, attacked to drive the Yankees out of Fort Harrison in vain; he then contented himself with blocking the hole in Richmond's defenses. He succeeded and the city was secure for the moment.

While the army was at nearby Petersburg during the last year of the war, General Lee could sometimes be seen in Richmond. A young boy of 12 remembered all his life that on December 14, 1864, he saw General Lee standing in front of the War Department. It was cold, the boy remembered, and the general was wearing a short blue cloak over his uniform. He looked robust; his face was ruddy and cheerful, and his hair and beard, white under a gray slouch hat. Waiting for his horse to be brought around, he stood patiently on the sidewalk, striking his gloved fists together absent-mindedly. Obviously his thoughts were far away.

71.

How the Evacuation Fire Was Put Out

As you drive up 9th Street toward Grace, Capitol Square is on your right. You may well wonder why it was not destroyed by the Evacuation Fire which burned unchecked for so long.

A little after 8:00 A.M. on April 3, 1865, Major General Godfrey Weitzel, the Union commander of forces entering Richmond, stood on the landing of the Capitol steps. He had just arrived, and he watched the approaching flames just beyond the southern fringes of Capitol Square. The Square, crowded with refugees, was in grave danger and nobody was doing anything to fight the fire.

Weitzel realized that if the city was to be saved it was up to him. At that moment General Ripley's Infantry Brigade (300 officers and 4,200 men) arrived, formed into line, and were stacking arms north of the Capitol. General Weitzel ordered Ripley to put out the fire. General Ripley feared the fire was uncheckable. How-

Ruins of Mechanic's Hall (Confederate War Department), a casualty of the Evacuation Fire, on 9th Street just opposite Bank Street. Meeting here in the spring of 1861, the Virginia State Convention decided to secede. *Virginia State Library*

FOURTH TOUR—AREA OF THE EVACUATION FIRE

Richmond firemen and Federal soldiers pulling down burned buildings on the fringes of Capitol Square as the cleanup from the Evacuation Fire begins.
Library of Congress

ever, he rang the alarm bell which brought few volunteers. A quick inspection of the city firefighting equipment revealed that someone had cut the hoses. Meanwhile, Weitzel's Engineer troops that Ripley had requested arrived with wagons of shovels, picks and gun powder.

After estimating the wind direction and determining the arrangement of vacant lots and structures in the path of the fire, a decision was made to create a firebreak across the whole front of the advancing flames as quickly as possible. The troops began to batter down walls and detonate buildings. It was touch and go, and as more Bluecoats arrived, General Weitzel committed them to reinforce Ripley's tiring men. Bucket brigades were formed to save the homes on the safe side of the firebreak which were endangered by flying sparks. The Governor's Mansion was saved, but the court building at the southeastern end of the Square was lost.

For a time the outcome was in doubt; then the troops began to prevail, helped greatly by the wind's dying down. The firebreak held, and backfires were successful in breaking the momentum of the fire. In six or seven hours, about midafternoon, the citizenry began to realize that most of the city away from the commercial district had been saved. People didn't like to admit it, but the discipline and courage of the Yankees had saved the city. One lady noticed, almost against her will, that under their bright blue uniforms they were only boys, just like their Confederate counterparts.

72.
St. Paul's Church

Continue on 9th Street and turn left into Grace Street. St. Paul's Church is on the southwest corner to your left. Designed by Thomas Stewart of Philadelphia and finished in 1845, the church has a restrained, classic exterior. During the war years it had the loftiest spire in Richmond, a city of many high spires. The steeple was taken down in 1911 for fear it would topple in a high wind.

A Mathew Brady photograph of the Washington Monument and St. Paul's Church in April 1865. An entry in Mary Chestnut's diary relates that someone reported 14 generals at Sunday services at St. Paul's on March 3, 1864. The same party suggested that less piety and more drilling of commands would suit the times better.

National Archives

President Davis and General Lee were parishioners as were most of the social elite of the city. By early May 1863, church attendance had increased in response to constant military crises. The Battle of Chancellorsville raged 50 miles to the north, and General Stoneman's Union cavalry also was threatening to enter vulnerable Richmond. Mrs. Chestnut, a parishioner at St. Paul's, reported what occurred one Sunday: "The rattling of ammunition wagons, the tramp of soldiers, the everlasting slamming of those iron gates to Capitol Square" just across the street scattered one's thoughts. Adding to the anxiety, were the notes the sexton would deliver during service to worshipers whose relatives had been brought in wounded or dead from Chancellorsville. The families would leave for the train station to look for their loved ones. Not even the Reverend Dr. Minnigerode was exempt. As he bent over the chancel rail, the sexton "whispered to him . . . then disappeared." Minnigerode left with him. After services, there at the door stood Mrs. Minnigerode "wretched and wild looking." Thankfully, the message was in error. Deeply agitated, Dr. Minnigerode explained on his return from the station, "Oh, it was not my son who was killed, but it came so near it aches my heart."[113]

In the winter of 1864–1865 when Richmond was short of everything but beautiful women, many weddings still occurred. On January 19, 1865, Major General John Pegram, one of Lee's best young generals, and Miss Hetty Cary, one of the loveliest belles of Richmond, stood at St. Paul's altar, in the company of social Richmond. Less than three weeks later Mrs. Pegram was back at St. Paul's, pale and wan; General Pegram's coffin was placed in the chancel where the two were joined in marriage such a short time before. He had fallen at the frozen field of Hatcher's Run on February 6, 1865.

Sunday, April 2, 1865 was a pleasant day, and President Davis was in his pew on the center aisle. The choir had just sung "Jesus, Lover of my Soul" when the sexton walked slowly down the aisle and handed the President a sealed note which he opened and read. Constance Cary, sitting behind him, saw Mr. Davis's face turn gray. Picking up his hat, he walked quietly from the church. To some, he seemed to walk a bit unsteadily. A murmur swept the congregation. Soon, notes were passed to other officials, and they left too. As they came out of church, the parishioners learned what had happened. The lines had broken at Petersburg, the President would have to flee that night, and Richmond would be given up. Confirming their worst fears were bundles of documents from the Second Auditor's office burning in the roadway.

Richmond belle, Miss Hetty Cary, who married General Pegram at St. Paul's in January 1865. A guest wrote that she was altogether the most beautiful woman of any land.

Virginia State Library

FOURTH TOUR—AREA OF THE EVACUATION FIRE

Brigadier General John Pegram of Richmond, division commander under Lee, was killed at the Battle of Hatcher's Run three weeks after his wedding to Hetty Cary at St. Paul's. *Virginia State Library*

Army of Northern Virginia. They served in the hallowed Pickett's Division and were among those who marched forward in the famous charge at Gettysburg.

Each Sunday St. Peter's, like all the churches in Richmond, offered a prayer for the chief of state. The war played havoc with this custom. On the sabbath of April 21, 1861, the prayer for the President of the United States, Abraham Lincoln, was omitted. The church authorities substituted a prayer for the Governor of Virginia, the Honorable John Lecher. After Virginia entered the Confederacy, the prayer was then said on behalf of the Honorable Jefferson C. Davis, Provisional President of the Confederacy. The use of this prayer became habit until April 3, 1865, the day the Federal army entered Richmond. An order came down to reinstate the name of Abraham Lincoln. In fact, the occupation commander, General Weitzel, didn't enforce the order fast enough, thus incurring the immediate wrath of Secretary of War Stanton. Within the week Weitzel was relieved of his command. After Lincoln's assassination on April 14, congregations found themselves praying for yet another president, this time the Honorable Andrew Johnson of Tennessee.

73.
St. Peter's Catholic Church

Continue west on Grace Street. St. Peter's Church is on your right at the northeast corner of Grace and 8th Streets. Built in 1834, this small church was the cathedral of the Richmond Diocese until 1906.

It was customary for parishes, towns, states and other social and economic groups to organize, man and equip military units and send them off proudly to defend the homeland. A rifle company was recruited from St. Peter's Parish in the spring of 1861. Called the "Montgomery Guards," it was actually Company C of the 1st Virginia Infantry Regiment, the oldest and most honored unit in the state. On a Sunday in May the Guards, in dress uniform and bearing symbolic medieval weapons, trooped into the basement of St. Peter's. Here, Bishop McGill of Richmond blessed them and prayed for their deliverance in the times ahead. On May 25, 1861, the Guards departed by rail for Manassas Gap. Their captain, John Dooley, wore a vivid green uniform to emphasize his Irish origins, and Father Teeling from the parish went along as chaplain. The Montgomery Guards fought for four years in Lee's

A building of the Greek Revival style, this small church was the Roman Catholic Cathedral of Richmond until 1906.
Virginia Historic Landmarks

Linden Row, built in 1847 and 1853, still suggests the appearance of the residential section of Franklin Street during the war years. Lined on both sides with fine Greek Revival and early Victorian homes, the dirt street was shaded by leafy trees and brightened by spring flowers. Often columns of Confederate troops traversed Franklin Street, drawing cheering crowds from their homes to the curbs.

Virginia Historic Landmarks

74.
Franklin Street

Still driving west on Grace turn left into 6th Street, then drive one block to Franklin Street. Turn left again on Franklin and park.

Like Main Street, Franklin was a central artery, running the length of the wartime city from east to west. West of Capitol Square, which bisected it, was a stretch of a dozen blocks where many of Richmond's well-to-do families lived in comfortable homes along this tranquil, tree-lined street.

Mrs. Mark Valentine, a resident of Franklin Street, recalled that several times "the Army of Northern Virginia passed down Franklin Street on their way to battle." One stirring occasion was on April 20, 1862, when 8,000 cavalry and artillery troops marched briskly east down Franklin, while at the same time many more thousands of infantry men marched down Main Street, one block south. The horsemen filled the streets to the curbs, creating a great commotion and "suffocating the crowds with sheer excitement." Their bugles sounded before them, and at their head rode the incomparable cavalier, Jeb Stuart himself.[114]

"Who could lose with such men?" thought Judith Brockenbrough McGuire, a refugee from Alexandria, now living in Richmond. She hurried to find a place on the sidewalk, her anxious eyes scanning for her nephew, Captain William B. Newton. A "halt" was given just as he, at the head of his company of cavalry, was passing her. She called him, but mounted and amid the din and tumult, he could not hear, but as he raised his cap to salute the ladies near him, his quick eye caught (hers); in an instance he was at (her) side. "Don't be uneasy," he said, ". . . we are going to the right place. . . ." His face glowed with animation. Then the "halt" was over; there were shouts and commands; he was back in his saddle and had moved on.

FOURTH TOUR—AREA OF THE EVACUATION FIRE

She had meant to be cheerful, but after he was gone she "found that her face was bathed with tears." He had looked as if "the world were bright before him,"[115] but hardly a month had passed before Captain Newton was captured near Williamsburg. After an exchange of prisoners he rejoined his regiment, but in October 1863 he was killed.

75.
Headquarters Department of Richmond

Drive east on Franklin one block to 7th Street. At this intersection stood a house which served in 1864–65 as the Headquarters Department of Richmond. This command was responsible for Richmond's defense, using local troops and a small contingent of Lee's men, although in crisis, Lee's regulars would move in quickly and take over.

At 10:00 A.M. on April 2, 1865, General Ewell returned to his headquarters from an all night ride to the lines south of the city and found orders on his desk directing Richmond's evacuation to begin that same evening at 8:00 P.M. The task seemed overwhelming. However, he sent men to prepare supplies and stores to be burned; others were sent to Libby and Belle Isle prisons to march the prisoners west—away from the path of Grant's army; still others were ordered to collect all the horses they could find. When all the preparations were finished, Ewell and his men would join Lee's retreat.

By 2:00 P.M. there were crowds around the headquarters seeking every scrap of news they could get and blocking the intersection and walkways. They saw one mud-covered officer ride wearily through the crowd, dismount and shoulder his way through the people to go inside. Shortly the news was spread, confirming their fears: He was one of Pickett's officers, fresh from the disaster of Five Forks the evening before. He had survived the fighting by simply riding west to the Burkeville depot of the Richmond and Danville Railroad. Here he loaded his horse on a flat car and "retreated" all the way into Richmond.

Later one of Richmond's citizens saw General Ewell coming out of his headquarters. The one-legged general was strapped into the saddle of his horse, Rifle. He rode over to the War Department at 9th and Bank Streets, where he was seen leaning across his saddle conferring animatedly with another horseman, General Breckenridge, the Secretary of War. Around them, hurried preparations were progressing for the Confederate evacuation that evening.

These two men left Richmond in different directions. Early next morning "Old Bald Head" rode across Mayo's Bridge with the last of his men to join General Lee and the final retreat. He was captured a short time later when the Federals cut off much of Lee's army at Sayler's Creek. Breckenridge rode out of Richmond that night along the canal path to the west to join Jefferson Davis at Danville and follow him for a time in his flight from the Federal authorities.

The Lee home, the middle house in the 700 block of Franklin Street. The houses on both sides of the street have now vanished, leaving the Lee home the single survivor of the old residential neighborhood.
Library of Congress

76.
General Lee's Richmond Home

As you drive from 7th to 8th along Franklin Street, you see in midblock on the right the brick home rented by General Lee. Mrs. Lee and her family lived here from early 1864 through the end of the war. After Appomattox Lee returned here, staying until September 1865, when he left for Lexington.

All along both sides of leafy Franklin Street were pleasant homes where wealthy families lived. On one side of the Lees was George W. Randolph's home; for a time he was the Confederate Secretary of War. The Randolphs entertained frequently, often at big receptions with many young officers and pretty girls. By contrast, the Lees were not very social. Not only was Mrs. Lee quite incapacitated by rheumatism, but also she was concerned about entertaining in such times of genuine hardship and scarcity. She "felt a sense of impropriety in the suggestion that the wife . . . of the commanding general of half-starved armies, himself sleeping in a tent and living on ascetic fare, should . . . lead in any entertainment of a social sort."[116] Instead of entertaining she and her daughters spent their days sewing clothing and socks for the soldiers. On a visit to the Lee home in early 1864, Mrs. Chestnut remarked that the place was like an industrial school. The Lee girls and other ladies were plying their needles.

Arriving in Richmond on the evening of the Evacuation, Percy Hawes, one of Lee's young couriers, stopped by the Lee's tall, brick home on Franklin Street. He found Mrs. Lee drinking tea with her daughter and two visiting officers. Though obviously suffering from her rheumatism, she was enjoying herself, voicing her firm decision to remain in Richmond and her home, no matter what.

Mid-morning the next day found her still at home. The Evacuation Fire was drawing fearfully close. The United Presbyterian Church went up in a flash of fire and smoke, just half a block to the east. The dwelling next to the Lee home caught fire briefly. Still Mrs. Lee would not leave. She sat quietly in her parlor, reassuring frantic callers. Her calmness and presence of mind matched her husband's. She proved to be right; the fire went no farther.

77.
The United Presbyterian Church Burns

Continue to 8th Street on Franklin. The United Presbyterian Church, built in 1821, once stood on the northwest corner of this intersection. The destruction of this fine brick building by the Evacuation Fire the morning of April 3, 1865, ended the fire's advance to the north.

Young Addison Hodge stood on the roof of his uncle's home at the corner of 5th and Main Streets, throwing buckets of water on sparks which had struck the roof and watching the wall of flames approach. His attention was caught by flames "dancing up the shingled steeple" of the United Presbyterian Church some three blocks northeast. Then the tall spire "swayed and tottered, falling backward on the main roof" with an explosion of fire. Soon the church was a flaming ruin.[117]

For Addison Hodge and all the homeowners in the Franklin Street neighborhood, it must have been an omen of approaching doom. They had just seen Dr. Reed's church destroyed. The War Department was falling in too; burning papers were being wafted about the smoking streets. The Commissary Department, with its desks and papers, was consumed already. Cary and Main Streets were an inferno; Bank Street was beginning to catch fire, and now it had reached Franklin. Judith McGuire, one of the residents, wrote later, "At any other time it would have horrified me, but I had ceased to feel anything."[118]

78.
The Fire and Mrs. Stannard

At the northeast corner of 8th and Franklin Streets was a fine home belonging to Mrs. Robert C. Stannard, directly across the street from the United Presbyterian Church.

Perhaps the closest thing that Richmond had to a Parisian salon was the home of the wealthy widow Mrs. Stannard. Her spacious, beautifully furnished home became the meeting place for notables of the Confederate government, celebrities, military heroes and the rich, powerful and beautiful people of Richmond. Such sought-after men as Secretary of State Judah Benjamin, Senator Semmes and Generals Wade Hampton, Jeb Stuart and John B. Gordon could be found at dinners and receptions here. Other guests could include the lovely Carys, Constance and her two cousins, Hetty and Jennie. Connie added brains and imagination, Hetty and Jennie offered great beauty and musical talent.

Mrs. Chestnut, often a visitor at Mrs. Stannard's, felt that Richmond needed diversion and entertainment as an antidote to the war that drained them all. "I do not see how sadness and despondency would help us," she observed. "If it would do any good, we could be sad enough." Besides, General Lee himself approved of dances and parties in the city for the morale of his men. To the very end of the war, there continued to be frequent social gatherings, if only to share some hard-to-come-by food or coffee. These parties acquired special names like "muffin matches" or "waffle worries."[119]

On the morning of April 3, 1865, not even Mrs. Stannard was immune from catastrophe. The Evacua-

FOURTH TOUR—AREA OF THE EVACUATION FIRE

Looking north on 8th Street at the farthest point of the Evacuation Fire's advance up Shockoe Hill. The ruins of the United Presbyterian Church can be seen on the left above Franklin Street (the first crossing), and opposite are the ruins of Mrs. Stannard's home, the site of many social gatherings.
Virginia State Library

tion Fire was headed directly toward her home. She went upstairs and packed a trunk with her favorite clothing and jewelry and had a servant carry it downstairs to the sidewalk. There she sat, watching coolly the fearsome scenes around her. Across the street the United Presbyterian Church suddenly burst into flames, then her own house went up. Meanwhile, from Capitol Square came great billows of smoke that seemed to announce the imminent destruction of the whole city. However, she assured a fleeing friend that she had no fears, and she remained sitting calmly on her trunk wearing a fine dress, her most fashionable bonnet, thin veil and long gloves, observing the chaos through her lorgnette.[120]

After the war, Mrs. Stannard resumed her career as a society hostess, this time in Washington, D.C.

79.
The Corner of Franklin and 9th Streets

As you drive east on Franklin Street, pause at the corner of 9th Street if the traffic permits; it was one of Richmond's busiest corners during the war. The War Department and the President's offices were a few doors down to the right; the Capitol and the Governor's Mansion were across the street in Capitol Square, and the bulk of the Confederate offices and bureaus were grouped in a nearby complex that stretched from 8th to 12th Street and between Grace and Cary Streets.

John Jones, clerk in the Confederate War Department, tells about an incident that he witnessed when passing this corner on a September day in 1864. Suddenly he heard a shout, "Halt!" From the direction of Franklin Street, a large man in civilian clothes ran by, obviously terrified. In pursuit came a hard-breathing, red-faced soldier who stopped, and taking deliberate aim with his rifle "burst a cap (misfired)!" He hurriedly fixed another cap into the nipple of the firing mechanism, and again the weapon misfired. By this time the civilian had escaped somewhere up 9th Street.[121] This incident was an example of the difficulties the government had with the conscription of civilians into the Confederate army. Many who remained in civilian life tried to avoid combat service at all costs, and even those serving in Richmond were fearful. One staff officer expressed a growing sentiment when he received orders to join Lee's army. To go into battle against Grant's large, well-equipped army in late 1864 was a "sentence of death."[122]

80.
Shoot-Out On Bank Street

Turn right on 9th Street, then turn left into Bank Street. Not more than three blocks long, Bank Street marks the southern boundary of Capitol Square. The Evacuation Fire burned out Bank Street completely except for the prewar, strongly built U.S. Customs House, used as the Confederate Treasury Department and Presidential offices.

A somber side of antebellum society was the custom of dueling, which persisted in Richmond during and even after the war. An unorthodox duel occurred on Bank Street on April 24, 1865. It happened that Mr. Dixon, Clerk of the House of Delegates, had dismissed one of his clerks, a Mr. Ford, from his position. Mr. Ford politely told Mr. Dixon of his intent to shoot him

Looking across Bank Street from Capitol Square into the burned business district, smoke is still discernible among the ruins. The horses hitched to the Square's iron fence probably belong to Federal officers with business at the Capitol. *Valentine Museum*

wherever they next met. About 2:00 P.M. the two men met on Bank Street near the Treasury. Both men drew revolvers. Mr. Ford shot a bystander, then killed Mr. Dixon with a shot through the chest.

81.
The Transportation Quartermaster

On the right side of Bank Street, between 9th and 10th Streets, were three buildings that held important bureaus of the Confederate government. In the one nearest 10th Street was the office of the Quartermaster in charge of Transportation.

Rail transportation was generally regarded as the most mismanaged, neglected department of the Confederate government. For a time control remained with headstrong railroad presidents who did as they pleased. Later, government intervened to draft railroad men and commandeer iron rails (for armor plate and ordance) and other equipment, but conditions did not improve. With demands on the system at an all-time high, soldiers and civilians habitually suffered from serious food shortages while thousands of bushels of grain rotted at one station and hundreds of barrels of meat at another. The quality of passenger traffic deteriorated as maintenance of the roadbeds and rolling stock was neglected. By 1864 the railroads were approaching collapse.

Miss Clara Lynn wrote of her efforts to depart by rail from Richmond to the family home in Norfolk in the spring of 1864. The government had requested that all able noncombatants leave Richmond, for food was growing scarcer and the city could soon be under siege.

"For the first two mornings we got no further than the (Richmond and Petersburg) depot. The train service was absolutely inadequate to carry such a crowd. On the third morning (by starting early) we secured a corner seat . . . I sat on an empty stove which had a round top . . . Two mortal hours it took the train to start. With the most unearthly groans and rattling of all the internal machinery, we'd get a little start, then something would break or threaten to break, so we'd back up again and be patched. In the meantime doors were locked, for every seat was full.

"Every now and then a soldier with one arm or on crutches, for every able-bodied man stayed in the city . . . well, one of these would put his head in the window and whisper to a mother . . . 'Madam, please lend me your baby.' The baby was . . . handed out of the window, and in a few moments soldier and baby appeared at the door and demanded admittance of the guard.

"The rule that prevailed on all the railroads . . . (was) that the ladies coaches were reserved strictly for women and children and only the men belonging to them . . . The guards must have been in on the secret, for I have seen the same baby act as door-opener to half a dozen soldiers in almost as many minutes; making a steady round, out at the window, and in at the door, as fast as it could be managed.

"At last we got off with many a thump and bump. . . ."[123]

82.
The Federal Courthouse

Continuing to drive east along Bank Street, you will see on your right the United States Post Office, occupying the block between 10th and 11th Streets. You saw the Main Street side of this building and read about it in selection No. 68.

It is common knowledge that the center block of the Post Office held the offices of President Davis and the Treasury and State Departments. Less well known is the fact that ironically President Davis was brought here, to the building so closely associated with his service to the Confederacy, to be arraigned on a charge of treason against the United States.

On May 15, 1867, pale and much enfeebled by his confinement in a cell at Fortress Monroe, Mr. Davis sat in the ground floor courtroom surrounded by his lawyers. Among them was Mr. Burton Harrison, his wartime private secretary. Richmond was outraged that the United States would proceed to such extremes, and even some Northerners shared these sentiments. What to do about Jefferson Davis continued to be a profoundly controversial issue two years after the war.

That morning the courtroom was jammed with uneasy onlookers, almost all supporters of Mr. Davis. Presiding Judge Underwood, a Northern man and partisan of Reconstruction, was much disliked and feared in Richmond circles.

Soon after the proceeding began, His Honor signaled the position of the U.S. government in a way that filled the courtroom with the wildest jubilation. "This case," he said, "is undoubtedly bailable."[124] That meant to the lawyers, and then instantly to everyone else, that the government was prepared to release Mr. Davis from confinement. Immediately, Horace Greeley, who had come down from New York, set about arranging bail. Since Mr. Davis was without funds, Greeley, six other prominent Northerners including Cornelius Vander-

After being discharged under bail, Jefferson Davis emerges from the Federal Court House, the same building that had held his wartime offices. He was accompanied by a joyful crowd to his hotel.
Virginia State Library

FOURTH TOUR—AREA OF THE EVACUATION FIRE

bilt and five Virginians jointly put up bail. Jefferson Davis was then dismissed by the court and escorted by a cheering crowd in his carriage in a triumphal parade to rooms in the Spottswood Hotel two blocks away. By either chance or design, he occupied the same suite that had been his when he arrived in Richmond in 1861 to take up his presidential duties.

Two years later the U.S. government withdrew from further legal action against Jefferson Davis by quashing the indictment for treason.

83.
Belvin Block

Bank Street becomes Franklin Street as you cross 12th Street. Belvin's Furniture Store probably occupied the right side of Franklin between 12th and 13th Streets. Destroyed in the Evacuation Fire, the store was part of a larger complex of office space known as Belvin's Block, which mostly housed Confederate offices.

Sometime after 2:00 A.M. on April 3, 1865, an ambulance pulled to a halt outside Belvin's Furniture Store. The body of Lt. General A. P. Hill, one of General Lee's corps commanders, lay inside. He had been killed early the previous morning in the fighting that

Bank Street looking east from 11th Street shortly after the Evacuation Fire. The ruined wall that juts out from the right in the middle distance is what is left of the Belvin Block. A few hours before its destruction, the Hill cousins found a coffin in Belvins Furniture Store for General Hill in the early morning hours of April 3, 1865.
Library of Congress

had broken the Confederate lines at Petersburg. The General's nephew, Henry Hill, Jr., had spent the previous day and a large part of the night trying to bring the body to Richmond. He now needed to find a coffin. He located his cousin, G. Powell Hill, who was in the process of burning papers in the Paymaster General's Office, and the two young men went searching for a coffin.

They found the business district being looted by a rampaging mob. Discovering Belvin's Furniture Store wide open and empty, they searched for a coffin on their own. After locating one, they carried the General's body to a nearby office. The two men washed his face and looked for his wounds. He had been shot through the heart. They placed him in the coffin, and loaded it into the ambulance and drove off through the mob and smoke.

Crossing Mayo's Bridge, probably not two hours before its destruction, the two Hills headed the horses toward the Winston family farm on southside where G. Powell Hill's parents were living as refugees. They arrived to interrupt the elder Hills at breakfast. They reported that General Hill had died, and that the whole Confederate position in front of Richmond and Petersburg had collapsed. The young men then went out to the Winston family burial grounds and, with the help of a black man, buried General Hill.

By a curious chance, both Generals Jackson and Lee spoke of General Hill in their final moments. Jackson's words in delirium were, "Order A.P. Hill to prepare for action; pass the infantry to the front." In a similar way, General Lee's final words were, "Strike the tent. Tell A.P. Hill to come up!"[125]

Lt. General Ambrose Powell Hill, savior of the day at Sharpsburg and one of Lee's top commanders, was killed at Petersburg trying to prevent the breakthrough of his defense lines.
Virginia State Library

GENERAL LEE'S CITY

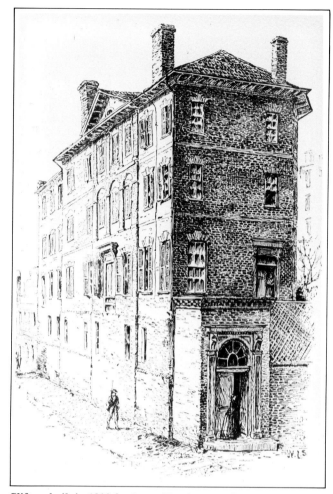

Clifton, built in 1808 for James Harris, was a fine home on ample lawns located on high ground above Shockoe Creek. It became a rooming house after 1843, and by the time the Cary girls lived here in 1861, it was much run down. *Virginia State Library*

84.
Clifton House

As you approach the intersection of Franklin and 14th Streets, look left on 14th Street. Half a block up the street is the site of an old rooming house, the Clifton House, which was demolished in 1905.

Connie Cary and her two cousins, Hetty and Jennie, war refugees from Maryland, lived here the first winter of the war. "A dismal old rookerie," Connie described it. Nevertheless, the three romantic girls, later known throughout Richmond as the "Cary Invincibles," tried to make the best of a bad situation, even giving the hotel their own name—"the Castle of Otranto."

One serious drawback for these socially minded girls was that Clifton House was so crowded with refugees it offered no place to entertain guests. The girls explored the building and discovered that it was honeycombed with subterranean passages, one leading to an unused doctor's office a few doors down steep 14th Street. This unlikely place they converted into a tasteful sitting room where they held frequent parties. The girls would lead their guests by candlelight from the hotel through the tunnel to the old office. It was not unusual to see a general enter "hugging a bottle of candied peaches," or a congressman bearing "his quota of sardines." The girls might provide a ham or turkey in those early days of the war.

Generally considered the chief beauty of the war, Hetty had talent as well, for she had written the stirring words to "Maryland, My Maryland." Recalling their days at the Clifton House, Connie observed, "We girls managed to extract sunbeams from cucumbers."[126]

85.
A Heroine Stops at the Ballard House

Also at this intersection of Franklin and 14th Streets were two prestigious hotels—the Ballard House on the northeast corner and the Exchange Hotel on the southeast corner—owned by John B. Ballard. An upstairs passage over Franklin Street connected the hotels. Both offered spacious parlors, wide hallways and high ceilinged rooms with marble mantles.

On an early June day in 1862, the attractive widow and zealous Southern partisan who lived in Washington, Mrs. Rose O'Neal Greenhow, registered at the Ballard House. She had just come through the lines on a truce boat. It was she who, in early summer 1861, had somehow discovered that the Union army would advance to Centreville, Virginia, during the third week of July. Through a sister conspirator she was able to smuggle the information out of Washington through the lines to General Beauregard, the Southern commander whose force stood west of Bull Run Creek. The timeliness and accuracy of her information enabled the Confederates to concentrate two armies in the area, and on July 21, the combined Confederate force routed the Union army inflicting severe losses, sending it pell-mell back to Washington. Mrs. Greenhow's espionage was discovered, and she was imprisoned for months at the Old Capitol Prison in Washington.

FOURTH TOUR—AREA OF THE EVACUATION FIRE

Mrs. Rose Greenhow, perhaps the most famous of the Confederate spies. This photograph was taken by Mathew Brady when Mrs. Greenhow and her daughter were imprisoned at the Old Capitol Prison in Washington. The Greenhows exasperated their captors and were eventually sent through the lines on the truce boat to Richmond in 1862. *National Archives*

Haughty Mrs. Greenhow was eventually sent through the lines to Richmond, having tried the patience of her jailers beyond endurance.

On the evening of her arrival at the Ballard House, the only reward she had ever wanted for her patriotism was given her. President Davis himself called on Mrs. Greenhow to express the gratitude of the whole Southern nation for her daring and successful espionage. "But for you," he told her, "there would have been no battle of Bull Run." She cherished his words and kindness "as the proudest moment" of her life.[127]

But her remaining days were limited. After her visit to Richmond, she left for England where she tried to publicize the plight of the South. In 1864, as the pressures against the Confederacy mounted, she sought to return home on a blockade runner. Off the shoreline at Fort Fisher, North Carolina, she tried to make her own way ashore in a small boat, because she greatly feared capture by a pursuing Federal ship. Her small boat swamped in the turbulent waters; and she drowned, carried under by the weight of a bag of $40,000 in gold coins tied around her waist.

GENERAL LEE'S CITY

The Ballard House (left), connected by an upstairs passage to the Exchange Hotel (obscured by buildings), in a wartime photograph. John P. Ballard is said to have built the former in 1855, angered because he couldn't get a room at the Exchange. General Lee customarily stayed at the Exchange Hotel after the war on his infrequent visits to Richmond. Both hotels were closed in 1896 and demolished some years later.
Library of Congress

86.
Vannerson Studio

Turn right into 14th Street and drive south one block to Main Street, then turn right again. At one of the corners of this intersection stood the studio of J. Vannerson which, like the other buildings of Main Street's business section, was consumed by the Evacuation Fire.

On a day in early 1864 General Lee dressed in his finest uniform and presented himself at Vannerson's photographic studio to have some portraits taken. Edward V. Valentine, a Virginia sculptor then studying in Germany, needed the portraits to model a small statue of the Southern hero. The likeness was to be sold at a Confederate bazaar in Liverpool, England, for the benefit of disabled Southern veterans. For such a purpose General Lee lent himself gladly.

Mr. Vannerson is thought to have taken four views. Although General Lee left no record of the event, Mrs. Lee did send a hastily worded note to Mr. Valentine's sister:

> "My Dear Madam:
>
> General Lee went to Vannerson's yesterday and had the photographs taken for you. I do not know if they are completed but you can see them or whether they will answer your purpose (sic). I should like to see them before you send them anyway."

The note's last sentence reflects Mrs. Lee's insistence on approving any likenesses of the General before they were made public.

The photographs were smuggled successfully through the Union naval blockade and reached Mr. Valentine in Germany. However, the sculptor was unable to complete the piece to his satisfaction in time for the bazaar. It was eventually completed, as photographs attest, but its whereabouts are now unknown.

The Vannerson photographs of General Lee are fine work, equal in quality to those produced by the Brady studios. Widely reproduced in daguerreotypes, paintings, prints and engravings, they provide the image of General Lee most often seen today.

FOURTH TOUR—AREA OF THE EVACUATION FIRE

General Lee in 1863—an etching made from one of the Vannerson photographs.

Library of Congress

FIFTH TOUR

Gamble's Hill, Hollywood Cemetery and Monroe Park

This final portion of the tour takes us through the city to its western fringes. We see more of Main Street, then drive south to view the settings of the Confederacy's largest industrial base. Outside the old city we visit Hollywood Cemetery. The tour closes with a drive down Monument Avenue with its statues of the Confederate great.

GENERAL LEE'S CITY

MAP 15

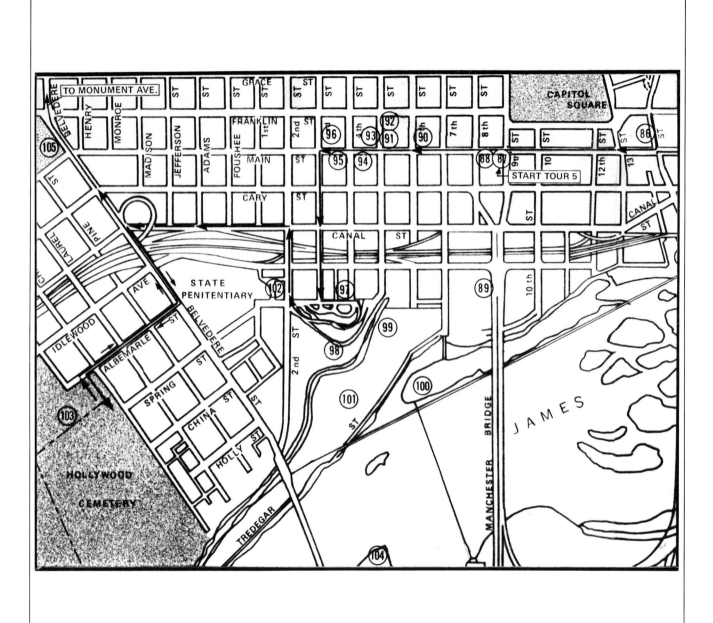

Fifth Tour—Gamble's Hill, Hollywood Cemetery and Monroe Park.

FIFTH TOUR—GAMBLE'S HILL, HOLLYWOOD CEMETERY AND MONROE PARK

87.
A Memorable Parade Down Main Street

As you drive west on Main Street you are retracing a four-block section you have already traveled, from 14th to 9th Streets. Before you is the most prosperous part of Richmond's business district, both now and during the war. The infantry corps of the Army of Northern Virginia paraded down this same street from west to east on April 20, 1862, a bright Sunday when the Confederacy was young and hopes were still high.

On this perfect spring day, jonquils, violets and hyacinths presented a spectacle of color in gardens and window boxes. Unexpectedly, Main Street was filled from curb to curb with the beloved army, bound for Yorktown to meet the immense force of Bluecoats under General McClellan. All day long and into the night, people stood transfixed upon the packed sidewalks, hypnotized by the ranks of marching men and the exhilarating blare of bands playing "Dixie," "Maryland, My Maryland," "The Bonnie Blue Flag" and other stirring marches—over and over again. One general, perhaps with political ambitions or just carried away with the excitement of it all, rode at the head of his men past the Spottswood Hotel where many of the high society watched. He retraced his path along his column several times leading different units past the

Materials from the American Hotel (foreground), which was destroyed in the Evacuation Fire, were salvaged and used to erect the Lexington Hotel, the first building constructed in the district after the Fire. *Valentine Museum*

same informal reviewing stand, and each time he was cheered for the encore.

Windows were full of girls throwing kisses and flowers at the ranks of young soldiers. Mounted officers who bore famous names, among them Longstreet, bowed over their saddles as they were recognized. Women set up tables of food along the street, and soon there were loaves of bread on the men's bayonets. Rifle muzzles held spring flowers, and some gray felt hats wore garlands. Anxious people stood rooted to sidewalks, searching for loved ones among the marching troops. Now and then a soldier would break ranks long enough for a hurried embrace, then run forward to regain his place.

As one regiment passed by, the men saw a lady and a young man in civilian clothes standing at a window waving their handkerchiefs. The soldiers called out, "Come right along, Sonny; the lady'll spare yer. Here's a musket for ye!" "All right, boys," came the shouted reply, "Have you got a leg for me too?" He placed on the sill the stump of a leg already given to the cause. Recognizing the man as an honorable veteran, the regimental commander called his men to a halt. The troops immediately stopped, oblivious to the oncoming columns behind them. Feet stamped the dirt street as the gray-clad men turned to face the window smartly, and all rifles came up in tribute to present arms. Then the wild scream of the "Rebel Yell" rattled the windowpanes as the ranks saluted a comrade. In a moment it was over; they were marching again, lost in a sea of soldiers.[128]

88.
The Spottswood Hotel

Driving west on Main Street, you arrive at 8th Street. The Spottswood Hotel sat on the southeast corner of 8th and Main. The hotel, new when the war began, had a handsome, classic iron facade on its Main Street front. It was the social and political center of Confederate Richmond. Jefferson Davis, his cabinet members and their families were guests here after their arrival in May 1861, until permanent homes could be found.

The Spottswood was the place to see and be seen; early in the war even captured Union generals on parole sometimes stayed here. They would stroll about the parlors in their blue uniforms, polite, talkative and at ease. After the surrender in 1865, Generals Meade, Sherman and Sheridan were overnight guests while their armies were passing through the city.

Mrs. Margaret McLean, a Maryland resident whose husband was fighting for the South, was a guest at the hotel on July 21, 1861. She noticed the anxious expressions on people's faces as her carriage drew up to the entrance late that Sunday afternoon. A gentleman responded to her query, "Yes, Madam, they have been fighting at Manassas since six o'clock this morning." She sat with a group of ladies in the lobby, all waiting impatiently for news from the battlefield. When a telegram arrived from President Davis with a list of some of the killed and wounded officers, most of the ladies were deeply relieved, but sorrow struck the wife of General Bartow and others, whose husbands had fallen. The lucky ones retired to their rooms with grateful hearts.

The next day was one of clouds and rain—and lack of information. People spoke softly to each other as they waited to learn the price of victory. Women who (had) talked so freely of their willingness to sacrifice their men on the "altar of freedom" were bowed down in the dust, fearing they might be called upon. "God help us," said one woman, "is this what we have prayed for?"[129]

By Tuesday the telegrams were coming in from Manassas, each one bearing its message of victory or its burden of sorrow. The President had returned from the field and spoke stirringly of the victory from a hotel window. For Mrs. McLean the saddest moment came "when the parlors were illuminated, friends were congratulating one another, and the street in front of the hotel was crowded with a cheering throng . . . while like a passage in a minor key in some brilliant piece of music . . . (she) heard at a distance the 'Dead March' and knew that the bodies of General Bartow and General Bee were being escorted to the Capitol."[130] She left the parlor. Hardly three months after the war began, its romance and glamour were gone.

89.
The Richmond and Petersburg Depot

As you drive through the intersection of Main and 8th Streets, look left three blocks to 8th and Byrd Streets. The Richmond and Petersburg Railway terminal was located here. It and the railway trestle that led south across the James River were lost in the Evacuation Fire. This area is now completely changed by new construction.

FIFTH TOUR—GAMBLE'S HILL, HOLLYWOOD CEMETERY AND MONROE PARK

The Spottswood Hotel as it looked when the war ended. A momentary shift of the wind spared the Spottswood from the Evacuation Fire. Note the debris from the Fire in the foreground. Five years later, the hotel burned to the ground on Christmas morning.

Library of Congress

On May 29, 1861, at the dawn of the Confederacy, President and Mrs. Jefferson Davis arrived at this depot to take up their duties in Richmond, a city that had become a national capital. Scores of "Stars and Bars" flew all over town, churchbells pealed, bands trumpeted, troops formed their ranks at the station, and a battery of artillery made ready to fire a presidential salute.

A special train from Petersburg whistled as it rounded the long turn through Manchester, clattered over the James River railroad trestle and drew slowly to a halt at the station. The President, with his wife, Varina Davis on his arm, dismounted from the cars, to be received by a formal delegation of welcome which included Virginia Governor Lecher, Mayor Mayo and the City Council. With gravity and military erectness he reviewed the honor guard, stood politely as his first presidential salute in his new capital boomed out over the town, then assisted Mrs. Davis into a ceremonial carriage.

The President and his lady drove up 8th Street toward the Spottswood Hotel with troops lining each side of the road, holding back the cheering crowds. Mr. Davis never would be so popular again, for his four year administration was clouded with acrimonious controversies over political and strategic issues. But this was the President's day. The slender, distinguished looking leader was at his gracious best. As the carriage moved along, someone threw a large bouquet of flowers to Mrs. Davis. It fell short into the street. The President halted the carriage, dismounted, picked up the bouquet and handed it to his wife. This graceful and charming gesture captured the crowd; it symbolized the civility and sensitivity of the Southern nation that set them apart from the supposed crassness, greed and commercialism of the "money-grubbing" North.

90.
Arlington House

Proceed west on Main Street and notice the northeast corner of Main and 6th Streets. The Arlington House, a small hotel built in 1837, once stood here. It was outside the path of the Fire but was demolished later in the 19th century.

Mrs. Nellie Gray stayed in the hotel during the winter and spring of 1864–65, and she left an account of conditions in Richmond during these last months of the war. Mrs. Fay, the proprietress, operated on the European plan. Nellie, her mother, and Miss Delie McArthur lived in one small room for $25 a month. At first, each woman cooked her own rations over a grate, but to save money and share food, they began to share their resources. Occasionally, other lodgers pooled their food to join the Grays for a meal, too. Coal was bought in common and kept up in the rooms. Nellie's husband at the front sent what he could, perhaps a rare sack of potatoes or peas, maybe a firkin of butter. The food, firewood, coal and clothing were stored under beds or about the room. Pots, pans, kettles and cooking utensils were arranged around the small hearth.

In spite of the crowded conditions, southern hospitality prevailed when company came, and somehow everyone was fed. If the guest was a soldier, he got the best part of what they had. Once Colonel Walter Taylor, Lee's young adjutant general, visited. "I confidently expect to come here some day and find a pig tied to the leg of the bed, and a brood or two of poultry. . . ." he said, after seeing how they lived.[131]

The ladies schemed to make enough money to survive from day to day. They knit socks and gloves to sell. One lady made neckties out of old pieces of silk. But inflation kept them on the verge of starvation. Lacking cash, they resorted to bartering possessions for peas, dried apples or rice.

Yet, Nellie "never remembers having more fun in her life than at the Arlington—while the country bristled with bayonets, and the air . . . shook with the thunder of guns." They were never in despair. "Our faith in Lee," she wrote, "and his ragged, starving army

Ruins of the Richmond and Danville Depot with Federal soldiers clambering about a destroyed engine. The roof of the Capitol (right) and the spires of St. Paul's and the Broad Street Methodist Church (left) can be seen in the background. *Library of Congress*

FIFTH TOUR—GAMBLE'S HILL, HOLLYWOOD CEMETERY AND MONROE PARK

amounted to a superstition. . . . There was hunger and nakedness and death and pestilence and fire and sword everywhere . . . but, somehow, we laughed and sang and played on the piano."[132]

Nellie was still at Arlington House when the end came on that unforgettable spring morning in 1865. Just after noon she saw a regiment of Blue horsemen ride up and quarter themselves in the homes next door on 6th Street. "We could hear them moving about . . . talking and rattling their sabres. . . . There was no unnecessary noise." Surprisingly, the presence of these orderly men was reassuring. Nellie remembered they gave the half-starved children all kinds of "sweets," making some of them quite sick.

This Bluecoat habit of giving candy to children immediately caused stories like this to circulate. "One little girl did not weep because the Yankees came. She clapped her hands and danced for joy, 'The Yankees have come! And now I have something to eat,' she cried. 'I'm going to have pickles and molasses and oranges and cheese and nuts and candy until I have a fit and die!'"[133]

91.
Hoge House

Go one block to 5th Street. The fine home which once stood on the northeast corner of Main and 5th Streets is now gone, but an excellent photograph remains. Early in the war, the Hatcher family lived there; later it was occupied by Dr. Moses D. Hoge and his family. Dr. Hoge served as minister of the Second Presbyterian Church next door. After Dr. Hoge's death in 1899, the house was torn down and replaced by a commercial building.

On a July afternoon in 1862, the Hatchers' butler looked doubtfully at a bearded caller wearing a faded, stained uniform that had obviously been through many campaigns. Probably a private, he thought. The man's hat was pulled low over his eyes, giving him the austere appearance of a country preacher. The caller wished to see Mrs. Hatcher. Before asking him in, the servant

The Hoge House, a representative upper-class home of the war period. Dr. Moses Hoge, minister of the Second Presbyterian Church next door, lived in the house some four decades and entertained many of the Confederate military and political leaders here. *Valentine Museum*

decided to check with his mistress. He left the soldier standing on the front porch—closing the door in his face.

When Mrs. Hatcher went to the door herself, imagine her embarrassment, "surprise and chagrin" to see the dusty figure of Stonewall Jackson, an idol of the South, waiting patiently.[134] Earlier that spring Jackson had defeated several Federal armies, one after the other, in record time and sent them scampering north from the Valley of Virginia. Then his army had been brought rapidly and secretly to Richmond where it contributed powerfully to General Lee's victories in the recent Seven Days Battles. Stonewall had simply dropped by to give Mrs. Hatcher news of one of her relatives who served on his staff.

92.
Second Presbyterian Church

Next to the Hoge house, near the northeast corner of Main and 5th Streets, stands one of Richmond's historic churches, the Second Presbyterian. Finished in 1847, it was designed in the Gothic style by Minard Lefner, a New Jersey architect, and still stands and serves its congregation today.

The pastor of the Second Presbyterian Church was one of Richmond's great orators and personalities. The Reverend Doctor Moses D. Hoge accepted a call to this

Dr. Moses D. Hoge, minister of the Second Presbyterian Church from 1847 until his death in 1899. A renowned orator, he was commanded by Queen Victoria to preach "in the royal presence" on a wartime trip to England. *Virginia State Library*

The Second Presbyterian Church (1847) was called the "Gothic Church" or "Dr. Hoge's Church." On Evacuation morning, Sunday, April 2, 1865, Dr. Hoge, with the eloquence for which he was famous, told his shocked parishioners that, in all probability, they would never again meet to worship at his church and bid them farewell. *Susan C. Lee*

church in 1847 and held the pastorate until his death in 1899. He was so famous that during a wartime trip to England he was "commanded by Queen Victoria to preach in the royal presence."[135]

On a Sunday morning in July 1862, General Stonewall Jackson and three aides mounted up at his headquarters on the Mechanicsville Road and rode into the city to Doctor Hoge's church. One of the aides, Major Henry Kyd Douglas, recalled that the general entered the church late and quietly took a seat without being recognized. But as the benediction was pronounced, "a general excitement and rising hum of voices indicated that he had been discovered." The congregation surrounded Stonewall's pew. "There was no relief in sight," remembers Kyd Douglas, "the staff was run over and squeezed into a corner." However, they escaped and

Stonewall Jackson in a photograph taken at Hamilton's Crossing near Fredericksburg, Virginia. He died about a month after this likeness was made.
Library of Congress

rescued the general, who took it all with a surprising meekness—totally at variance with his sternness and forcefulness in the field.[136]

Once they got Jackson safely outside, the aides drew a sigh of relief. Repulsing one more attempt by the crowd to carry the general off, Jackson and his staff mounted up and rode slowly back to camp. He left shortly thereafter on campaign. His next appearance in the city, ten months later, was his last. His body was brought by train from Guinea Station for a state funeral—he had died of wounds received at Chancellorsville.

"Sad and low
As fits an universal woe,
Did the long, long procession go."[137]

Palmer-Caskie House on the northwest corner of Main and 5th Streets. This fine city mansion with its octagonal shape is a rarity in Richmond.
Virginia State Library

93.
Palmer-Caskie House

On the northwest corner of 5th and Main Streets is the Palmer-Caskie House, a handsome brick mansion built in 1802–04.

This home was owned by Mr. and Mrs. William Palmer during the war. One of their sons, Colonel William H. Palmer, was a well-known Confederate officer who served as Adjutant General and Chief of Staff to General A.P. Hill, the Commander of the Confederate 3rd Corps.

As told in selection No. 83, General Hill was killed on the final day of fighting at Petersburg, and buried the following day at the Winston family farm near Richmond on southside. Sometime after the war, General Palmer had General Hill's remains removed to Hollywood Cemetery from where they were moved again in 1892 to lie beneath the equestrian statue of the general on Hermitage Avenue.

It is known that General Lee visited at the Palmer-Caskie House.

94.
The Harold Home

Drive west on Main Street one block to 4th Street. The Harold home once stood at this intersection.

At the height of the Evacuation Fire the Harold family was in serious peril of losing their home from flying sparks. A shell from the exploding dump at the Armory struck near the house, shattering its windows. Eventually the house did catch on fire, forcing the family to pack a few things and walk to their uncle's home uptown. Jennie, one of the daughters, carried a bag over her shoulder containing two dresses and a wheat straw hat. With her other arm she carried her dog, Frank.

When word came that the fire was out, they quickly returned to their home. Worried about the mob still in the streets, the Harolds asked the Union troops now in the city for a military guard. When he arrived he told them that his name was Harry Bluff from New Jersey, and that he was 16 years old. He also told them that he was almost starved. When the family made him the best lunch they could from their meager supplies, he took one look at it and blurted out, "Do you think I would eat a thing you Rebs gave me? Why, you would poison me." Notwithstanding their request for guarding, the Harolds "were equally afraid of his gun."[138]

95.
Secretary Mallory's Home

About halfway between 4th and 3rd Streets on the left side of Main Street, was the house in which Confederate Secretary of the Navy and former U.S. Senator Stephen R. Mallory lived during the war. The house was demolished long ago.

FIFTH TOUR—GAMBLE'S HILL, HOLLYWOOD CEMETERY AND MONROE PARK

Stephen R. Mallory, Secretary of the Navy. When Richmond fell, Mr. Mallory accompanied Mr. Davis on his flight and was captured in Georgia. For a time he was imprisoned at Fort Lafayette in New York Harbor.
Virginia State Library

An attractive, wealthy man, Secretary Mallory did his able best with a frustrating job—trying to create a navy for the Confederacy in spite of shortages in materials, manufacturing capacity and manpower, while his enemies in the North built a powerful, modern navy that grew stronger each month.

From 1862 to 1864, with great effort and much delay, three powerful Confederate ironclad warships (*Virginia II*, *Richmond* and *Fredericksburg*) were completed at the Richmond Navy Yard. In the spring of 1864, Mr. Mallory held a luncheon on board one of the new warships for some prominent Richmond ladies. The guests were full of praise for these formidable vessels. Gratified, Mr. Mallory added, "Well, ladies, I have shown you everything about them." Still stung by the disappointment that all Richmonders felt when the first *Virginia* was blown up in Norfolk to prevent its capture in 1862, Miss Howell spoke up. "Everything but one," she quietly asked, "the place where you blow them up?"[139] She recognized the problem: the gunboats were locked in the upper James River by the Federal blockade—vulnerable to capture by the Federal army.

Her question proved to be prophetic. On the night of April 2–3, 1865, with the Federal army nearing Richmond, these gunboats had to be destroyed without ever having gone to battle. The crews of the gunboats, which were anchored upriver from Drewry's Bluff, packed the vessels with kegs of gunpowder; shells and cartridges already jammed the magazines. Shortly after 2:00 A.M. on April 3, the three ironclads went up with shattering explosions; buildings in Richmond swayed and windows shattered. Hundreds of shells from their magazines were hurled into the air with fuses lighted; "they exploded by 2s and 3s and by the dozen."[140]

96.
Robertson Home/Hospital

Continue on Main Street to the intersection of 3rd Street. On the northwest corner stood the large home of Judge John Robertson, which throughout the war was known as Robertson Hospital.

In mid-1861 Aunt Sally Tompkins, as she was known in the city, was determined to have her own hospital to care for incapacitated soldiers. She first approached Judge Robertson and with a fervid appeal to his patriotism, persuaded him to donate his home. Ten days after the First Battle of Manassas in July of 1861, she

Captain Sally Tompkins, matron of Robertson Hospital.
Valentine Museum

began to take patients and soon reached her capacity of 21. Ladies who met her exacting standards served as nurses, and private donations supported the hospital for a time.

Right from the start, Robertson's was a hospital with a difference. It became famous for its food, cleanliness and nursing care. The authorities noticed that even seriously wounded patients thrived at Aunt Sally's. She rarely lost a patient.

In 1863 the government closed the private hospitals in the city and transferred their patients to the larger military hospitals—with the single exception of Robertson Hospital. It was simply too good to close.

The exception was made as a result of President Davis's intervention. He sent Aunt Sally the commission and pay of a Confederate Captain of Cavalry; this insured financial support for the hospital. She returned the pay but kept the rank, and continued to run her hospital flawlessly until April 1865. A total of 1,333 sick and wounded men were lucky enough to come under Captain Aunt Sally's care during the war, and only 73 deaths were listed.

97.
Pratt's Castle and Snyder House on Gamble's Hill

Turn left on 3rd Street, going south along the high ground that leads to Gamble's Hill. On the right near Canal Street, you will pass the Cabell Mansion, one of Richmond's fine antebellum homes. Continue over the Expressway Bridge into the Ethyl Corporation complex on Gamble's Hill. Drive south of the buildings to Arch Street; turn left on Arch and continue to 4th Street where you turn right into the park. Park on this road. You are very close to the site of Pratt's Castle, and three doors north on the same side of 4th Street was the Snyder home.

William B. Pratt built Pratt's Castle shortly before the war. Possibly as a reaction to the classic simplicity of Richmond's Greek Revival homes, he sought, with

Robertson Hospital on the northeast corner of 3rd and Main Streets. The frame building is long since gone, but a plaque on the wall of the building now there marks the location.
Virginia State Library

FIFTH TOUR—GAMBLE'S HILL, HOLLYWOOD CEMETERY AND MONROE PARK

A view of Richmond to the northeast taken from near Pratt's Castle right after the Evacuation Fire.

Library of Congress

some success, to recreate a medieval castle. In 1862 Mr. Pratt went to Europe to buy ammunition for the Confederate government and remained there for much of the war. However, his neighbors, the Snyder family, stayed in Richmond throughout the war and recorded the events on Gamble's Hill the morning of the Evacuation Fire.

The homes were perched on the crest of Gamble's Hill, separated by no more than 300 yards from the Confederate Arsenal and its stockpile of over 100,000 shells and stocks of rifle ammunition. A little after 8:00 A.M., the Fire reached the Arsenal complex, immediately engulfing it in flames. The ammunition began to explode, hurling hundreds of shells into the air with lighted fuses. They seemed to hover over the city before falling. They exploded all over town, adding fresh terror to the fire. The Snyder family, on the roof trying to extinguish sparks with blankets, looked directly down the hill on this inferno and feared for their safety. Although the James River and Kanawha Canal and the steepness of the hill created a firebreak, there was still acute danger from flying sparks and shells. One large shell could demolish a house.

In the midst of the uproar, an escaped convict, still in Penitentiary garb, appeared at the front door. When the Snyder children recovered from their fright, they recognized the man as a former employee of their father. The father was away at the time and the prisoner had come to see if he could help them. After changing clothes, he went to work trying to save the house. At the height of the crisis, some of the family gathered in the parlor. Mrs. Snyder and her infant daughter were hugged protectively by their black cook, who was announcing loudly that the Judgment Day had come. When they sighted some blue-coated soldiers fighting the flames on the shingled roofs of houses across 4th Street, they realized the fire would be contained. The Snyder home and Pratt's Castle were

Pratt's Castle, a longtime Richmond landmark now demolished, was built in 1853, an example of the craze for Gothic, Romanesque and Byzantine architecture that swept America in the 1850s.

Library of Congress

157

spared, but hardly a home on Gamble's Hill escaped some blast and fire damage.

Pratt's Castle was sold shortly after the war. Fifteen years later Mrs. Corrick, the daughter of the late Mayor Mayo, lived here. She never forgot the hardships of the Federal naval blockade, especially the shortages. To her dying day this woman, despite her wealth, saved everything she could, down to odd stockings and coffee pots.

98.
The James River and Kanawha Canal

Almost beneath you at the foot of Gamble's Hill is the James River and Kanawha Canal.

Confederate troops moving to the front in western Virginia in 1861 by the canal boats of the James River and Kanawha Canal.
Virginia State Library

The idea of a canal connecting the tidewater at Richmond to the Ohio River goes back to the dawn of the republic. George Washington helped launch the project in 1784, and after many vicissitudes the canal was finished in 1854. It never reached the Ohio River, but proceeded some 222 miles to Lynchburg and the eastern edge of the upper Valley of Virginia. As late as 1860, well into the railroad age, it was the leading freight carrier in Virginia. By 1880 the railroads had forced it into bankruptcy. Today, the main line of the Chesapeake and Ohio Railroad follows much of its trace.

Passenger packet boats left Richmond every other day; passengers thought it marvelous that it took only 30 hours to reach Lynchburg. When Richmond fell, fleeing citizens used the canal and its towpath as escape routes.

On an afternoon in late June 1865, after the end of hostilities, General and Mrs. Lee and members of the family went down to the Canal Basin, a few blocks from their Franklin Street home. Planning a brief escape from the inconveniences and hardships of occupied Richmond, they boarded a packet boat a little before sunset, bound for a visit to Mrs. Elizabeth Randolph Cocke's country home Oakland.

With a 55-mile journey ahead, the ladies shortly retired into a long cabin below. After supper, it was divided into two sleeping compartments—one for men and another for women. The packet boat captain, honored by General Lee's presence, prepared the best bed he had for him. "But Lee would not accept special favors. Instead he spread his military cloak and slept on deck—the last night that he ever spent under the open sky.... It was not an unpleasant journey, with the boat moving slowly along the canal, pulled by a stout horse on the towpath, while the water swished against the sides of the laden craft, and the driver's horn sounded musically every few miles to warn the lock-keeper of their approach."[141]

99.
The Confederate Armory and Shops

Look at the foot of the hill directly east to the other side of the canal where the Confederate Armory (or arsenal) was located. It was a large brick building in the center of a sprawl of private businesses and ordnance and arsenal shops stretching from 4th Street to 7th Street.

The Virginia State Armory became known as the Confederate State Armory after Virginia seceded. Built in 1797, it was a long two-story brick building that was still turning out flintlock muskets in 1806, but then sat unused for many years. Hardly had the Ordinance of Secession been passed (May 1861) when Governor Lecher ordered Virginia troops to seize the U.S. Arsenal at Harpers Ferry to obtain modern machinery for making caplock rifle muskets. Although the Federal commander had burned most of the small arms, this priceless machinery, unavailable anywhere in the South, was captured intact and moved immediately to

FIFTH TOUR—GAMBLE'S HILL, HOLLYWOOD CEMETERY AND MONROE PARK

the Armory in Richmond. For the balance of the war the Armory was able to turn out large quantities of small arms, rifles, carbines and pistols.

Together with the adjacent Tredegar Iron Works and its satellite shops and foundries, the Armory produced up to half of all the supplies, armament and ammunition used in the Confederate war effort: by war's end 341 heavy siege guns, 1,306 field artillery pieces, more than 350,000 small arms and about 72 million rounds of ammunition, plus shells for heavy cannon and field artillery and many other supplies.

The person whose duty it was to maintain arms production was General Josiah Gorgas, the Chief of Ordnance. Because of his dedication and energy, he was a fortunate choice for a country saddled with limited industrial capacity and economic scarcity. With attention focused on the unabating crises at the battlefields, Gorgas's performance often has gone unnoticed. Gorgas somehow made a lot of things come about and in time. In late 1863, when the authorities were demanding heavy projectiles for Charleston's defense, he got them manufactured and shipped, even though the Federals had taken the high quality coal in eastern Tennessee he needed to make them. There was a severe shortage of saltpeter for producing gunpowder in January 1864, but he got enough from blockade runners and other sources to keep ammunition flowing to the front. Copper, an essential ingredient in making ignition caps, also became hard to get. He overcame this shortage by raiding North Carolina whiskey stills.

General Gorgas had a thankless job. Even General Lee, a considerate man, complained that his powder was bad at Fredericksburg and some of the new field artillery pieces had blown up in battle. In early 1865, Lee admonished General Gorgas for trying to keep essential war-production artisans out of the trenches. At this point in the war General Lee quite rightly believed he needed every pair of hands in the trenches to hold the Federals back.

Sometime around eight o'clock in the morning when Richmond fell, the Fire reached the Arsenal and the heavy ammunition, which included 100,000 shells stockpiled in the yard. The Gorgas family had left their living quarters at the Armory the previous evening. The Armory and all its ammunition went up in an explosion that lasted four hours. When the fire burned itself out, the Armory complex was demolished; only its smoking ruins remained.

Ruins of the Armory, April 1865. The canal is in the immediate foreground. *Library of Congress*

100.
Explosion at the Confederate Laboratory

Still on Gamble's Hill, look southeast across the site of the Confederate Armory and you will see in the distance a strip of water and then more land. This is Brown's Island where the Confederate Laboratory (or powder loading plant) was located, separated from the city by water because of the hazardous work being done there.

An entry dated March 14, 1863, in the diary of General Josiah Gorgas, Chief of the Confederate Ordnance Department, read: "Mama has been untiring in aiding, visiting and relieving these poor sufferers and has fatigued herself very much."[142] He was referring to his wife's efforts and those of others to cope with the aftermath of a "fearful accident" that happened the previous day. Without warning, the Cartridge Loading Factory, where women, girls and boys were working to turn out great quantities of small arms ammunition in anticipation of the spring campaign, had blown up in a terrific explosion. Ten women close to the accident had been killed outright, their bodies so torn and mutilated they could not be identified. Thirty other workers were mortally wounded, and another 20 had serious injuries and burns, but would eventually recover. Almost all the casualties were women whom the hard times had forced into such dangerous work.

The eastern half of Brown's Island is seen just behind the burned arsenal in the spring of 1865. The group of white frame buildings on the island is the powder loading plant which appears intact. Although historical consensus is that the Evacuation Fire reached the island and that the explosives stored at the plant detonated, this photograph casts doubt on that belief, since the buildings seem neither damaged nor destroyed.

Library of Congress

FIFTH TOUR—GAMBLE'S HILL, HOLLYWOOD CEMETERY AND MONROE PARK

A well-known Alexander Gardner photograph of the Tredegar Iron Works taken in April 1865. The bridge leads from the Tredegar plant to the western tip of Brown's Island, the location of the Confederate Laboratory.
Library of Congress

101.
Tredegar Iron Works

Before moving on, look directly south across the canal to the mostly bare plain between the canal and the river. Here was the site of the most important iron foundry and manufacturer of heavy armaments in the South—the Tredegar Iron Works. Almost all of this large plant is now gone; however, thanks to the present owner, the Albemarle Paper Company, some buildings have been preserved including its cannon foundry, with "1861" over the door and a store fronting on the canal which sold supplies and fittings to canal boats.

The Tredegar operated throughout the war on a contractual basis in support of the Confederate Armory, the Navy Yard and a number of large private businesses, such as the railroads.

One day on a run to Petersburg, a conductor on the Richmond and Petersburg Line found a laborer riding without a ticket. "Are you working for the government?" he inquired. "No," was the response, "for t'uther consarn."[143] "T'uther consarn" was the Tredegar Iron Works, its importance to the war effort acknowledged by all as equal to that of the Confederate government. So important was it that its employees were apparently given free passage on the railroad.

Under General J.R. Anderson, its president, the Tredegar produced well over a thousand cannon of differing calibers and ammunition; one of them, the seven-inch "Brooke gun," was a new rifled cannon that was entirely developed, tested and produced here. Iron plates, sometimes recycled from railroad tracks, were rolled at Tredegar for the heavy ironclad warships that served in the James River Squadron. Some new, exotic weapons, such as naval torpedoes, also were successfully designed and produced.

Like other war-related enterprises the Tredegar was scheduled for destruction before the Federal army took the city, but General Anderson wanted to preserve it. The Tredegar Works, notwithstanding a serious fire in 1863, had expanded and even modernized during the war unlike most Southern industry. Before the Yankees entered the city, he armed his workers and prevented both the authorities and the mob from setting fire to the place. His was the only business south of Main Street to survive the fire and luckily so, for the South needed the Tredegar for the rebuilding of its economy. By August 1865, it was turning out rails to rebuild the South's railroads.

102.
The State Penitentiary

Return to your car, then drive slowly through Gamble's Hill Park, circling to your right toward the bottom of the hill where you intersect 2nd Street. Drive right on 2nd a few yards and you will see the entrance to the Virginia State Penitentiary on your left. Although many of the wartime buildings have been replaced, the Penitentiary still looks much the same as it did during the war. You are now outside the wartime city.

A northern view of the Virginia State Penitentiary as it looked during the war.
National Archives

Early in the morning of April 3, 1865, the day of the Federal occupation, the convicts awakened to the sounds of explosions from the destruction of the Powder Magazine and the James River Squadron. When they realized that guards were no longer at their posts, the convicts broke out of their cells and set themselves free. They stole civilian clothes from the prison store house, plundered some buildings, set the prison workshop on fire, then left to join the mobs in search of food and booty.

They rampaged while they could, and a few got away.

However for most, freedom was short-lived. With the Union came provost marshal and infantry troops who restored order as fast as possible. Later that morning a dragnet was thrown over the city, and all suspicious characters were rounded up. By nightfall most of the convicts were back behind bars. More than a hundred were held in Libby Prison or Castle Thunder until the Penitentiary could be repaired.

MAP 16

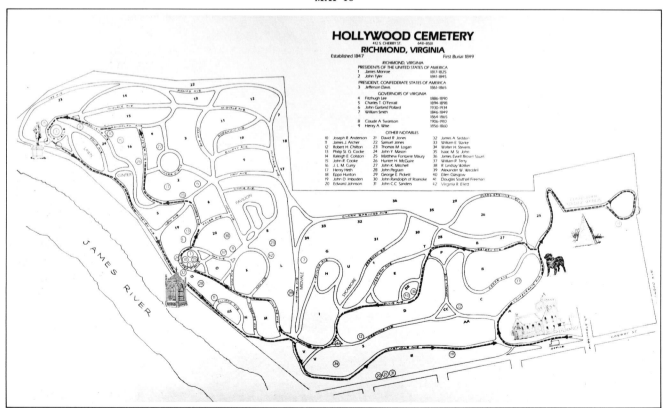

The dotted line shows the circular route to follow to see numbered grave sites of Confederate notables including the Davis graves at extreme left.
Hollywood Cemetery

FIFTH TOUR—GAMBLE'S HILL, HOLLYWOOD CEMETERY AND MONROE PARK

The northern military section of Hollywood Cemetery as it looked during the war. The cemetery was intended to have a wooded, rustic appearance, but the war changed that with its hurried burials. Today the grounds appear as originally planned.
Valentine Museum

103.
Hollywood Cemetery

Drive north on 2nd Street to Canal Street. Turn left into Canal; go four blocks, then turn left onto the ramp leading to Belvidere Street. Turn left into Belvidere Street, for half a block, then right on Albemarle and go three blocks to the entrance of Hollywood Cemetery. The high, flat ground you traversed on Albemarle Street was a Confederate Camp of Instruction during the first year and a half of the war. At a parade here in the spring of 1862, President Davis presented the new Confederate battle flag to the troops. This was not the Stars and Bars of 1861, but the well known battle flag with the diagonal cross bars of stars on a red field.

Stop momentarily at the Gate House to receive directions and a map. Drive first to your right (northwest), then swing to your left in a great circle that will bring you back to the entrance. This route will allow you to see the graves of the 18,000 Confederate war dead here, and also those of General Pickett, General J.E.B. Stuart, Jefferson Davis and his family, General Fitzhugh Lee, General John Pegram and others.

In the heat of July 1862, grave diggers could not dig graves fast enough. Sometimes, bodies taken from hearses or wagons had to be placed on the ground and left overnight. The odor was appalling. To obviate a health problem, the City Council adopted a plan of digging long trenches in which the dead could be laid side by side. Of course, people still preferred individual graves for loved ones and this was continued whenever possible.

Although the fighting moved farther north, the death toll mounted as the months passed, since Richmond had the most hospitals in the Confederacy. Citizens of the city mourned, "Our best and brightest young men are passing away." On one occasion a lady came by train from Ashland, bringing a basket of food to a sick soldier at Camp Winder Hospital. On arriving she found he had died and had been buried that same morning at Hollywood. She walked to Hollywood, followed the directions of the cemetery officials and found the grave. On a small wooden headboard she found this inscription, "I leave my boy at 4:00 A.M. for my North Carolina home. His father."[144]

This granite pyramid commemorates the 18,000 Confederate dead buried at Hollywood Cemetery, most of whom died at Richmond's military hospitals. A sailor incarcerated at the State Penitentiary gained his freedom by climbing the pyramid to place a metal cap at the apex.
Virginia State Library

GENERAL LEE'S CITY

Belle Isle Prison with Richmond in the background. This print was apparently made late in the war, for the cannon emplaced during the winter of 1863–64 are seen in position.
National Archives

104.
Belle Isle Prisoner of War Camp

After looking at the Jefferson Davis family graves, drive some 300 yards on the designated route (Map 16) back to the cemetery entrance. You are near the bank of James River. Where the bushes do not conceal your view to the right, look across the James and you will see the bushy, wooded shoreline of Belle Isle. The camp was near the island's northern tip.

After the Seven Days Battles in late June 1862, the Confederate army near Richmond was left with as many as 10,000 Federal prisoners of war who everyone called "live Yankees." In view of the scarcity of space and the need to keep them from escaping, the enlisted prisoners were moved to Belle Isle, an island in the middle of the James River across from Richmond. At first Belle Isle was intended as a transient camp. Prisoners would be moved on to more secure camps farther south or they would be exchanged for captured Southern soldiers. But things didn't work out as planned.

Belle Isle began as a well-run camp, with orderly streets, precise lines of tents and carefully regulated sanitary conditions. But Southern victories in the battles of 1862–63 produced such a steady flow of prisoners into Belle Isle that by the winter of 1863–64 the

FIFTH TOUR—GAMBLE'S HILL, HOLLYWOOD CEMETERY AND MONROE PARK

camp held nearly 12,000 men—far too many for the island to hold or to be supported with adequate food supplies and tents. The rail lines that connected Richmond to the south were far too busy carrying war materials and supplies to move prisoners of war.

There were major outbreaks of diarrhea, dysentery, typhoid and pneumonia. Large numbers of prisoners died, deprived of basic needs in the midst of a very cold winter. The Confederate intention was not to mistreat the prisoners, but even Lee's army and the civilian population were suffering deprivations. People justified the terrible conditions by pointing to Northern prisons, which in some cases were not much better.

General Winder, the Provost Marshal in charge of prisons at Richmond, feared a serious prison outbreak. Cannon were positioned on Belle Isle on the high ground behind the camp and on Oregon Hill to the west of Richmond. These guns could sweep the prison in case of a mass escape attempt. Rescue for the prisoners came only with the fall of Richmond, too late for hundreds who did not survive the ordeal. Their remains, first buried at Belle Isle, were reburied in the federal cemetery near Richmond on the Williamsburg Road, where they rest today.

105.
Monroe Park and Stuart Hospital

You leave Hollywood Cemetery at the Albemarle Street entrance. Drive east on Albemarle Street, then turn left into Belvidere. Follow Belvidere Street four blocks to Monroe Park on your left.

This city park, outside wartime Richmond, was in antebellum days the City Fair Grounds. In 1861 it became a Camp of Instruction where VMI cadets trained the new Confederate soldiers arriving in Richmond. The first soldiers to arrive were from South Carolina, both officers and men from the best families of the state who naturally brought their body servants with them. What a stir these bluebloods made in Richmond society. Young Richmond girls, many with matrimony on their minds, drove to the camp in their carriages and strolled around in their crinolines and parasols to see and be seen. They watched the novel sights of training, mock battles and shooting matches and afterwards attended regimental receptions.

After Richmond settled into the day-to-day business of war, 16 wooden barracks and three support buildings were erected at the park to house the Richmond City Guard, part of the local security force. Later the barracks were converted into a military hospital, named for the lamented Jeb Stuart, to house the casualties from the battles of attrition in the spring of 1864.

Mrs. Eliza Middleton Huger Smith of Charleston, South Carolina, spent two months at Stuart Hospital nursing her son, Mason, who had been wounded at Cold Harbor. She reported on her ordeal in letters home:

"June 11, 1864—Dr. Meredith says it is his opinion that he will recover . . . the ball meandered so as just to avoid the intestines, also the bladder . . . He has been moved into a private room much to my relief, for in the ward there are three men desperately ill with typhoid fever in the same corner with him. . . ."

"June 30—Mason suffers dreadfully . . . Oh, this hospital experience is subduing indeed . . . Those whose friends are 'passed instantaneously' have much to be thankful for; some linger and suffer and die after all, and often times the sufferings are so aggravated. . . . Whenever I feel depressed about him I go into one of the other wards and there see such aggravated suffering that I come back cheerful . . . what a mercy it is that I came."

"July 2—Mason is better and able to put things together . . . I shall get him home just as soon as I can. . . ."

"July 4—The doctors speak hopefully, but I feel discouraged—31 days and this his present state! . . . The poor boy is worn out . . . About 80 wounded were brought in yesterday; it is very fearful. I see dead bodies carried by the windows two or three times a day and have seen worse scenes than that . . . Some part of hospital practice I do abhor— they bury the dead like animals, without any religious service and without clothes 'almost' if not entirely. They say the Confederacy cannot afford to lose the clothes. . . ."

"July 10— . . . I thought Mason's hours numbered . . . His pulse sunk so, that I made up my mind to be prepared to see God do his own work and prayed it might be a gentle departure . . . He told me a few days ago that he did not wish to die, but was not afraid if so God willed it. . . ."

"August 16 . . . I could not bring him home. He lies in Hollywood."[145]

106. Monument Avenue

Continue on Belvidere past Monroe Park to Broad Street. Turn left on Broad and go two blocks to Laurel Street. Turn left on Laurel; drive one block to Grace Street and turn right. Proceed four blocks on Grace Street to Lombardy Street and turn left. Go one block and then turn right on Monument Avenue.

Monument is a distinctive avenue whose generous width and lush landscaping complement the five large monuments to the Confederacy's greats that give it its name and the gracious homes on either side. A slow drive along Monument Avenue is the perfect end for your tour of wartime Richmond.

At Stuart Circle, appropriately, stands the fine statue of General J.E.B. Stuart, commander of the Confederate Cavalry Corps. Fred Moynihan's statue seems to portray the man perfectly. Stuart's sword is drawn; he is obviously in the presence of the enemy. He is searching the ground carefully, as a good cavalryman does, his reins in his left hand—unconscious that he is on a prancing horse. He wears the flamboyant Stuart uniform. Both he and his horse are caught in a moment of restless, vigorous movement.

Further on, at the intersection of Allen and Monument Avenues, is Jean Antoine Mercie's superb equestrian statue of Robert E. Lee. The General has removed his hat, as if receiving the cheers of his men. He is in full uniform with sword, something he rarely wore as he usually dressed simply in the field. However, this could have been the Lee both sides saw at Appomattox. He was described by one writer as looking like "an elderly major of dignity."

Several blocks later, you'll see a cannon placed on the median strip between the east and west lanes of Monument. This cannon marks the location of Star Fort No. 10, one of the small artillery forts of the Inner Defense Line (see map No. 17).

The next monument you see is the statue of Jefferson Davis with its elaborate flanking stonework. The grandeur of the monument is fully in keeping with the memory of the man who was the only president of the Confederacy during its four years of travail. The actual likeness does seem like the man his neighbors in Richmond might have seen taking the daily stroll from his office to his home on Clay Street.

On the southeast corner of Monument and Boulevard sits the First Baptist Church (moved here from its original location at Broad and 12th Streets). To the left of the brick church is a loggia built to hold the bronze bell that the church gave to the Confederacy to be made into a cannon. Mr. Thomas, a parishioner, bought it back for gold coins. (See selection No. 19.)

Just beyond the church at this same intersection, facing north as if still in defiance of the Union, stands the sculpture of Stonewall Jackson, sitting erectly on his horse as if reviewing one of his divisions. His stern face is especially realistic, but he seems too well dressed to be in the field. Contemporaries described him as rumpled, like a country preacher. Perhaps he looked like this when dressed up to attend Sunday services at the Second Presbyterian Church in Richmond.

The Mercie statue of Lee on Monument Avenue which was executed in Paris, shipped to New York and then arrived by train in Richmond. On the afternoon of May 7, 1890 the disassembled pieces were pulled through the streets to the site by thousands of school children and veterans. The statue was unveiled on May 29, 1890, with over 200 Confederate generals and two of Lee's daughters, Mildred and Mary, in attendance. *Virginia State Library*

FIFTH TOUR—GAMBLE'S HILL, HOLLYWOOD CEMETERY AND MONROE PARK

A photograph of General Lee on Traveller taken by Michael Miley of Lexington, Virginia in 1868, offering yet another equestrian view of the general—a posture believed by many to be his most flattering. *Library of Congress*

APPENDIX

MAP 17

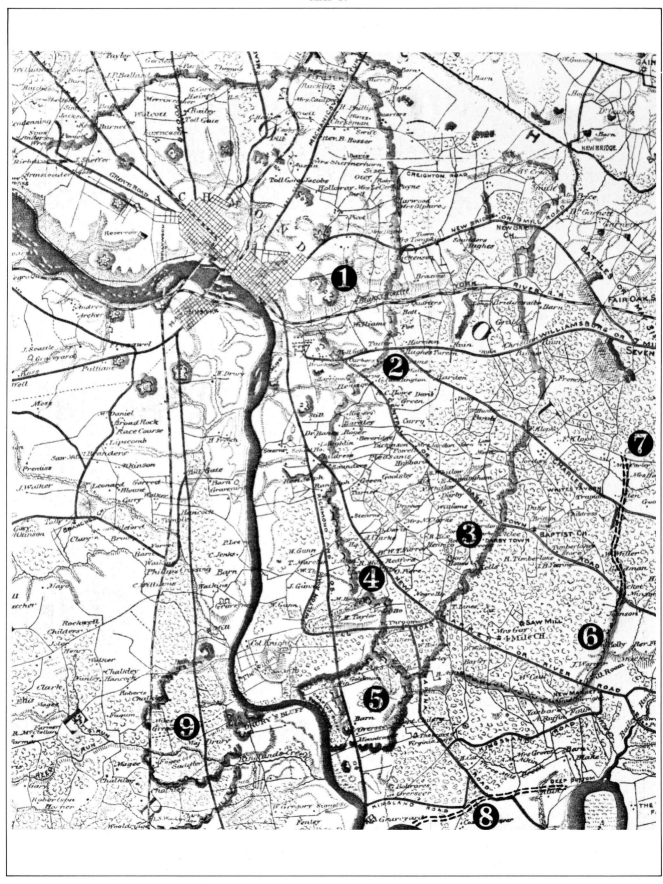

APPENDIX

THE DEFENSES OF RICHMOND*

The Beginnings

On May 9, 1861, a committee from Richmond's City Council called on General Robert E. Lee, new commander of the Armed Forces of Virginia, at his temporary offices in the old U.S. Customs Building. Aware of the need to defend Richmond, they asked his opinion on the possibility of building "batteries around or near the city."[146] Lee and his Chief Engineer, Colonel Andrew A. Talcott, were aware of Richmond's vulnerability: The Confederate capital was slightly over 100 miles from Washington, so close that Federal forces would inevitably attack this "Center of Rebellion." Furthermore, the Federal fleet's control of the Atlantic and the navigable waters of Virginia would enable the Union to move a large army from Washington, via the Potomac River and Chesapeake Bay, to positions close to Richmond.

Richmond was not without certain strengths, however. It lay behind natural obstacles, and it was surrounded by many low hills excellent for field fortifications and densely wooded areas difficult to penetrate. And although the James River allowed a water approach to Richmond, its meandering course, tributaries and swamps made the route difficult. The countryside was poorly mapped and its dirt road system rudimentary—two other obstacles for an enemy.

On May 25, General Lee advised the committee that the first defense positions had been chosen on the south side of the city to cover the Osborn and Darby Town Roads.[147] (Four years later, these two small forts, probably Star Fort Nos. 2 and 3, were positioned to block the very roads used by the Federals to march into Richmond.)

---

* Though the lines connecting Richmond to Petersburg and those around Petersburg are all properly part of a single defense system, this appendix discusses only the lines north of the James designed to hold Richmond itself.

The Defense Lines of Richmond.

(1) The Inner Defense Line.
(2) The Intermediate Defense Line.
(3) The Outer Defense Line.
(4) A switch or special defense line to hold the Osborn Road.
(5) A complex of heavy defense positions or fortified camps which included Fort Harrison.
(6) The New Market Line.
(7) & (8) Unfinished lines captured before completion.
(9) Drewry's Bluff defenses which held the James against naval attack.

Library of Congress

The Defense Lines

In the four years of the war, Richmond's defenses developed into a very powerful and sophisticated system. Although President Davis and others were fully committed to the task, there seems little doubt that the driving force behind the achievement was General Lee himself. His persistence and convictions about the value of the defenses strengthened the government's resolve to continue with this enormous and expensive undertaking. Maintenance of fortifications already built was difficult with the rapid destruction caused by freezes, thaws and rains; and construction of new lines was essential. But Lee's letters from the field prodded the Richmond authorities to persevere; the safety of the city was ever on his mind. On his brief trips to Richmond, he liked to ride out and inspect the progress of the works.

The two forts Lee discussed with the City Council were the first of a ring of 24 Star Forts, as they were called, that surrounded Richmond and Manchester and were located about a mile beyond the populated areas. The Star Forts were small but strongly built with earthen walls strengthened by timbers. Sited on high ground to provide a good field of fire, each had a few heavy cannon and was garrisoned with one officer and nine or ten artillery men. Four battalions of heavy artillery maintained in Richmond could reinforce the forts if necessary. The Star Forts were manned and maintained until the end of the war as they constituted the city's Inner Defense Line (Map No. 17[1]).

At a five mile radius from the Capitol building was another circle of field fortifications that did not extend south of the James. Consisting primarily of a continuous line of rifle pits (trenches) running along the crests of the low hills with intermittent locations for batteries of field artillery, these field works were not occupied; they were a reserve line to be defended in case of emergency. This was the Intermediate Defense Line (Map No. 17[2]).

Still farther out, seven to nine miles from Capitol Square, was a third belt of fortifications. Known as the Outer Defense Line (Map No. 17[3]), it made a 65-mile circuit around the city. Its perimeter did not extend south of the James River except for a very heavy fort at Drewry's Bluff (Map No. 17[9]), which helped to anchor the Outer Line and blocked Union gunboats from coming up the river to Richmond. This line was Lee's main position in the battle for Richmond and was the front line during most of the last year of the war. It was not given up until Richmond itself had to be aban-

MAP 18

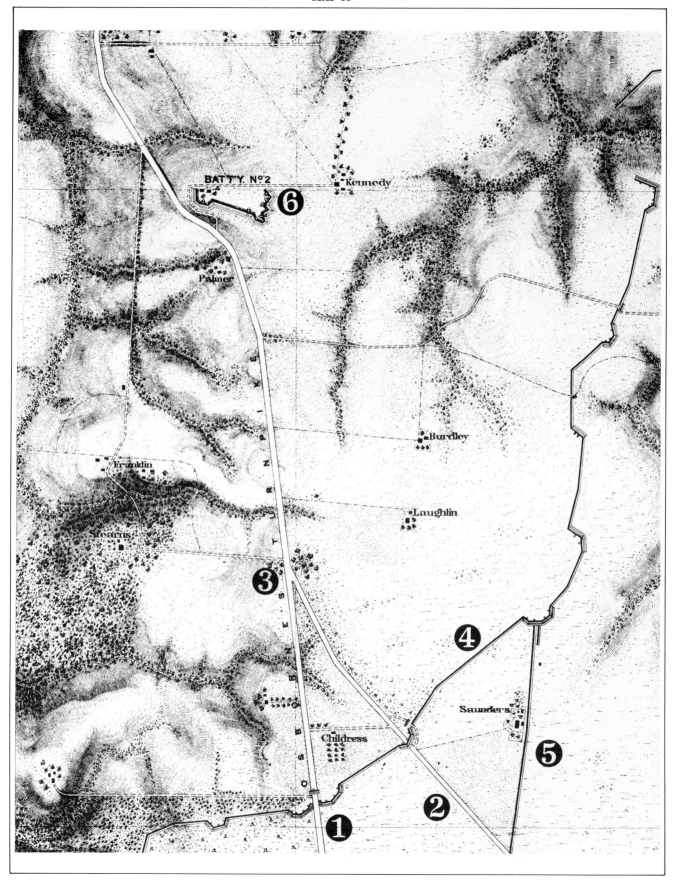

APPENDIX

doned in 1865. Consequently the two inner lines never sustained major attacks, although the Intermediate Line occasionally repulsed surprise enemy cavalry raids.

Between the Intermediate Line and the great armed camp of which Fort Harrison is a part (Map No. 17[5]), another line was built parallel to and east of the Osborn Road (Map No. 17[4]). It appears this line was designed to protect the Osborn Road in the event the Federals broke through the Outer Defense Line on one of the several roads to the east.

Not satisfied, General Lee constructed yet another line, called the New Market Line (Map No. 17[6]), two to four miles to the southeast of the Outer Defense Line. Its purpose was to block an attack coming from Aiken's Landing or Deep Bottom on the James River, two probable crossing sites for an offensive against Fort Harrison. Unfinished lines of trenches joined the New Market Line to the north and south (Map No. 17[8]). They suggest an extension of this outermost position had time permitted.

Building the Lines

Lee assumed command of the Army of Northern Virginia on June 1, 1862. His army was deployed east and south of Richmond generally along much of what later became the Outer Defense Line. Two days later, he ordered the construction of field works all along his front with much of the army providing the manual labor. Digging trenches was so unpopular with the troops that the General became known as "Old Spade Lee" or "The King of Spades."[148] Their objections did not dissuade him, however, and after the Seven Days Battles (June 26–July 1, 1862), the more discerning of his men realized what he was up to. The trenches were to economize—to save men. He could leave a small portion of his army in the new trenches to protect Richmond, and take the bulk of his troops north of the Chickahominy River to attack an exposed and smaller Union flank.

Portions of Three Defense Lines, U.S. Army Corps of Engineers Map, 1865.

(1) **The Osborn Road.**
(2) **The New Market Road**—used by Federal troops marching north to Richmond.
(3) **Junction of Osborn and New Market Roads**—about 2½ miles south of Richmond where Mayor Mayo surrendered the city.
(4) **The Intermediate Defense Line.**
(5) **A switch defense line covering the Osborn Road.**
(6) **Battery No. 2**—one of the Star Forts of the Inner Defense Line.

Library of Congress

In August of 1862, Lee left Richmond with his army, but the city's defense was constantly on his mind. He wrote to his Engineer in Richmond, "I desire you to use every exertion to perfect and complete the defenses . . . of Richmond by land and water. I wish to place them in such a condition that troops can be withdrawn with a proper guard, and again restored when necessary."[149] This system, requiring good timing and careful preparation, would provide for Richmond's defense, but with a minimum commitment of troops.

When Lee's army was away, the job of building the lines fell to local black labor. Early in the war, about 2,000 slaves were recruited from their owners in nearby counties for the daily work. Townspeople became accustomed to columns of black men marching through Richmond with shovels and picks over their shoulders.

Progress was slow and was sometimes reversed by the freezing and thaws of winter and by spring rains. In early 1862, inspecting officers found the Outer Line "thoroughly inadequate. . . . Three feet of water flooded some of the gun emplacements, only 25 of 218 gun positions were in place."[150]

As the danger to Richmond mounted, the numbers of black laborers increased, reaching 10,000 men by spring 1864.[151] In late September as the battle for Richmond reached crisis stage, the Provost Marshal's men arrested all blacks they could find in the streets and marched them to work on the defenses.

A Federal lookout tower on high ground. One of these was located on Signal Hill near Dutch Gap. From it the Federal observers watched Richmond burning the night of April 2–3, 1865.

National Archives

Using the Lines

General Lee only kept troops in the fortifications to repel attacks. Otherwise, the troops were located near Richmond at Drewry's Bluff and Petersburg in reserve positions which allowed them to defend Richmond or move north rapidly by rail to join his army along the Rappahannock River. By June of 1863, the beginning of the Gettysburg campaign, Lee had no regular forces to spare. Marching north, he left only reserve and local volunteer forces at Richmond. Although this seemed risky, for there were a number of Union raids against the city that summer and fall, the advantage of the trenches became obvious. The militia and locals, protected in the trenches, could and did hold off attacking regular Federal troops who were obliged to come at them across open fields.

In June 1864, Lee's whole army returned to the trenches of Richmond. His troop dispositions in September, just before the great attack against Fort Harrison, are instructive. Lee could spare only 8,700 men for the enormous Richmond defense lines. He deployed some 4,400 regular and reservists on the New Market Line and at Fort Harrison. The remainder were artillerymen and local volunteer forces. Of these, 2,700 were in battalions from the War, Navy and Treasury Departments, the Post Office, the Tredegar Iron Works and the Armory. The final reserves were convalescent battalions from the hospitals. These armed civilians were positioned in the lines or near the city, available to be mobilized as needed.

Lee's plan was for this small force of 8,700 men, properly placed at the point of attack and in the trenches, to absorb the first blow, gaining time for his larger forces to come up from Petersburg, reinforce and counterattack. The fact that Richmond almost fell at this time suggests that the initial force was too small and ill prepared for the task. Subsequently and continuing until the final evacuation of Richmond, General Lee had to position General Longstreet's Corps of three divisions (by this time perhaps 15,000 men) along the Outer Defense Line.

The End

When the Federals broke the lines at Petersburg during the early morning hours of April 2, 1865, General Lee was forced to abandon both the Petersburg and Richmond lines in order to extricate his army. That evening Confederate bands began to serenade their enemies. As was fairly common, the Union bands joined in, and soon the night was full of music. The melodies were, of course, to drown out the noises of the troop withdrawal going on behind the Confederate lines. By 10:00 P.M. they were gone. Only General Gary's small South Carolina Cavalry Brigade remained in position as a thin screen, providing the rear guard. They kept the fires lit and made noise in an attempt to keep the Federals from knowing what had happened.

At three in the morning when a black teamster crept through the lines to the Federal side to tell them the Confederates were gone, Gary's men set fire to the tents and whatever else they could and pulled out. The awakened Union leaders knew that Richmond would fall without a fight, for the sounds of explosions in the city were audible, and the skies were lit with reflections of fires.

The Union forces, about 12,000 soldiers commanded by Major General Godfrey Weitzel, were concentrated about six miles south of the city along a front covering the Osborn, New Market and Darby Town Roads. They began their advance through the Outer Defense Line after daylight so they could see the thousands of formidable obstacles, mines, torpedoes (booby traps), ditches and barriers planted between the lines. Also the size and complexity of the works could cause confusion or delays.

Around 6:00 A.M. long ribbons of Bluecoats filed between the lines, following the paths that Confederate troops had used the night before. Once through the Outer Defense Line, the infantry formed into columns on the three roads. They marched rapidly north towards Richmond in high spirits; there was no opposition. It became a race to see who could be first in the city.

General Weitzel's engineers examined the Confederate fortifications they were passing with great interest, impressed with their complexity and strength. One observer wrote that the army had passed through seven distinct lines of defensive positions before it reached Richmond.[152] What they were seeing were actually elaborations of the Outer and Intermediate Defense Lines and the position which lay between them (Map No. 17[4]). Some men took time to scavenge the camps; the defenders had departed so quickly that many weapons and personal effects were left behind.

After General Weitzel had ridden past the junction of the Osborn and New Market Roads, he reached Star Fort No. 2 of the Inner Defense Line. Standing guard on the parapet was a lone, armed Confederate soldier, dressed in a gorgeous militia uniform, hypnotized by the thousands of Bluecoats marching past him. He was the last defender of Richmond. General Weitzel sent an aide to tell the man to put down his gun and go home to his family.[153] With his departure, the defense lines of Richmond passed into history.

APPENDIX

Comparing the Richmond and Washington Defense Lines

Some similarities existed between the two capitals' defense lines. Both systems formed a perimeter around the capitals; both were heavily armed with cannon. They both consisted of field fortifications, well planned by trained army engineers.

But there were more differences than similarities. Richmond had no less than *three* concentric lines of fortifications around it, not counting the New Market line, while Washington had but a single fortified line. Washington's lines were 35-miles around, while Richmond's lines were longer, making a 65-mile circuit around the city. Richmond's lines were also more developed than those of Washington, containing reserve positions, switch lines and communication trenches. In front of the Richmond lines was a complicated barrier of felled trees, sharpened stakes, torpedoes, moats, ditches, traps, listening posts, etc. Its purpose was to slow attacking troops to inflict heavy fire. Nothing in the Washington lines approached the sophistication of this barrier system.

There is no doubt that the Richmond defenses of concentric, heavily built lines were by far the more formidable and dangerous to an attacking force. They were so strong that General Grant gave up frontal attacks and settled down to a siege. Why did the South develop a much more advanced system than the North? Because in truth, they had to.

With the North having the advantage in men and resources, Southerners knew an attack against Richmond was inevitable. This provided the incentive to build strong fortifications quickly. On the other hand few people expected Washington to be besieged. Most of its defensive lines were finished in the spring of 1862, and in fact it was only threatened once.

Another reason for the stronger Richmond defenses was that the whole Army of Northern Virginia was concentrated in the Richmond–Petersburg Lines for most of the last year of the war. Thus, a large labor force was available to create the most formidable lines of fortifications they could to hold back their enemy.

After the city fell, the Confederate cannon from the Richmond fortifications were gathered at Rocketts Landing, then shipped north as part of the postwar disarmament of the city.
National Archives

CHRONOLOGY 1861–65

Since the tours are arranged geographically, the accompanying narratives are not in chronological order. This chronology of the war years is provided to place the stories in historical perspective.

1861

Jan. 19	– Following South Carolina's secession on Dec. 20, 1860, Mississippi, Florida, Georgia, Louisiana and Texas secede from the Union.
Feb. 4	– Seceding states meet to form Confederacy at Montgomery, Alabama.
Feb. 9	– Jefferson Davis is elected Provisional President of Confederacy.
Mar. 4	– Abraham Lincoln is inaugurated as President of the United States.
Mar. 14	– First Confederate flag flown in Richmond from tower of Richmond Female Institute.
Apr. 13	– Fort Sumter in Charleston Harbor falls.
Apr. 14	– President Lincoln calls for 75,000 volunteers to suppress the insurrection in South Carolina.
Apr. 17	– Virginia State Convention passes Ordinance of Secession; "Stars and Bars" flies over Capitol building.
Apr. 18	– Colonel Robert E. Lee turns down the command of the Union army in Washington.
Apr. 19	– Giant torchlight procession in Richmond celebrates secession.
Apr. 19	– Virginia troops capture Federal Arsenal at Harpers Ferry.
Apr. 19	– President Lincoln orders a blockade on all ports in the Confederate states.
Apr. 20	– Unionist supporters from western Virginia meet in Powhatan House, Richmond; start plans to secede from Virginia and form a new state.
Apr. 21	– Richmond is traumatized by "Pawnee Sunday."
Apr. 22	– Colonel Robert E. Lee arrives in Richmond to command Virginia troops.
Apr. 27	– Virginia invites Confederate Provisional Government to make its capital in Richmond.
Late Apr.	– Richmond, a city of 38,000, begins rapid growth—nearly doubling in size by late summer.
Late Apr.	– Northern press exhorts Union troops "Forward to Richmond."
May 23	– Virginia voters ratify secession.
May 24	– Union troops occupy Alexandria, Va. and Arlington Heights, Va.
May 25	– General Robert E. Lee informs City Council of first steps to defend Richmond.
May 29	– President and Mrs. Davis arrive in Richmond; stop at Spottswood Hotel.
Jun. 5	– More than 10,000 Confederate troops train in Richmond.
Jun. 8	– Transfer of Virginia forces to Confederate control.
Jun. 10	– Confederates' first victory at Big Bethel.
Jul. 13	– Union forces win at Carricksford and kill General Garnett.
Jul. 21	– Confederates win important victory at First Manassas.
Jul. 23	– Wounded arrive from Manassas at Virginia Central Depot.
Sep. 4	– Richmond begins brief use of horse cars on Main and 9th Streets.
Oct. 21	– Confederate victory at Ball's Bluff near Leesburg, Va.
Late Oct.	– Confederate campaign in western Virginia a failure.
Nov. 7	– Federal fleet captures Port Royal, S.C., securing a naval base.
Nov. 8	– Removal of Confederate envoys Mason and Slidell from British Ship *Trent* by Federal war vessel *San Jacinto* has international complications for Union.
Nov. 21	– Confederate Secretary of War Walker resigns; Judah Benjamin takes his place.

1862

Jan. 19	– Confederates suffer defeat at Mill Springs, Ky.
Feb. 6	– General Grant captures Fort Henry in Tennessee.
Feb. 8	– Capt. O. Jennings Wise of Richmond Blues is killed at the fall of Roanoke Island, N.C.
Feb. 16	– General Grant captures Fort Donelson in Tennessee.
Feb. 16	– First meeting in Richmond of the First Congress of the CSA.
Feb. 22	– Jefferson Davis takes oath of office as President of Confederacy on Capitol Square.
Mar. 1	– Richmond under martial law.
Mar. 8	– Ironclad *CSS Virginia* sinks *USS Cumberland* and *USS Congress* at Hampton Roads.
Mar. 9	– Drawn battle between *USS Monitor* and *CSS Virginia* at Hampton Roads.
Mar. 14	– Union General Burnside captures New Bern, N.C.
Mar. 17	– 120,000 troops from Washington begin arriving at Fortress Monroe.
Mar. 18	– Judah Benjamin resigns as Secretary of War; becomes Secretary of State.

APPENDIX

Mar. 19	George Washington Randolph is appointed Secretary of War.
Mar. 23	General Stonewall Jackson fights drawn battle at Kernstorn in Valley of Virginia.
Apr. 6–7	South loses hardfought battle of Shiloh; General A.S. Johnston killed.
Apr. 8	Confederates give up Island No. 10 on Mississippi River.
Apr. 10	Fall of Fort Pulaski at Savannah, Ga.
Apr. 20	Confederate army passes through Richmond enroute to Yorktown.
Apr. 25	Surrender of Fort Macon, N.C.
Apr. 29	New Orleans formally surrenders to Federal fleet under Admiral Farragut.
Late. Apr.	Government prepares to leave Richmond due to military failures on Peninsula.
May–Jul.	Richmond serves as forward base for army fighting on Virginia Peninsula.
May 3	Confederate Commander, General J.E. Johnston abandons Yorktown line.
May 5	Battle at Williamsburg, Va.; Confederates fall back on Richmond.
May 6–7	Badly wounded from Williamsburg arrive in Richmond.
May 8	General Jackson wins battle at McDowell in Valley of Virginia.
May 10	Confederates abandon Norfolk.
May 11	*CSS Virginia* blown up to prevent capture.
May 13	President Davis sends wife and children to safety at Raleigh, N.C.
May 15	Confederate army arrives eight to ten miles outside of Richmond.
May 15	Federal naval attack on Fort Darling at Drewry's Bluff is repulsed; city is saved.
May 20	General Jackson begins victorious campaign in Valley; wins at Front Royal.
May 25	Jackson takes Winchester; threatens Harpers Ferry.
May 31	Army of Northern Virginia attacks Union army at Seven Pines and Fair Oaks; Confederate Commander General Johnston wounded in indecisive battle.
Jun. 1	President Davis makes General Lee commander of Army of Northern Virginia.
Jun. 6	Memphis falls to Union.
Jun. 12	General Jeb Stuart starts reconnaissance around Union army.
Jun. 26–July 1	Lee attacks in Seven Days Battles. Victories at Mechanicsville, Gaine's Mill, Savage Station, Frayser's Farm and Malvern Hill. Richmond sees war close up.
Jun. 27	Confederates use balloon over Seven Days Battles to observe Federals.
Jun. 30	General Lee orders first use of cannon on rail car at Savage Station.
Jul. 4	Confederate ship *Teaser* with balloon attached observes Federals; captured near Malvern Hill on James by *USS Monitor*.
Jul. 14	U.S. Congress passes law creating state of West Virginia.
Early Aug.	Lee shifts army north.
Aug. 9	Jackson wins at Cedar Mountain.
Aug. 29	General Lee wins great victory at Second Manassas.
Sep. 1	Jackson wins victory at Chantilly in Northern Virginia.
Sep. 14	Confederates fight defensive battle at South Mountain.
Sep. 15	Confederates capture Harpers Ferry.
Sep. 17	Drawn Battle of Sharpsburg causes great losses on both sides; Lee withdraws to Virginia.
Sep. 24	President Lincoln issues Emancipation Proclamation.
Oct. 8	Confederates lose at Perryville in Kentucky.
Oct. 10	General Stuart raids western Maryland to Chambersburg, Pa.
Dec. 13	General Lee wins another great victory at Fredericksburg; fighting can be heard in Richmond.

1863

Jan. 1	Confederates recapture Galveston, Texas; seize *USS Harriet Lane*.
Jan. 2	Drawn battle at Murfreesboro, Tenn. turns into Confederate defeat.
Jan. 30	Large Federal naval attack on Charleston, S.C. fails.
Jan.–Mar.	Smallpox epidemic in Richmond.
Mar. 13	Explosion at Richmond's Confederate Ordnance Laboratory (power loading plant) wounds and kills 69 employees.
Apr. 2	Richmond bread riots occur downtown on Main and Cary Streets.
Apr. 7	Federal fleet is repulsed again in attack on Charleston, S.C.
Apr. 29–May 3	General Lee wins another great triumph at Chancellorsville.
Apr. 30–May 6	General Stoneman raids Richmond area and returns.
May 12	Richmond holds state funeral for General Jackson in Capitol.
May 14	Fire seriously damages Tredegar Iron Works.
Jun. 9	General Stuart holds off Federals in cavalry battle near Brandy Station, Va.
Jun. 15	Confederates capture Winchester, Va., then invade Maryland.
Jun. 26	Series of small cavalry raids plague Richmond and vicinity all summer.
Jul. 1–3	Lee retreats after Confederate defeat at Gettysburg.
Jul. 4	Confederacy cut in two after fall of Vicksburg, Miss.
Jul. 8	Port Hudson, La. falls to Union forces.
Sep. 19–20	South wins major victory at Chickamauga, Tenn.
Sep. 19	General Lee in Richmond for first time since Gettysburg campaign.

Oct. 16	– Union army checks Lee's attack near Centreville, Va.
Oct. 28	– British government seizes Confederate arms building in Britain.
Nov. 18	– General Longstreet's forces fail to capture Knoxville in eastern Tennessee.
Nov. 25	– General Grant wins battle of Missionary Ridge, Tenn. and Chattanooga Campaign.

1864

Jan. 8	– General Morgan, celebrated Confederate cavalry raider, visits Richmond.
Jan. 17	– Confederate Congress passes law abolishing conscription substitution.
Jan.–Mar.	– Richmond suffers coldest winter in many years.
Feb. 9	– 109 Federal officers escape from Libby Prison, Richmond; 48 recaptured and 59 reach Federal lines (2 drown).
Feb. 29	– Strong Union cavalry force under General Kilpatrick and Colonel Dahlgren fails to capture Richmond or free prisoners of war.
Feb.–Mar.	– Richmond authorities begin frequent shipments of prisoners further south, mostly to Georgia.
Mar. 9	– General Grant assumes command of all Union forces; takes position at Culpeper with General Meade's army.
Mar.–May	– Confederates prepare for spring campaign; noncombatants and nonessential personnel urged to leave city.
Mar. 10–May 2	– Federal General Banks defeated in Red River expedition; Louisiana preserved.
May 1	– Funeral at St. Paul's church for President Davis's young son Joe.
May 4–7	– Grant's army crosses Rapidan River; Battle of Wilderness takes place.
May 8–18	– Grant and Lee fight again at Battle of Spotsylvania Courthouse.
May 11	– Battle of Yellow Tavern checks General Sheridan on the Richmond defenses; General Stuart mortally wounded.
May 13	– General Stuart's funeral is held at St. James Episcopal Church in Richmond.
May 15	– Federal army under General Sigel suffers defeat in Valley of Virginia at New Market.
May 16	– General Butler's Army is beaten near Drewry's Bluff; shuts itself up at Bermuda Hundred.
May 23–25	– Lee's troops repulse Federal army at Hanover Junction.
May 27	– VMI cadets, fresh from victory at New Market, parade at Capitol Square.
Jun. 3	– General Lee's army wins large defensive battle at Cold Harbor.
Jun. 11–12	– Generals Hampton and Sheridan fight cavalry battle at Trevelian Station; Sheridan retreats to Grant's army.
Jun. 13–18	– General Grant shifts army south, secretly crosses James River and strikes at Petersburg, but fails to capture it; siege begins.
Jun. 18–July 12	– General Early conducts brilliant raid down Valley of Virginia; enters Maryland; is victorious at Monocacy; raids outskirts of Washington; returns safely to Valley.
Jun. 19	– General Early, Lee's 2nd Corps commander, defeats General Hunter's army at Lynchburg; drives it into West Virginia.
Jun. 19	– *USS Kearsarge* sinks Confederate raider *CSS Alabama*.
Jul. 30	– Confederates defeat Federals at Battle of the Crater near Petersburg.
Aug. 5	– Confederate fleet suffers defeat at Mobile Bay.
Aug. 18	– General Grant refuses to exchange prisoners of war.
Sep. 2	– Atlanta falls to General Sherman's army.
Sep. 4	– General Morgan, Confederate raider and hero, is surprised and killed.
Sep. 19	– General Sheridan defeats General Early's forces at Winchester in the Valley.
Sep. 22	– Another defeat for General Early's forces at Fisher's Hill; Union cavalry begins burning the Valley of Virginia; deprives Richmond of needed food.
Sep. 24	– General Sheridan begins the destruction of food supplies in Valley of Virginia.
Sep. 29	– Federal forces capture Fort Harrison, key point in Richmond's defenses; great scare in Richmond, but General Lee shores up defensive line.
Oct. 16	– Federal forces fail to take Richmond, driving west on Charles City Road.
Oct. 19	– General Sheridan defeats General Early's forces again at Cedar Creek.
Oct. 27	– Federals threaten Richmond again on Williamsburg and Boynton Roads.
Nov. 8	– President Lincoln is elected for a second term.
Nov. 16	– General Sherman's army begins march through Georgia to sea.
Nov. 30	– General Hood drives Federals from Franklin, but at heavy cost.
Dec. 16	– General Hood's Army of the Tennessee is defeated at Nashville.
Dec. 21	– General Sherman's army captures Savannah.

1865

Jan. 15	– Fort Fisher falls, closing last open port in Confederacy.
Jan. 19	– One of Lee's generals, John Pegram, marries Hettie Cary at St. Paul's.
Jan. 30	– General Lee is appointed Commander-in-Chief of all Confederate forces.
Feb. 1	– General John Breckenridge, former U.S. Vice

APPENDIX

	President, becomes Confederate Secretary of War.	Apr. 1	– Strong infantry and cavalry forces under Sheridan overwhelm Confederate flank at Five Forks; many prisoners taken, and Lee's right flank open.
Feb. 3	– Confederate peace commissioners led by Vice President Stevens meet with President Lincoln at Hampton Roads; no result.	Apr. 2	– Grant's army breaks through the Petersburg lines in several places; Lee abandons Petersburg that night.
Feb. 6	– General Pegram dies at Hatcher's Run near Petersburg.		
Feb. 7	– President Davis speaks at patriotic rally at African Church in Richmond.	Apr. 2	– President Davis flees Richmond by train late in evening; Confederate forces evacuate Richmond and Petersburg.
Feb. 16	– Exchange of prisoners of war resumes between North and South.	Apr. 3	– Richmond falls to Federal army in midst of great fire in city; Confederates destroy all bridges over James River.
Feb. 17	– Fall of Charleston, S.C. to Sherman's troops.		
Feb. 17	– Sherman's army burns Columbia, S.C.		
Mar. 2	– Sheridan scatters remainder of General Early's army at Waynesville, Va.	Apr. 4	– President Lincoln visits Richmond briefly.
Mar. 6	– General Sheridan's forces take Charlottesville, Va.; Union forces closing in on all sides of Richmond.	Apr. 5	– Federal Engineers complete pontoon bridge across James River at 17th Street.
		Apr. 9	– General Lee surrenders at Appomattox Courthouse, Va.
Mar. 18	– Last Confederate Congress in Richmond adjourns.	Apr. 12	– First of surrendered officers and men arrive in Richmond.
Mar. 19	– General Sheridan's forces join Grant's army, preparing for the final blow.	Apr. 13	– General Lee returns from Appomattox to home in Richmond.
Mar. 25	– General Lee's final attack of war on Fort Steadman at Petersburg fails.	Apr. 14	– President Lincoln is assassinated in Washington.
Mar. 25	– General Lee sends letter to Richmond's pastors asking parishioners to seek food in the countryside for his starving men.		

ACKNOWLEDGMENTS

My task of putting together this book was made easier by the contributions of a number of people who have lent their special skills. My thanks for their assistance goes to:

Dr. Hugo J. Mueller, Professor Emeritus of Linguistics and German at American University, Washington, DC. Throughout the writing and research of the book, he read drafts, made comments and corrections. For his generosity, wisdom, philosophical views and the sheer pleasure of our long collaboration, I dedicate this book to him.

My busy daughter Susan who, as in the case of my first book (*Mr. Lincoln's City*), was my mentor on graphics. When needed pictures were not forthcoming, she went to Richmond and photographed a number of sites herself.

John Ozimina, talented commercial artist, old friend and neighbor, who prepared 18 maps for publication. He accepted my many revisions with equanimity, and in one case redrew a large map of the center of modern Richmond. The precision and artistic quality of his work enhances the book.

For help in selecting and locating photographs and maps, I am particularly indebted to Richard Stevenson, head of the Reference, Geography and Map Division, Library of Congress, whose specialty is maps of the Civil War period.

At the Virginia State Library, Leslie Ann Tuttle, Pictorial Assistant, was most patient and helpful in locating and ordering needed photographs, as was Jane Sumpter, Picture Librarian. Rick Eck, Supervisor of Photographic Laboratories, went out of his way to provide the prints I had ordered.

Margaret Peters of the Virginia Historical Landmarks gave permission to the Virginia State Library to use the Landmarks' negatives to reproduce some prints for the book.

Thanks also goes to the staff at the Valentine Museum. Dwana Saunders, Curator of Photos, Gregg Kimball, Curator of Books and Manuscripts and Betti David, Volunteer, all assisted with photographic research and offered enthusiastic support. Lacy W. Dick, Supervisor of the Reading Room, responded promptly to my last minute requests.

I also owe thanks to Kay Lawson, Photographic Assistant at the Museum of the Confederacy, for her help in obtaining one picture that had long eluded me.

Most importantly, I must thank my publisher and trusted friend, Evelyn Metzger. I have relied on her ideas, suggestions and experience. Among her staff, Peter Exton made thoughtful comments after reading the manuscript from a conceptual point of view. These were most helpful in surmounting a number of difficulties. Equally, I must thank Judy Heit and Janet Nelson, for they possess skills I do not have. They subjected the book to a rigorous, detailed editorial scrubbing that has proved no less than invaluable.

In closing, I acknowledge my debt to my wife, Marianne, for bearing with me during the months of preparation, and especially through the final hectic weeks, when it seemed that everything had to be done at once.

R.M.L.

SOURCE NOTES

Introduction

1. Freeman, *R.E. Lee* 4:464.
2. DeLeon, *Four Years in Rebel Capitals*, 404.

Richmond in Wartime—An Overview

3. Ibid., 104.
4. Thomas, *Wartime Richmond*, 5.
5. Chestnut, *Diary from Dixie*, 91.
6. Catton, *The Coming Fury*, 191.
7. K. Jones, *Ladies of Richmond*, 67.
8. Churchill, *History of English Speaking Peoples*, 430.
9. Freeman, *R.E. Lee* 2:86.
10. C. Harrison, *Recollections Grave and Gay*, 82.
11. Bill, *Beleaguered City*, 128.
12. K. Jones, *Ladies of Richmond*, 124.
13. J.B. Jones, *Rebel War Clerk's Diary* 1:257.
14. S. Putnam, *Richmond During the War*, 320.
15. K. Jones, *Ladies of Richmond*, 168.
16. S. Putnam, *Richmond During the War*, 228.
17. J.B. Jones, *Rebel War Clerk's Diary* 2:100.
18. C. Harrison, *Recollections Grave and Gay*, 150.
19. S. Putnam, *Richmond During the War*, 192.
20. Chestnut, *Diary from Dixie*, 196.
21. Ibid., 199.
22. S. Putnam, *Richmond During the War*, 315.
23. K. Jones, *Ladies of Richmond*, 231–2.
24. Ibid., 224.
25. Ibid., 235.
26. Chestnut, *Diary from Dixie*, 196.
27. C. Harrison, *Recollections Grave and Gay*, 190.
28. K. Jones, *Ladies of Richmond*, 254.
29. Ibid., 263.
30. Ibid., 270.
31. Ibid.
32. Manarin, ed., *Richmond at War*, 595.
33. Patrick, *Fall of Richmond*, 65.
34. Ibid., 68.
35. Ibid., 58.
36. J.B. Jones, *Rebel War Clerk's Diary* 2:208.
37. K. Jones, *Ladies of Richmond*, 291.

First Tour—Capitol Square

38. Bill, *Beleaguered City*, 181.
39. Chestnut, *Diary from Dixie*, 301.
40. Bill, *Beleaguered City*, 277.
41. DeLeon, *Four Years in Rebel Capitals*, 108.
42. C. Harrison, *Recollections Grave and Gay*, 68.
43. S. Putnam, *Richmond During the War*, 218.
44. B. Davis, *To Appomattox*, 186.
45. C. Harrison, *Recollections Grave and Gay*, 141.
46. Bill, *Beleaguered City*, 42.

Second Tour—Broad Street, Shockoe Hill and Court End

47. Ibid., 148.
48. Ibid., 24.
49. Munford, *Richmond Homes and Memories*, 220.
50. Eggleston, *A Rebel's Recollections*, 220–2.
51. B. Davis, *To Appomattox*, 123.
52. Bill, *Beleaguered City*, 221.
53. Ibid., 222.
54. K. Jones, *Ladies of Richmond*, 278.
55. S. Putnam, *Richmond During the War*, 146.
56. Ibid., 226.
57. K. Jones, *Ladies of Richmond*, 221.
58. J.B. Jones, *Rebel War Clerk's Diary* 2:411.
59. Bill, *Beleaguered City*, 253.
60. Rhodes, *Landmarks of Richmond*, 21.
61. B. Davis, *To Appomattox*, 141.
62. K. Jones, *Ladies of Richmond*, 67.
63. Ibid., 164.
64. Ibid., 268.
65. Patrick, *Fall of Richmond*, 130.
66. B. Davis, *To Appomattox*, 187.
67. Chestnut, *Diary from Dixie*, 292.
68. Freeman, *R.E. Lee* 2:253.
69. Ibid., 252.
70. Ibid. 4:470.
71. Munford, *Richmond Homes and Memories*, 98.
72. J.B. Jones, *Rebel War Clerk's Diary* 1:114.
73. S. Putnam, *Richmond During the War*, 192.
74. Freeman, *Lee's Lieutenants* 2:19.
75. Hoehling, *Day Richmond Died*, 68.

Third Tour—Eastern Quarter

76. Freeman, *R.E. Lee* 1:450.
77. Ibid. 4:464.
78. K. Jones, *Ladies of Richmond*, 120.
79. Freeman, *R.E. Lee* 2:130.
80. Ibid. 2:74.
81. DeLeon, *Four Years in Rebel Capitals*, 400–1.
82. V. Jones, *Eight Hours Before Richmond*, 131–5.
83. Ibid., 134.
84. Pember, *Southern Woman's Story*, 28–9.
85. Ibid., 92.
86. B. Davis, *To Appomattox*, 183.
87. Ibid., 184.
88. Wilkins, *War Boy*, 28.
89. K. Jones, *Ladies of Richmond*, 134.
90. Bill, *Beleaguered City*, 12.

91. Ibid.
92. K. Jones, *Ladies of Richmond*, 264.
93. Waitt, *Confederate Military Hospitals*, 10, 14.
94. V. Jones, *Eight Hours Before Richmond*, 14.
95. B. Davis, *To Appomattox*, 185.
96. Weitzel, *Richmond Occupied*, 56.
97. Dowdey and Manarin, eds., *Wartime Papers R.E. Lee*, 185.
98. Bill, *Beleaguered City*, 184.
99. Manarin, *Richmond at War*, 66.
100. Freeman, *R.E. Lee* 4:191.
101. K. Jones, *Ladies of Richmond*, 154.
102. Bill, *Beleaguered City*, 165.

Fourth Tour—Area of the Evacuation Fire

103. B. Davis, *To Appomattox*, 129.
104. Patrick, *Jefferson Davis*, 40.
105. Campbell, *Evacuation of Richmond*, 4.
106. Hoehling, *Day Richmond Died*, 221.
107. K. Jones, *Ladies of Richmond*, 126.
108. Ibid., 132.
109. Kimmel, *Mr. Davis' Richmond*, 85–7.
110. C. Harrison, *Recollections Grave and Gay*, 211.
111. Bill, *Beleaguered City*, 105.
112. J.B. Jones, *Rebel War Clerk's Diary* 2:269–97.
113. K. Jones, *Ladies of Richmond*, 162–3.
114. Bill, *Beleaguered City*, 118.
115. K. Jones, *Ladies of Richmond*, 162–3.
116. J.B. Jones, *Rebel War Clerk's Diary* 2:196.
117. Hoehling, *Day Richmond Died*, 222.
118. Thomas, *Wartime Richmond*, 39.
119. Ibid.
120. Patrick, *Fall of Richmond*, 61.
121. J.B. Jones, *Rebel War Clerk's Diary* 2:292.
122. Ibid.
123. K. Jones, *Ladies of Richmond*, 208–9.
124. C. Harrison, *Recollections Grave and Gay*, 266–7.
125. Rhodes, *Richmond Guide Book*, 49.
126. C. Harrison, *Battles and Leaders* 2:439.
127. K. Jones, *Ladies of Richmond*, 118.

Fifth Tour—Gamble's Hill, Hollywood Cemetery and Monroe Park

128. DeLeon, *Four Years in Rebel Capitals*, 220.
129. K. Jones, *Ladies of Richmond*, 75.
130. Ibid., 76.
131. Ibid., 261.
132. Ibid.
133. Patrick, *Fall of Richmond*, 116.
134. Munford, *Richmond Homes and Memories*, 98.
135. C.R. Harrison, *Historic Guide*, 21.
136. Douglas, *I Rode With Stonewall*, 119.
137. Ibid.
138. K. Jones, *Ladies of Richmond*, 288.
139. DeLeon, *Four Years in Rebel Capitals*, 415.
140. Hoehling, *Day Richmond Died*, 167.
141. Freeman, *R.E. Lee* 4:210.
142. K. Jones, *Ladies of Richmond*, 152.
143. DeLeon, *Four Years in Rebel Capitals* 110.
144. K. Jones, *Ladies of Richmond*, 135.
145. Ibid., 223–8.

Appendix—The Defenses of Richmond

146. Manarin, *Richmond at War*, 35.
147. Ibid., 59.
148. Bill, *Beleaguered City*, 130.
149. Dowdey and Manarin, *Wartime Papers*, 265.
150. Thomas, *Wartime Richmond*, 24.
151. J.B. Jones, *Rebel War Clerk's Diary* 2:233.
152. Hoehling, *Day Richmond Died*, 204.
153. Weitzel, *Richmond Occupied*, 52.

BIBLIOGRAPHY

Bailey, James Henry II. *History of St. Peter's Church, 1834–1929*. Richmond: Lewis Printing Co., 1959.

Bartges, D.C., Jr. "Five in Bronze." *Richmond*, February 1975, 32.

Battles and Leaders of the Civil War. 4 vols. New York: The Century Co., 1887.

Bill, Alfred Hoyt. *Beleaguered City, Richmond 1861–1865*. New York: Alfred A. Knopf, 1946.

Blackford, Wm. W. *War Years with Jeb. Stuart*. New York: Chas. Scribner's Sons, 1945.

Boykin, E.M. *The Falling Flag—Evacuation of Richmond, Retreat and Surrender at Appomattox*. New York: E.J. Hale & Son, 1874.

Bowman, John S., ed. *The Civil War Almanac*. New York: Gallery Books, 1983.

Cadwallader, Silvanus. *Three Years With Grant*. New York: Alfred A. Knopf, 1955.

Campbell, John A. *Recollections of the Evacuation of Richmond, April 2, 1865*. Baltimore: John Murphy & Co., 1880.

Catton, Bruce. *Bruce Catton's Civil War*. New York: Fairfax Press, 1984.

———. *The Coming Fury*. Garden City, N.Y.: Doubleday & Co., 1961.

———. *Grant Takes Command*. Boston: Little Brown & Co., 1968.

———. *Terrible Swift Sword*. Garden City, N.Y.: Doubleday & Co., 1963.

Cavada, Frederic F. *Libby Life, Experiences of a Prisoner of War in Richmond, Va*. Philadelphia: J.B. Lippencott & Co., 1865.

Chamberlayne, C.G., ed. *Letters and Papers of an Artillery Officer in the War for Southern Independence, 1861–1865*. Richmond: Dietz Printing Co., 1932.

Chesson, Michael B. *Richmond After the War*. Richmond: Virginia State Library, 1981.

Chesterman, William D. *Guide to Richmond and the Battlefields*. Richmond: J. L. Hill Printing Co., 1894.

Chestnut, Mary Boykin. *A Diary from Dixie*. Edited by Isabella D. Martin and Myrta Lockett Avary. New York: Appleton & Co., 1905.

Christian, George L. *Confederate Memories and Experiences*. Richmond: Clayton Printing Co.

Christian, W. Asbury. *Richmond Her Past and Present*. Richmond: L.H. Jenkins Co., 1912.

Churchill, Winston S. *History of the English Speaking Peoples*. New York: Dodd Meade Co., 1965.

Coggins, Jack. *Arms and Equipment of the Civil War*. New York: Fairfax Press, 1983.

Commager, Henry Steele, ed. *The Blue and the Gray*. New York: Bobbs-Merrill Co., 1950.

Cornish, J. Jenkins III. *The Air Arm of the Confederacy*. Richmond: Official Publication No. 11, Richmond Civil War Centennial Commission, 1963.

Cullen, Joseph P. *Richmond National Battlefield Park*. Washington: National Park Service Historical Handbook Series No. 33, 1961.

Cunningham, H.H. *Ceremonies at the Unveiling of the Statue of General Lee*. Richmond: Virginia General Assembly, House Document No. 6., 1932.

———. *Doctors in Gray—The Confederate Medical Service*. Baton Rouge, La.: Louisiana State University Press, 1958.

Cutchins, John A. *A Famous Command—The Light Infantry Blues*. Richmond: Garrett & Massie, 1934.

Dabney, Virginius. *Richmond—The Story of a City*. Garden City, N.Y.: Doubleday & Co., 1976.

Dade, Virginia E. *One Woman in the War*. Charleston, S.C.: News & Courier Book Press, 1885.

Davis, Burke. *The Civil War—Strange and Exciting Facts*. New York: Fairfax Press, 1982.

———. *Gray Fox*. New York: Fairfax Press, 1981.

———. *To Appomattox—Nine Days in April 1865*. New York: Rinehart & Co., 1959.

Davis, George B., et al. *The Official Military Atlas of the Civil War*. New York: Arno Press, 1978. (Original publication Washington, D.C.: GPO, 1891–1895).

Dawson, Henry B. *The First Flag Over Richmond, Virginia, April 3, 1865*. Morrisiana, N.Y.: Privately Printed, 1866.

De Leon, Thomas Cooper. *Belles, Beaux and Brains in the Sixties*. New York: G.W. Dillingham Co., 1909.

———. *Four Years in Rebel Capitals*. New York: Crowell Collier Publishing Co., 1962 (Reprint).

Department of Henrico and Richmond. Record Group 109. U.S. National Archives, Washington.

De Peyster, Livingston. *The Colors of the United States First Raised over the Capitol of the Confederate States*. Morrisiana, N.Y.: Privately Printed, 1866.

Douglas, Henry Kyd. *I Rode with Stonewall*. Chapel Hill, N.C.: University of North Carolina Press, 1940.

Dowdey, Clifford. *Experiment in Rebellion*. Freeport, N.Y.: Books for Libraries Press, 1946.

Dowdey, Clifford, and Manarin, Lewis H., eds. *The Wartime Papers of R.E.Lee*. Virginia Civil War Centennial Commission. New York: Bramwell House, 1961.

Dulaney, Paul S. *The Architecture of Richmond*. 2d. ed. Charlottesville, Va.: University of Virginia Press, 1976.

Dunham, William C., et al. *Memorial to the Congress of the United States: Removal of Obstructions on James River*. Richmond: Evening State Journal Printing House, 1870.

Eggleston, George C. *A Rebel's Recollections*. Bloomington, Ind.: Indiana University Press, 1959.

Evans, Mrs. James. *Our Women of the War*. Charleston, S.C.: News & Courier Book Press, 1885.

Ewell, Richard S. "Evacuation of Richmond." *Southern Historical Society Papers* 13 (1885): 247–252.

Ezekiel, Herbert T. *The Recollections of a Virginia Newspaper Man*. Richmond: Privately Printed, 1920.

Fisher, George D. *History and Reminiscences of the Monumental Church from 1814 to 1878*. Richmond: Whittet & Shepperson, 1880.

Foote, Shelby. *The Civil War—A Narrative—Red River to Appomattox*. New York: Random House, 1974.

Freeman, Douglas S. *Lee's Lieutenants*. 3 vols. New York: Chas. Scribner's Sons, 1947.

———. *Robert E. Lee*. 4 vols. New York: Chas. Scribner's Sons, 1947.

Fuller, J.F.C. *The Generalship of Ulysses S. Grant*. New York: Dodd, Meade & Co., 1929.

Garnett, Theodore S. "J.E.B. Stuart." Address delivered at the unveiling of the equestrian statue of Gen. Stuart at Richmond, Va., May 30, 1907. New York: Neale Publishing Co., 1907.

Giesy, Rev. Samuel H. *A Discourse on the Fall of Richmond*. Christ Evangelical Reformed Church. Philadelphia: James B. Rodgers, Printer, 1865.

Gorgas, Amelia. "As I Saw It—One Woman's Account of the Fall of Richmond." *Civil War Times, Illustrated*, May 1986, 40–43.

Gorgas, Josiah. *The Civil War Diary of . . .* Edited by Frank E. Vandiver. Tuscaloosa, Ala.: University of Alabama Press, 1947.

Goss, Warren Lee. *A Soldier's Story of His Captivity, Belle Isle*. Boston: Richardson Co., 1871.

Harrison, Caroline Rivers. *Historic Guide—Richmond and James River*. Richmond: Cussons, May & Co., 1966.

Harrison, Constance Cary (Mrs. Burton). *Battles and Leaders of the Civil War*. vol. 2. New York: The Century Co., 1887.

———. *Recollections Grave and Gay*. New York: Charles Scribner's Sons, 1911.

—"War Days in Richmond." *Appelton's Journal*, 6 July 1872.

Hattaway, Herman, and James, Arthur. *How the North Won*. Urbana, Ill.: University of Illinois Press, 1983.

Hill, J.P. *Souvenir Unveiling of Soldiers and Sailors Monument*. Richmond: J.L. Hill Printing Co., 1894.

Hoehling, A.A. and Mary. *The Day Richmond Died*. New York: A.S. Barnes & Co., 1981.

Holmes, J.T. *Richmond Revisited By a Federal Soldier*. Columbus, Ohio: Berlin Printing Co., 1905.

James, G. Watson, Jr. "Richmond's Three Lines of Breastworks." *Sunday Journal*, 13 June 1920, 1.

Jeffrey, William H. *Richmond Prisons 1861–1862*. St. Johnsbury, Vermont: The Republican Press, 1893.

Johnson, J. Ambler. *Echoes of 1861–1865*. Richmond: Privately Printed, 1971.

Jones, John Beauchamp. *A Rebel War Clerk's Diary at the Confederate States Capital*. 2 vols. New York: Old Hickory Bookshop, 1935.

Jones, Katharine M. *Ladies of Richmond—Confederate Capital*. New York: Bobbs Merrill Co., 1962.

Jones, Virgil Carrington. *Eight Hours Before Richmond*. New York: Henry Holt & Co., 1957.

Ketchum, Richard M., and Catton, Bruce. *American Heritage Picture History of the Civil War*. New York: American Heritage Publishing Co., 1960.

Kimball, William J. "As Richmond Girded for War in Spring of 1861." *Civil War Times, Illustrated*, November 1963, 36–40.

———. *Starve or Fall—Richmond and Its People, 1861–1865*. Ann Arbor, Mich.: University of Michigan Press, 1976.

—ed. *Richmond in Time of War*. Boston: Houghton Mifflin Co., 1960.

Kimmel, Stanley P. *Mr. Davis' Richmond*. New York: Coward-McCann, 1958.

Kunhardt, Philip B., Jr. "Images of Which History Was Made Bore the Mathew Brady Label." *Smithsonian*, July 1977, 24–34.

Langston, Loomis J. "The First Federal to Enter Richmond." *Richmond Dispatch*, 10 February 1893.

Lecour-Gayet, Robert. *Everyday Life in the United States Before the Civil War*. New York: Frederick Unger Publishing Co., 1972.

Leslie, Frank. *Illustrated History of the Civil War*. New York: The Fairfax Press, 1977 (Reprint).

Lightfoot, Mrs. William B. "The Evacuation of Richmond." *The Virginia Magazine*, January 1933, 215–222.

Little, John P. *History of Richmond*. Richmond: The Dietz Publishing Co., 1933.

Lutz, Francis Earle. "Federal Raids on the Confederate Capital." *Richmond Magazine* 18 (1932): 31, 58–60.

———. *A Richmond Album*. Richmond: Garrett & Massie, 1937.

Manarin, Louis H., ed. *Richmond at War—The Minutes of the City Council 1861–1865*. Chapel Hill, N.C.: University of North Carolina Press, 1966.

McCarthy, C. *Walks About Richmond*. Richmond: McCarthy & Ellyson, 1870.

McClellan, H.B. *I Rode With Jeb Stuart*. Bloomington, Ind.: University of Indiana Press, 1958.

McGuire, Judith W. Brockenbrough. *Diary of a Southern Refugee During the War*. New York: E.J. Hale & Son, 1868.

Meridith, Roy. *The Face of Robert E. Lee*. New York: Fairfax Press, 1981.

Miller, Francis Trevelyan, ed. *The Photographic History of the Civil War*. New York: Fairfax Press, 1983 (Reprint).

Moore, Samuel J.T., Jr. *Moore's Complete Civil War Guide to Richmond*. Revised Edition. Richmond: Published Privately, 1978.

Mordicai, Samuel. *Richmond in Bygone Days*. 2d. ed. New York: Arno Press, 1975 (Reprint).

Munford, Robert Beverley, Jr. *Richmond Homes and Memories*. Richmond: Garrett & Massie, 1936.

Mustian, Thomas F. *Facts and Legends of Richmond Street Areas*. Richmond: Carroll Publishing Co., 1977.

Myers, Gustavus A. "Abraham Lincoln in Richmond." *The Virginia Magazine*, October 1933.

Patrick, Rembert W. *The Fall of Richmond*. Baton Rouge, La.: Louisiana State University Press, 1960.

———. *Jefferson Davis and His Cabinet*. Baton Rouge, La.: Louisiana State University Press, 1961.

Pember, Phoebe Yates. *A Southern Woman's Story*. Jackson, Tenn.: McCowat-Mercer Press, 1959 (Reprint).

Pickett, Mrs. George E. *Pickett and His Men*. Philadelphia: J.B. Lippencott Co., 1913.

———. *What Happened to Me*. New York: Brentanos, 1917.

Pollard, E.A. *Southern History of the War*. New York: Fairfax Press, 1982 (Reprint).

Porter, Horace. *Campaigning with Grant*. New York: Bonanza Books, 1961 (Reprint).

Putnam, George Haven. *A Prisoner of War in Virginia 1864–1865*. New York: G.P. Putnam Sons, 1912.

Putnam, Sally A. Brock. *In Richmond During the Confederacy*. New York: Robert McBride Co., 1961 (Reprint).

———. *Richmond During the War*. New York: G.W. Carleton & Co., 1867.

Reed, Charles W., and Sheppard, William. *Soldier Life in the Union & Confederate Armies*. Greenwich, Conn.: Fawcett Publications, Inc. 1961.

Rhodes, M. *Richmond Guide Book*. Richmond: M.A. Burgess Publisher, 1909.

———. *Richmond Howitzer Battalion*. Richmond: Carlton McCarthy & Co., 1883.

———. *Richmond, Virginia—Colonial, Revolutionary, Confederate and the Present*. Richmond: Baptist & Saunders, 1896.

Rhodes, Mary Lou. *Landmarks of Richmond*. Richmond: Garrett & Massie, 1938.

"The Richmond Campaign." *War of the Rebellion*. Official Records of the Union and Confederate Armies, Series 1, Vol. 46 (Parts 1, 2 and 3). Washington: National Archives, U.S. Government Printing Office, 1894–95.

Ripley, Edward H. "The Burning of Richmond, April 3, 1865." *Southern Historical Society Papers* 32 (1904):73–76.

Sandberg, Carl. *Abraham Lincoln—The War Years*. 4 vols. New York: Barcourt, Brace & Co., 1939.

Sanders, C.W., and Bowers, C.W. *Illustrated Richmond*. Richmond: Richmond News Co., 1908.

Scott, Mary Wingfield. *Houses of Old Richmond*. Richmond: The Valentine Museum, 1941.

———. *Old Richmond Neighborhoods*. Richmond: Whittet & Shepperson, 1950.

Scott, Mary Wingfield, and Catterall, Louis F. *Virginia's Capitol Square*. Richmond: The Valentine Museum, 1957.

Scott, W.W., and Stannard, W.G. *The Capital of Virginia and the Confederate States*. Richmond: James E. Goode, Printer, 1894.

Semmes, Raphael. *Memoirs of Service Afloat*. Baltimore: Kelley & Co., 1869.

Shover, Mrs. D. *Our Women in the War*. Charleston, S.C.: S.C. News & Courier Book Press, 1885.

Skoch, George. "War Along Southern Lines: The Great Locomotive March." *Civil War Times, Illustrated*, December 1986, 12–16.

Sommers, Richard J. *Richmond Redeemed*. Garden City, N.Y.: Doubleday & Co., 1981.

Souvenir Unveiling Soldiers and Sailors Monument. Richmond: Hill Printing Co., 1894.

Spencer, W.F. "A French View of the Fall of Richmond." *The Virginia Magazine*, April 1965, 178–188.

Stannard, Mary Newton. *Richmond, Its People and Its Story*. Philadelphia: J.B. Lippincott Co., 1923.

Stuart, Meriwether. "Of Spies and Borrowed Names." *The Virginia Magazine*, July 1981, 308–327.

Sublette, Emily. "A Little Girl's Story." *Richmond Times Dispatch Sunday Magazine*, 22 May 1958.

Sulivane, Clement. "Who Was the Last Soldier to Leave the Burning City?" *Southern Historical Society Papers* 37 (1909):317.

Thomas, Emory M. *The Confederate State of Richmond*. Austin: University of Texas Press, 1971.

———. "Wartime Richmond." *Civil War Times, Illustrated*, (Special Pamphlet), 1977.

Tucker, Dallas. "The Fall of Richmond." *Virginia Society Papers* 29 (1901):152.

Waitt, Robert W., Jr. *Confederate Military Hospitals in Richmond*. Official Publication No. 22. Richmond: Richmond Civil War Centennial Commission, 1964.

Wallace, Charles M. *Boy Gangs in Richmond*. Richmond: Richmond Press, 1938.

Walthall, Earnest T. *Hidden Things Brought to Light*. Richmond: Dietz Printing Co., 1933.

Weddell, Elizabeth W. *St. Paul's Church*. Richmond: The William Byrd Press, 1931.

Weinert, R.P. "Federal Spies in Richmond." *Civil War Times, Illustrated*, February 1965, 28–35.

Weitzel, Godfrey. *Richmond Occupied*. Edited by Louis H. Manarin. Official Publication No. 16. Richmond: Richmond Civil War Centennial Commission, 1965.

White, Wm. S. *Contributions to a History of the Richmond Howitzer Battalion*. Pamphlet No. 2—A Diary of the War. Richmond: Carlton, McCarthy & Co., 1883.

———. "Stray Leaves from a Soldier's Journal." *Southern Historical Society Papers* 2 (1883):552.

Wilkins, B.F. *War Boy*. Tullahoma, Tenn.: Wilson Bros. Printing Co., 1938.

Young, William H. *Journal of an Excursion from Troy, New York to General Carr's Headquarters at Wilson's Landing (Fort Pocahontas) on the James River During the Month of May 1865*. Troy, N.Y.: Privately Printed, 1871.